Stonewall Jackson's

VALLEY CAMPAIGN

Stonewall Jackson's

VALLEY CAMPAIGN

FROM NOVEMBER 4, 1861 TO JUNE 17, 1862

BY

WILLIAM ALLAN

SMITHMARK

This edition published in 1995 by SMITHMARK Publishers, Inc.
16 East 32nd Street, New York, NY 10016.

SMITHMARK books are available for bulk purchase for sales
promotion and premium use. For details write or call the
manager of special sales, SMITHMARK Publishers, Inc.,
16 East 32nd Street, New York, NY 10016; (212) 532-6600.

This edition published by arrangement
with W.S. Konecky Associates, Inc.

ISBN: 0-8317-1432-8

Printed in the United States of America

10 9 8 7 6 5 4 3 2 1

Dedication

TO

THE PEOPLE OF LEXINGTON, VIRGINIA

IN WHOSE MIDST

JACKSON MADE HIS HOME IN LIFE

AND CHOSE HIS RESTING-PLACE IN DEATH

PREFACE

THE operations of General T. J. Jackson in the Valley of Virginia, during the first half of the year 1862, constitute one of the most brilliant and interesting episodes of the great Civil War. The theatre on which they took place afforded a quick and easy approach to the Federal capital and to the Northern States. The mountains and rivers of the Valley gave to an active and skilful commander many opportunities of neutralizing great disparity of force. The celerity, energy, and skill which Jackson manifested on this field excited the admiration of his countrymen and produced a feeling nearly akin to consternation among his foes. His campaign had a most important bearing upon all the military operations in Virginia in the spring and summer of 1862, for he caused to be detained, for the defence of Washington and Maryland, forces in the aggregate four or five times as numerous as his own, and thus in a fatal degree hampered and paralyzed McClellan. The story of this campaign will always be interesting to the actors in it on both sides, and not merely to them; to the student of military art it affords an admirable

PREFACE

example of an aggressive-defensive campaign, and one of the best instances in modern times of the degree to which skill and daring may neutralize superiority of numbers and resources.

Our aim has been to give an accurate history of this campaign from official sources. Dr. Dabney's *Life of Jackson* was written during the war, and without access to the Federal sources of information. Much has been written since, but generally in the shape of personal narratives, or of statements based upon the newspaper correspondence of the time. Such accounts are of course imperfect, and some of them are so partisan in character as to be of no value. Until recently the official reports were in a large degree inaccessible, but this is no longer the case. As will be seen by the notes at the foot of text pages and those collated at the end of the volume, we have been at pains to verify all important statements about numbers—in a great many instances from the original MS. returns themselves.

Our thanks are due to Adj.-Gen. Townsend and to Gen. M. W. Wright for facilities extended to us in the examination of papers in their offices, to Dr. Jones, secretary of the Southern Historical Society, for many favours, and to A. P. Tasker, Esq., of the Confederate Archive Office, and J. W. Kirkly, Esq., of the Adjutant-General's Office (the well-known historian of the First Federal Maryland regiment), for frequent and valued courtesies.

In addition to the official reports, we have

PREFACE

been indebted to the various lives of Jackson by Maj. J. Esten Cooke, Miss Randolph, and an " Ex-Cadet," and especially to the earliest and very valuable biography of Jackson by his former chief of staff, Dr. R. L. Dabney. We have also drawn from the Historical Papers of Gen. G. H. Gordon, of Massachusetts, and the reminiscences of Gen. Strother, and from many others, to whom our obligations are acknowledged in the text or notes.

A full diary kept by Maj. Hotchkiss during the greater part of this campaign has been of great value. We are also indebted to a diary kept by J. A. Waddell, Esq., of Staunton, Virginia.

The maps have been prepared by D. C. Humphreys, C.E. of the United States River Surveys, under the direction of, and from the material furnished by, Maj. Jed. Hotchkiss, of Staunton, Virginia. Maj. Hotchkiss was topographical engineer for Gen. Jackson during this and his subsequent campaigns, and possesses by far the most valuable mass of topographical data now in existence relating to these campaigns. Maj. Hotchkiss has also furnished much valuable information besides that directly credited in the narrative.

W. A.

McDONOGH, IND.,

May 1, 1880.

CONTENTS

CHAPTER I

STONEWALL JACKSON'S CAMPAIGN

IN THE

SHENANDOAH VALLEY OF VIRGINIA

CHAPTER I

ROMNEY

THE long struggle between the two great sections of the United States came to an issue of arms in the spring of 1861. For years the course of events had tended to this result. The North, great and growing, filled with the most advanced ideas as to popular government, human rights, universal equality and fraternity, and tending, because of the immense expansion of commerce and manufactures, to a centralized government, chafed and fretted against the barriers interposed by a strict construction of the Constitution to an extension of its civilization over the entire country. The foundations on which the Union had been reared seemed narrow and antiquated to a people whose growth had been unprecedented, and who, by an immense infusion of un-English immigration,

had lost much of their reverence for the tradi-
tions and principles of the Fathers of the Republic. The South, more conservative in principle and practice ; less changed by immigration ; believing slavery the best relation for the
negro, and a necessary condition of permanence
in a purely democratic state ; saw no safety for
its institutions, except in strict adherence to
constitutional guarantees, and watched with the
utmost jealousy any encroachments attempted
upon the defences which the Constitution had
thrown around the weaker party. When the
long political struggle culminated in the election
of Mr. Lincoln to the presidency in 1860, some
of the Southern States thought it time to dis-
solve the Union, and seek safety in a separate
government from the anti-slavery deluge which
seemed to them about to spread over the land.
The border slave States held back for a time,
and Virginia especially, which had contributed
so largely to the formation of the Union originally, exerted all her influence to bring about a
peace between the conflicting sections, but in
vain. Meantime, Mr. Lincoln entered upon
office March 4, 1861. In a few weeks his
conciliatory sentiments yielded to the pressure
of the public opinion of his political associates
in the North. Early in April a decided stand
was taken against further concession to the
seceding States. It was determined to reinforce
Fort Sumter, in Charleston harbour. On
April 13 the fort was attacked by the Confederates and taken. On April 15, President

Lincoln issued his call for seventy-five thousand
troops to suppress "insurrectionary combina-
tions." On April 17, Governor Letcher, of
Virginia, refused to obey the President's call
for troops, and on the same day the Virginia
Convention, all its efforts for peace having failed,
and the issue being now war on the one side or
the other, repealed the ordinance by which the
State had originally adopted the Federal constitution, and seceded from the Union.

The authorities of Virginia at once took steps
to organize such military force as she possessed.
Volunteers were called for, and such as were
not ready for immediate service were ordered
to Richmond, where a camp of instruction was
established. In a few days it was determined
to bring down the senior cadets from the Virginia Military Institute, at Lexington, to be
used in drilling the recruits. On Sunday morning, April 21, the order reached Lexington,
Virginia, requiring those cadets to report at
Richmond, under command of Maj. T. J.
Jackson, then Professor of Natural and Experi-
mental Philosophy in the Virginia Military
Institute.

Maj. Jackson was born at Clarksburg, Western
Virginia, January, 1824, entered West Point in
1842, graduated in 1846, distinguished himself
in the march on the city of Mexico in 1847 as a
lieutenant in Magruder's battery, was breveted
captain for gallant and meritorious conduct at
Churubusco, August 20, and major at Chapulte-
pec, September 13, 1847. He accompanied his

command after the close of the Mexican war to
Fort Hamilton, whence he was sent to Fort
Meade, near Tampa Bay, Florida. While here
he was elected, in 1851, to the above-named
professorship in the Virginia Military Institute,
and resigning from the army he removed to
Lexington. Here he resided for the next ten
years.

At one o'clock on Sunday, April 21, 1861,
the cadets, under Maj. Jackson, took up their
line of march for Staunton, *en route* to Richmond. He then left his home for the last
time. A little more than two years afterwards
all that was mortal of " Stonewall " Jackson
was borne, amid the tears and lamentations of
his countrymen, to the simple village church-
yard of Lexington. Maj. Jackson was first
assigned to duty at the camp of instruction,
near Richmond, but at the end of a week he
was commissioned as colonel by the State of
Virginia, and ordered to take command at
Harper's Ferry, Virginia. He arrived there on
April 29, and held command until superseded
by Gen. Joseph E. Johnston,* who, upon the
adhesion of Virginia to the Confederate State,
was sent by the authorities of the latter to take
charge of this important post. Col. Jackson
was then placed in command of one of the
brigades of the army gradually collecting under
Gen. Johnston. He was made brigadier-general
on July 3, and marched to Manassas on the
18th and 19th, when Gen. Johnston moved to

* Gen. Johnston assumed command on May 23.

the assistance of Beauregard. At Manassas,
July 21, Jackson contributed materially to the
victory won by the Confederates, his brigade
checking the tide of Federal success, and rendering conspicuous service. It was on this
occasion that he received the sobriquet of
" Stonewall," from an expression used by Gen.
Bee in reference to Jackson's brigade [1].

On October 7 he was made major-general, in
recognition of his services at the battle of
Manassas, and soon after was assigned, under
Gen. Johnston, to the command of the Valley
district, with headquarters at Winchester, Virginia. (Map No. I.) On November 4 he left
Manassas for the latter place. He held this
command, in a considerable degree an independent one, until the middle of the following
June. This period in his career is in many
respects the most interesting. It embraces the
difficulties and struggles through which he rose
to fame, and covers that wonderful campaign in
the Valley of Virginia which filled the South
with unbounded admiration of his genius, and
has placed his name, in the estimation of the
world, high on the roll of captains. It is a
sketch of Jackson's career during this period
that we propose now to give.

The birthplace and early home of Gen. Jackson was Clarksburg, in Western Virginia, and
from the opening of the war he had burned
with a desire to be ordered to service in that

[1] The figures in brackets—[1], [2], [3], etc.—refer to the
Explanatory Notes following the text.

region. He had frequently expressed his wish to aid in expelling the Federal troops from the home of his childhood, and when assigned to the Valley district his first thoughts were turned towards the execution of such a design.

The campaign of the summer and fall in Western Virginia had not been favourable to the South. Gen. Robert S. Garnett, who had commanded the first considerable force in that region, had been out-manœuvred by Gen. McClellan, compelled to retreat from his positions at Leedsville and Rich Mountain with loss, and when overtaken at Carrick's Ford, on Cheat River, July 13, had been defeated and killed. This gave the Federals control of the greater part of the State of Virginia, west of the Alleghanies and north of the Great Kanawha River. In the valley of this river an effort was made a month later, by Gen. Floyd, with a Confederate brigade, to wrest a portion of this territory from them, but because of his small force, and the want of co-operation on the part of Gen. Wise (commanding a part of the Confederate troops in that region), he failed to effect any results of permanent value.

Gen. Lee, who had been sent to take command after the death of Garnett [2], with a considerable reinforcement, either through the difficulties of the country, or the inexperience of his subordinates, or both, failed to regain the advantages lost by Garnett, and was reduced to merely preventing any further encroachments of the enemy. He directed an advance upon the Federal positions on Cheat Mountain and at Elkwater on September 12, but it miscarried because the column under Col. Rust failed to attack. He then drew off a large part of Loring's force to unite with Floyd and Wise in opposing Rosecrans's movement up the Kanawha Valley, but the Federal Commander withdrew, and active operations ceased. About November 1 Gen. Lee was ordered elsewhere, and the approach of winter and the inaccessible character of the country rendered further operations almost impossible.

When, therefore, Gen. Jackson was assigned to the command of the Valley of Virginia, the enemy had possession of all the State north of the Great Kanawha and west of the Alleghanies, and had pushed their outposts into that mountain region itself, and, in some cases, eastward of the main range. Thus Gen. Kelly, under direction of Gen. Rosecrans, who commanded all the Federal forces in Western Virginia, had captured Romney, the county-seat of Hampshire, forty miles west of Winchester, and now occupied it with a force of five thousand (5000) men. This movement gave the Federals control of the fertile valley of the South Branch of the Potomac. Another force occupied Bath, the county-seat of Morgan, almost due north of Winchester, while the north bank of the Potomac was everywhere guarded by Union troops.

The Baltimore and Ohio railroad was open, and available for the supply of the Union troops

from Baltimore to Harper's Ferry, and again
from a point opposite Hancock westward. The
section of about forty miles, from Harper's
Ferry to Hancock, lying for the most part some
distance within the Virginia border, had been
interrupted and rendered useless by the Confederates, but this gap was supplied by the
Chesapeake and Ohio Canal, which was open all
the way from Cumberland, Maryland, to George-
town, in the District of Columbia.

Jackson recommended a bold plan of operations to dispossess the enemy and recover the
territory that had been lost. He had seen how
his predecessors had been hampered in trying
to operate from Staunton westward, by the
difficult and inaccessible nature of the country.
On that route a wide belt of mountains, destitute of supplies and for the most part penetrated
by nothing but indifferent wagon roads, intervened between the scene of operations and the
Confederate base of supplies. This had proved
a most serious hindrance. Jackson proposed
now to move along the Baltimore and Ohio
railroad and the turnpikes parallel to it, and
thus enter Western Virginia from the north-
east. In this way he could turn the left flank
of the enemy's forces, place himself on their
communications, and force them to evacuate,
or fight under circumstances of his own selection.
This mode of approach, it was true, was far
more exposed to the enemy, but it was easier;
it lay through a much more populous and
cultivated region; it would afford, to some ex-

tent, the use of a railroad for supplies ; and it would soon place him in the midst of some of the most fertile parts of Western Virginia. To carry out this plan he asked that his old brigade, which had been left at Manassas, and all the forces operating along the line of the Alleghanies, south-west of Winchester, should be concentrated under his command. This would have given him fifteen or sixteen thousand (15,000 or 16,000) men, the least force with which he thought it possible to undertake so considerable an enterprise.

The Confederate authorities deemed it impossible to comply fully with his wishes. His own brigade was promptly sent to him, and one of the brigades of Loring's troops reached him early in December [3]. Subsequently two more brigades, under Gen. Loring himself, were added, but all these troops only increased the small force of two or three thousand State militia, which had been assembled in the district itself, to about eleven thousand (11,000) men [4]. The greater part of Gen. Loring's force did not arrive until Christmas, thus preventing any important movements during November and December.

But meantime Gen. Jackson was not idle. When he entered upon his new command there were but three fragmentary brigades of State militia and a few detached companies of cavalry in the Valley district. These troops were poorly armed, and the militia was almost entirely without discipline or experience. In order to

increase this force he first caused the militia
which had not yet been summoned, or which
had been released, to be called out, and in a
short time the brigades under Brig.-Gens. Carson, Meem, and Boggs were increased in the
aggregate to about three thousand (3000) men.
He consolidated the cavalry companies into a
regiment, under the command of Lieut.-Col.
Ashby. Prompt measures were taken to equip
and discipline these troops. About the middle
of November, the first brigade—his own—was
sent up from Manassas, and by December 1 he
had at hand some four thousand (4000) troops,
and knew that a part of Loring's command was
en route to join him [5].

While waiting for the reinforcements that
would enable him to strike a blow, he determined to annoy the enemy by preventing any
attempt to reconstruct the Baltimore and Ohio
railroad, and by doing such damage as was
possible to the Chesapeake and Ohio Canal,
which runs along the north bank of the Potomac.
For this purpose the cavalry was actively engaged in scouting the country along that river,
and early in December a small force of infantry
and a battery were sent down to break Dam
No. 5, seven miles above Williamsport, which
supplied a long level of the canal with water.
This force appeared at Dam No. 5 on the afternoon of December 6, and during the next two
days kept up an active skirmish with the
Federal troops on the north side of the river.
Under cover of this fire the Confederates

attempted to break the dam on the night of the 7th, but effected little or no damage. The next evening they retired. Not satisfied with the result, Jackson made another effort a few days later to break Dam No. 5. Taking the cavalry, a part of the militia, and his old brigade (" Stonewall "), he left Winchester on the 16th. Next day, having disposed troops between Falling Waters and Dam No. 5, so as to provide against a flank movement, and having sent forces to make demonstrations at Dam No. 4 and at Williamsport, he collected the main body for an attack on Dam No. 5. Under cover of the infantry and artillery stationed on the hills on the south side of the river, parties were sent to break away this dam at the end nearest the Virginia side. Col. Leonard, with a part of the Thirteenth Massachusetts, the Fifth Connecticut, and a battery, was guarding this part of the Federal line. He kept up a vigorous and annoying fire on the working parties. Not much was accomplished by the Confederates until Capt. Holliday,* of the Thirty-third Virginia, and Capt. Robinson, of the Twenty-seventh Virginia, volunteered to go down by night with their companies and cut out the cribs. They made brave efforts to do this, standing waist-deep in the cold water, and under the constant fire of the enemy. A partial breach was effected, and the cribs so loosened that the next freshet made a wide gap in the

* Afterwards colonel of the Thirty-third Virginia regiment, and subsequently Governor of Virginia.

dam, and rendered useless, for the time, a long stretch in the canal. While this attack was in progress several regiments were sent up from Frederick, Maryland, to reinforce Col. Leonard [6], and the short time in which the whole of Banks's command, at the latter place, could reach Williamsport, rendered it inadvisable for Jackson to cross the river. Having done all the damage he could to the canal from the south side, he withdrew on the 21st, and returned to Winchester.

While engaged in this expedition, news had come of the decisive repulse by Gen. Edward Johnson of the attack made by the Federals upon his position at Camp Alleghany. This occurred on December 13 [7]. Gen. Jackson advised that this force be now sent to reinforce him or be moved towards Moorefield so as to co-operate with him in an advance on Romney [8]. This was not done, and later in the winter Johnson was forced to fall back to the Shenandoah Mountain, to avoid the danger of a flank movement against him from Romney.

Jackson, soon after his return to Winchester, was gratified to meet Gen. Loring, the last two of whose brigades arrived there at Christmas.*

Gen. Loring, who was to retain command of his own troops and to be second to Jackson, had three infantry brigades, under Col. W. B. Taliaferro, Col. Wm. Gilham, and Brig.-Gen.

---

* Loring arrived December 26. The same day the Hon. C. J. Faulkner, but recently released from a northern prison, offered his services to Gen. Jackson, and was appointed aide-de-camp.

S. R. Anderson respectively, and Mayre's and Shumaker's batteries. These troops numbered nearly six thousand (6000), and increased Jackson's entire force to about eleven thousand (11,000) men.*

Jackson had now all the troops that his superiors thought it judicious to spare him. He had been most anxious to make an effort to recover Western Virginia from the Federals, but the force at hand was felt to be inadequate to so large an undertaking. The season, too, was so far advanced that a mountain campaign would be attended with very great difficulties. He, nevertheless, decided to persevere. An immediate movement was determined upon against the forces stationed within the limits of his military district. This district extended over the region bounded on the south-east by the Blue Ridge, on the north and north-east by the Potomac, from Harper's Ferry to its source, and on the north-west by the crest of the Alleghanies, until it joins the district recently commanded by Gen. Lee, and still held by the troops left there under Gen. Edward Johnson. He would first clear his own district of the foe, do all possible damage to the railroad and canal, and then be guided by circumstances. The preparations were hurried forward, and by the last day of the year all was in readiness to move. (Map No. I.)

* Jackson reports his strength on January 10 to Gen. J. E. Johnston as 10,178 infantry and 648 cavalry. He had also 26 pieces of artillery.

The forces and positions of the enemy opposed to Jackson at the beginning of 1862 were as follows : Gen. Banks, commanding the Fifth corps of McClellan's army, with headquarters at Frederick, Maryland, had sixteen thousand (16,000) effective men,* the greater part of whom were in winter quarters near that city, while the remainder guarded the Potomac from Harper's Ferry to Williamsport. Gen. Rosecrans, still holding command of the Department of Western Virginia, had twenty-two thousand (22,000) men scattered over that region,† but was concentrating them on the Baltimore and Ohio railroad. He says in his report ‡ : " On December 6, satisfied that the condition of the roads over the Alleghanies into Western Virginia, as well as the scarcity of subsistence and horse-feed, would preclude any serious operations of the enemy against us until the opening of spring, I began quietly and secretly to assemble all the spare troops of the department in the neighbourhood of the Baltimore and Ohio railroad, under cover of about five thousand men I had posted at Romney, with the design of obtaining Gen. McClellan's permission to take nearly all these troops and suddenly seize, fortify, and hold Winchester, whereby I should at once more effectually cover the north-eastern

* *See Federal Congressional Report on Conduct of the War, 1863, Part II. p. 414, Gen. Banks's testimony.*

† See same Report, Part I. p. 202, Rosecrans's testimony, given December 31, 1861.

‡ See *Report on Conduct of the War,* 1865, vol. iii. p. 14, of Rosecrans's campaigns.

and central parts of Western Virginia, and at
the same time threatening the left of the enemy's
position at Manassas, compel him to lengthen
his line of defence in front of the Army of the
Potomac, and throw it farther south. That I
might more fully lay my views before the
general commanding, I requested his permission
to visit him at Washington, whither I proceeded
about December 28, and found Gen. Mc-
Clellan sick of typhoid fever. Before an inter-
view could be had with him on the subject,
Stonewall Jackson, with a column of ten thousand men, began an advance in the direction of
Cumberland, which threatened such serious
consequences that, although ordered to send all
my troops to Gen. Lander and to remain per-
sonally idle, I was obliged to return to Wheeling
for the purpose of seeing this order executed,
and supplies and subsistence sent to Gen.
Lander."

The same plan of Federal operations was
urged by Gen. Lander, who, in his testimony
before the Committee on the Conduct of the
War, December 27, 1861, says : " I have also
stated to gentlemen high in authority that if I
could be furnished with three hundred pack-
mules and with five thousand men, with liberty
in the quartermaster's department to purchase
beef cattle, and to employ some of my old
mountaineers, so that I could move with celerity
—such men now being in this city—I would engage to penetrate the Blue Ridge mountains,
and endeavour to take the town of Winchester,

and break the northern branch of the Manassas Gap railway. In all these matters I rely fully and completely on the co-operation of Gen. Kelly, now at Romney." * A few days after this Gen. Lander was ordered to duty on the line of the Baltimore and Ohio railroad, and the troops at Hancock, Cumberland, and Romney, and the intermediate points, were placed under his command.

Such was the condition of affairs, and such the plans of his enemy, when, on January 1, 1862, Jackson set out from Winchester in the direction of Bath. With him were Garnett's (the " Stonewall ") brigade,† the three brigades under Gen. Loring,‡ a part of the militia, five batteries, and Ashby's regiment of cavalry, the whole numbering some eight or nine thousand (8000 or 9000) men. His movement disconcerted all plans for an aggressive campaign against Winchester, and threw his opponents on the defensive. By moving against Bath, and dispersing the force there and at Hancock, he hoped to destroy communications between Banks and Kelly, threaten the latter's rear, and force him to evacuate Romney or fight single-handed. The weather during December had been fine, and the roads were in good condition. The morning of New Year's day was bright and pleasant, and the army set forth in fine spirits.

* *Report on the Conduct of the War*, 1863, Part I. p. 160.

† Brig.-Gen. Richard B. Garnett had been assigned to the command of Jackson's old brigade.

‡ The troops brought by Loring were known as the " Army of the North-west."

But the fine weather was, unfortunately, of short duration. Before the evening of the first day a cold storm arrived from the north-west. This was the beginning of a violent and protracted spell of bad weather, which continued for the next three weeks, and interfered most seriously with the expedition. The second day was cold and stormy, and the wagons being delayed by difficult roads,—by-ways being selected to conceal the movement,—the troops passed the night without anything to eat,* and, in many cases, without covering. Next morning, when the wagons had caught up, a short time was allowed for cooking and eating, and the march was renewed. Snow and sleet during the latter part of the day added much to the discomfort of the soldiers, and rendered the roads so slippery that the wagons were again unable to keep up with the troops. The night of January 3 was passed in the midst of the storm, about four miles from Bath. A scouting party of the enemy had been dispersed and partly captured during the afternoon. Next morning, Saturday, January 4, as soon as it was possible, Gen. Jackson made his dispositions to surround the town. A detachment was sent over the mountain to the left, with orders to approach the place from the west. The main body pushed along the road, while a regiment was thrown forward on the right and another on the left of the village. But the troops moved

* The first night the army camped near Pughtown, the second at Unger's.

slowly. They were exhausted by the cold and suffering of the preceding night, the ground was covered with ice, and a large part of the day was consumed before the Confederates, headed by Col. Baylor, of the general's staff, dashed into the town. The enemy, after skirmishing for some hours, had retired hastily. The village had been held by a part of the Thirty-ninth Illinois regiment, with a squadron of cavalry and a section of artillery. These troops had been reinforced on the morning of the 4th by the Eighty-fourth Pennsylvania regiment from Hancock, and at mid-day the Thirteenth Indiana had arrived at Sir John's Run, on the cars, and had marched towards Bath. But in the presence of a large hostile force, Col. Murray, of the Eighty-fourth Pennsylvania, who was in command, decided not to wait for an attack. Under his orders the Thirteenth Indiana was turned back, and the Eighty-fourth Pennsylvania and the Illinois troops both retreated to Hancock, leaving the stores and camp equipage of the force that had been stationed at Bath to be captured. From Bath two principal roads lead to the Potomac, one in the direction of Hancock, which is about six miles distant, on the Maryland side of the river; the other, farther west, to Sir John's Run, a station on the Baltimore and Ohio railroad, which is only three miles away. A road, still farther to the west, leads to the Great Cacapon River, at the railroad bridge over that stream.

Finding the enemy gone, Jackson ordered an

immediate pursuit. With the main body of his command he pushed on towards Hancock, driving the rear of the retreating enemy over the river. Gilham's brigade was sent towards Sir John's Run, but did not succeed in inflicting any damage on the forces retreating by that route. The road led along the narrow and precipitous defile of Sir John's Run, where a few men were easily able to check Gilham's advance until dark, and after nightfall the Federals retreated over the river. Col. Rust, with the Third Arkansas and the Thirty-seventh Virginia regiments, and two guns, was sent to destroy the railroad bridge over the Great Cacapon. The guard made a stout resistance, but the next morning were driven off, and the bridge, railroad station, and telegraph were destroyed.

The main Confederate force bivouacked on the night of the 4th opposite Hancock. Next morning Jackson sent Col. Ashby to demand the surrender of that town, and in the event of a refusal, to give notice that two hours would be allowed for the removal of non-combatants before the Confederate batteries would open upon it. Gen. Lander had just arrived and assumed command at Hancock, and he refused to surrender, and prepared to resist until reinforcements could reach him. Jackson placed several pieces of artillery in position, and kept up a brisk cannonade during the remainder of the day, which he renewed on the morrow. Meantime, an effort was made to construct a bridge at a point two miles above, with the view of crossing to the Maryland side. But it was found that this work would consume several days, in which time Gen. Lander might be reinforced to such an extent as to render the movement impracticable [9]. Hence the Confederate leader, having freed this part of his district from the enemy, after destroying such of the captured stores as he could not carry off, left the vicinity of Hancock on the morning of the 7th and marched in the direction of Romney, the head of his column reaching Unger's Store the same evening.

This march was a trying one. The severity of the weather continued without abatement. The snow and sleet, under the tramp of the soldiers, soon became as smooth as glass, so that marching was painful and difficult, while the road was filled with the falling horses of the wagons and artillery, that were unable to stand on their smooth-shod feet. Numbers of horses were disabled and some killed by this day's march. The intense cold added to the suffering of the troops, and caused the bivouac on the night of January 7, 1862, to be long remembered by many of them. The privations endured began to cause discontent and murmuring, especially among the troops which had recently joined Jackson. It was impossible to continue the march until the horses had been rough-shod, and Jackson, though reluctant, was obliged to remain some days at Unger's for this purpose.

On the day that the Confederates retired
from Hancock, January 7, a portion of the
Federal force at Romney made a successful reconnaissance on the Winchester road.   Just east
of the North River, a branch of the Great
Cacapon, runs a high ridge, through which, at
a narrow and precipitous gap called Hanging
Rock, passes the main road from Winchester to
Romney. This point, distant about fifteen
miles from the latter place, was held by about
seven hundred militia and a section of artillery,
under Col. Munroe.*   On the night of the 6th,
Col. Dunning, of the Fifth Ohio, under orders
from Gen. Kelly, set out from Romney with a
portion of the Fourth, Fifth, Seventh, and
Eighth Ohio, Fourteenth Indiana, and First
Virginia regiments, five companies of cavalry,
and six pieces of artillery, in all about two
thousand (2000) men [10].   They reached the
vicinity of Hanging Rock about daylight, and,
having captured the Confederate pickets, took
the main body by surprise.   Col. Munroe's main
force was on the bluff to the north of the road.
The hill on the south was deemed inaccessible,
and so was left comparatively undefended.
Munroe's artillery, under Lieut. Cutshaw, commanded the road, and the advance was instructed to burn the bridge over North River
upon retiring.   Col. Dunning, however, pressed
forward so quickly and with such overwhelming

* The force consisted of 650 militia infantry, Capt. Sheets's
company of cavalry of 56 men, and 2 pieces of artillery and 30
men under Lieut. Cutshaw. (Jackson's letter to Gen. J. E.
Johnston, January 10.)

force, that he drove the Confederates away from the bridge and seized it before it was materially injured. Having crossed the stream, he deployed his force, and while he sent one regiment over the hill south of the road by an unfrequented path, and another along the road itself, he led another to attack Munroe's force on the north hill. The Confederates were soon overpowered, and, seeing themselves flanked, fled, to escape capture [11]. The two guns fell into the enemy's hands, with a part of the baggage of the troops and seven prisoners [12]. The Federal troops set fire to the private houses, mills, etc., in the vicinity, and then returned to Romney, burning many houses and killing much cattle on the way. Of this conduct a northern correspondent, writing from Romney at the time, says : " The burning of dwellings along the road was a piece of vandalism which should be punished with the death, not only of the men who did it, but of the officers who countenanced and encouraged it" [13].

Jackson got his troops all up and into camp at Unger's on Wednesday, the 8th. Here, while he rested, the teams were prepared for better service on the ice. He was not ready to move the main body until the morning of Monday, the 13th, when the march to Romney was resumed. While waiting, however, Gen. Meem, with part of his militia, was sent on the 10th towards Moorefield, and Gen. Carson towards Bath, for the purpose of distracting the enemy ; while Ashby, with a small force of cavalry, watched the movements of the Federal forces in Romney [14].   Meantime, Gen. Lander, who had been placed in command of all the Federal forces in this vicinity, evacuated Romney on the 10th, and fell back to the railroad at Patterson's Creek.   At this point he concentrated the troops from Hancock and Cumberland, as well as those from Romney and Springfield.   The advance of the Confederates camped for the night of the 13th near Slanesville, headquarters being at Sherrard's, at Bloomery Gap. Next day the march was continued through a cold and driving sleet.   Jackson and the advance entered Romney in the evening.   The retreating enemy had left some stores and equipage, which fell into his hands.   (Map No. I.)

On the 15th, the troops being all up, Jackson began to prepare for another forward movement.   At Cumberland [15] the Potomac, which approaches that town from the south-west, makes a sharp bend, and, though tortuous, pursues, after leaving it, a direction but little east of south until it receives the waters of Patterson's Creek.   At the latter point the Baltimore and Ohio railroad crosses the creek going westward on an extensive bridge, and a short distance up the river crosses the Potomac itself to the north bank, on which side it continues past Cumberland to New Creek, where it recrosses to the Virginia side.   The bridges over the Potomac were important and valuable structures, and the demolition of them would render the railroad useless from New Creek (now called Keyser) eastward. This Jackson desired to accomplish, and at the same time to do such damage as he could to the forces guarding them. As a first step he determined to destroy the bridge at New Creek, so as to break Lander's western communications and threaten his flank and rear. The " Stonewall " brigade and that of Col. Taliaferro were selected for this undertaking.

Now it was that a new difficulty confronted the Confederate leader, and forced him to relinquish for the time all further movements. The severe privations of the soldiers at Bath and Hancock had not been endured without murmuring ; the painful march to Unger's Store had not allayed the dissatisfaction, and that to Romney, in still more severe weather, had caused the discontent, especially in Gen. Loring's command, to become open and outspoken. Many men were in hospital from the effects of the exposure. It was commonly declared that the cold was more fatal than the enemy. A campaign at such a season, among inhospitable mountains, was pronounced madness. This feeling was not confined to the men. Many of the officers, under Jackson for the first time, sympathized with it, or did nothing to repress it. Rain and a partial thaw were converting the ice-bound roads into slush and mire. The sufferings of the march, now proposed, promised to be greater than those already endured. The result was that when Jackson was ready to set out he found the troops, and especially Taliaferro's brigade, so discontented, and opposition to further movements with the present roads and weather so wide-spread, as to render his proposed undertaking inexpedient. " With deep mortification and reluctance," * says his biographer, " he therefore relinquished further aggressive movements, and prepared to defend what he had already won."

In two weeks, and with trifling loss, he had placed the troops opposed to him, while preparing for an aggressive movement, upon the defensive ; had expelled them virtually from his whole district ; had liberated three counties from their rule, and secured the supplies in them for the subsistence of his own troops.

He now proceeded to place his army in winter quarters. Gen. Loring's three brigades, and thirteen pieces of artillery, were quartered around Romney ; Boggs's brigade of militia was spread along the South Branch of the Potomac, as far as Moorefield, and his pickets joined those of Gen. Edward Johnson on the Alleghany, while three companies of cavalry were left with Loring for outpost duty. Carson's brigade of militia was stationed at Bath ; Meem's brigade at and beyond Martinsburg ; and Ashby with the greater part of his cavalry regiment on the line of the Potomac. Garnett's brigade was ordered to Winchester to watch and oppose Banks, and to this place Gen. Jackson removed his own headquarters on January 24. He thus left the larger part of his

* Dr. Dabney.

force at Romney, where it could subsist from the rich valley of the South Branch, and where it would be in position to meet an advance of the enemy from the north-west, or be ready to take advantage of the return of good weather to resume the offensive. A line of telegraph from Winchester was to put Jackson in communication with Romney. Garnett's brigade was stationed at the former place that it might be at hand to resist any movement of Gen. Banks, who menaced his front from Harper's Ferry to Williamsport, or might go to the assistance of Loring, if circumstances required [16].

When Jackson returned to Winchester, on January 24, everything betokened some weeks of quiet, undisturbed by any important military movements. He was not aware, however, of the extent of the discontent excited among Gen. Loring's troops, and did not imagine that by leaving them at Romney this feeling would be increased. Yet such was the case. They complained bitterly of the campaign which had been conducted at the expense of so much suffering; a campaign now suspended, they said, only to leave *them* in an exposed and dangerous position, in the midst of an inhospitable mountain region, out of reach of adequate supplies and of timely succour. They declared their position untenable in case of an attack, and even attributed the removal of the " Stonewall " (Garnett's) brigade to Winchester to favouritism. Jackson, silent and reserved in manner, never taking counsel even with his next in command as to his plans, most rigid and exacting as a commander, had not yet acquired that wonderful control over his soldiers which a few months later would have rendered such murmuring impossible. Indeed, it is difficult to realize the feeling of distrust then manifested when we consider the unbounded enthusiasm and devotion with which many of these same men afterwards followed Jackson to victory and death.

As soon as the troops had gone into winter quarters furloughs were freely given, and in the course of a few days the complaints and criticisms which had become so rife at Romney were carried to Richmond, and were pressed upon the attention of the War Department. The Secretary was beset with accounts of what was termed Jackson's rash and ill-advised campaign, and his interference was most earnestly invoked in behalf of a gallant body of troops now, it was said, in danger of being overwhelmed in Romney by Gen. Lander's largely superior forces, whenever the latter should choose to make a dash at them from the Baltimore and Ohio railroad. The Secretary, far from the scene of operations, with no information as to the real state of the case, except such as reached him in the above way, and with little knowledge of Jackson's character and capacity, unfortunately yielded to the pressure brought upon him.

On January 31, just one week after his return to Winchester, Gen. Jackson received the following telegram from the Secretary of War:

" Our news indicates that a movement is making
to cut off Gen. Loring's command ; order him
back to Winchester immediately." This order
was sent without consultation with Gen. J. E.
Johnston, then in chief command in Virginia,
or with Gen. Jackson himself, and of course reflected upon the latter's judgment and capacity.
Gen. Jackson at once complied with the order,
at the same time ordering back Carson's militia
from Bath to Bloomery Gap, and directing the
troops on the left of Loring, in the South Branch
Valley, to fall back if the enemy should advance. He then wrote to the Secretary as
follows :

" HON. J. P. BENJAMIN, etc.

" SIR :—Your order, requiring me to direct
Gen. Loring to return with his command to
Winchester immediately, has been received and
promptly complied with.

" With such interference in my command I
cannot expect to be of much service in the field,
and, accordingly, respectfully request to be
ordered to report for duty to the Superintendent
of the Virginia Military Institute at Lexington,
as has been done in the case of other professors.
Should this application not be granted, I respectfully request that the President will accept
my resignation from the army.

" Respectfully, etc., your obed't servant,
" T. J. JACKSON."

This letter was forwarded through Gen. Johnston, to whose adjutant he at the same time

wrote : " The Secretary of War stated in the
order requiring Gen. Loring's command to fall
back to this place immediately that he had been
informed the command was in danger of being
cut off. Such danger, I am well satisfied, does
not exist, nor did it, in my opinion, exist at the
time the order was given, and I therefore respectfully recommend that the order be countermanded, and that Gen. Loring be required to
return with his command to the neighbourhood
of Romney."   But the Commander-in-Chief,
though concurring in Jackson's opinion of the
campaign, did not think it best to assume the
responsibility of giving the order, and all of
Loring's troops returned to the vicinity of
Winchester.*   In regard to the resignation, Gen.
Johnston detained it for a time, and wrote
urging Jackson to reconsider it [17].

On the same day Jackson wrote to Governor
Letcher as follows :

" WINCHESTER, *January* 31, 1862.

" GOVERNOR :—This morning I received an
order from the Secretary of War to order Gen.
Loring and his command to fall back from
Romney to this place immediately. The order
was promptly complied with ; but as the order
was given without consulting me, and is aban-
doning to the enemy what has cost much preparation, expense, and exposure to secure, and
is in direct conflict with my military plans, and
implies a want of confidence in my capacity to

* Dabney's *Life of Jackson.*

judge when Gen. Loring's troops should fall back, and is an attempt to control military operations in detail from the Secretary's desk at a distance, I have, for the reasons set forth in the accompanying paper, requested to be ordered back to the Institute, and if this is denied me, then to have my resignation accepted. I ask as a special favour that you will have me ordered back to the Institute.

" As a single order like that of the Secretary may destroy the entire fruits of a campaign, I cannot reasonably expect, if my operations are thus to be interfered with, to be of much service in the field. A sense of duty brought me into the field, and has thus far kept me. It now appears to be my duty to return to the Institute, and I hope that you will leave no stone unturned to get me there. If I have ever acquired, through the blessing of Providence, any influence over troops, this undoing of my work by the Secretary may greatly diminish that influence.

" I regard this recent expedition as a great success. Before our troops left here on the 1st instant, there was not, so far as I have been able to ascertain, a single loyal man in Morgan county who could remain at home in safety. In four days that county was entirely evacuated by the enemy. Romney and the most valuable portion of Hampshire county was recovered without firing a gun, and before we had even entered the county.

" I desire to say nothing against the Secretary

of War. I take it for granted that he has done what he believed to be best, but I regard such a policy as ruinous.

"Very truly, your friend,
"T. J. Jackson.
"His Excellency John Letcher, Gov. of Va."

The Governor says : "The Secretary of War received the General's resignation before the General's letter reached me, and having been informed of the fact by one of my aides, to whom Mr. Benjamin communicated it, I at once went to the War Department, and after some conversation between the Secretary and myself, it was agreed that no action should be taken until I should have an opportunity to write to Gen. Jackson and receive his reply. I accordingly went to my office and wrote him a long and earnest letter, informing him of what had taken place, and urging such reasons as I thought would induce him to remain in the field, and concluding with the request that he would sanction what I had done and permit me to withdraw his resignation. This letter was sent by my aide, Col. Boteler, and I was greatly gratified, on his return, to find that the General acceded to my wishes, and gave me his full consent to the withdrawal of his letter of resignation from the files of the War Department " [18].

CHAPTER II

KERNSTOWN

THE withdrawal of the Confederate troops from Romney was a surrender of whatever had been gained by the expedition, for it soon resulted in the reoccupation by the enemy of all the territory that had been recovered from him.

Various causes combined to prevent any further movement on the part of Gen. Jackson for some weeks. After the events narrated at the close of the last chapter it was deemed expedient to make some changes. Gen. Loring was ordered to a new command in the southwest, and all his troops that were not Virginians were gradually removed to the other wing of Gen. Johnston's army. This took away Anderson's brigade, composed of the First, Seventh, and Fourteenth Tennessee regiments, and the First Georgia and Third Arkansas from Taliaferro's, and left to Gen. Jackson, besides Garnett's brigade, Gilham's brigade (now commanded by Col. J. S. Burks) [19], composed of the Twenty-first, Forty-second, and Forty-eighth Virginia regiments, and the First battalion of regulars (commonly known as the Irish battalion), and the Twenty-third and Thirty-seventh Virginia regiments, under Col. Taliaferro. The militia commands had never been well organized, and they were now dwindling rapidly by details and enlistments in the volunteer forces [20]. In accordance with a law passed by the Confederate Congress to encourage re-enlistments, furloughs for thirty days were now given to those soldiers who re-enlisted, and a large number of men were permitted to be absent in this way. On February 7 orders were issued to authorize the giving of furloughs to re-enlisted men to the extent of one-third of the number present for duty. The diminution of his force from these causes would have kept Jackson inactive, even had not the condition of the roads, which broke up as soon as the weather moderated, put a stop to any important movements. The opening of an aggressive campaign by the Federal armies in Virginia, involving as it did an advance of the greatly superior force in his front, was soon to throw him on the defensive.

Gen. Lander, finding that the Confederates had withdrawn from Romney and the South Branch Valley, reoccupied the former place without opposition on February 7, and a few days later sent an expedition as far south as Moorefield. This party, under Col. Dunning, of the Fifth Ohio, met with no serious resistance, and brought off more than two hundred cattle. Work was busily resumed on the railroad, Gen. Carson having fallen back from Bath to Bloomery Gap, and by the 14th the bridge over the Great Cacapon was rebuilt, and the railroad open once more from the west to Hancock.

On this day Lander made a bold dash, with four hundred cavalry and several regiments of infantry, at the militia forces stationed at Bloomery. Leaving Paw-Paw on the evening of the 13th, he constructed, during the night, a temporary bridge of wagons over the Great Cacapon River, at a point about seven miles south of the railroad, and, crossing over, moved rapidly towards Bloomery, where he took Col. Sincindiver * by surprise. Leading the charge of his cavalry himself, Gen. Lander dashed in among the Confederates before they had fully formed, and captured some seventy-five prisoners, of whom seventeen were officers. The Confederates, rallying after their first panic, checked the Federals until the trains could be gotten away, when they retreated. The loss in killed and wounded was insignificant on both sides. On the same day a reconnaissance in force was made by Col. Carroll and two regiments of Federal infantry to Unger's Store. As soon as Jackson knew of this affair he ordered Ashby from Martinsburg, with what force he had at hand, to check the enemy. On the 16th, Col. Ashby drove out the detachment which Lander had left at Bloomery Gap, but the territory beyond remained in Federal possession, and this rendered the railroad secure from Hancock westward. Jackson ceased to give furloughs for the time, and took steps, by sending a detachment with boats to Castleman's Ferry, on the Shenandoah, to make good his

* Commanding in the absence of Gen. Carson.

communications with Gen. D. H. Hill, at Leesburg, on the eastern side of the Blue Ridge.
(Map No. I.) These precautions were taken
against the advance of the enemy in force, but
no further movements were made by Gen.
Lander. That gallant officer was soon disabled
by the effects of a wound received the preceding
fall, which had been aggravated by active service. He sank rapidly, and died at his headquarters at Paw-Paw on March 2.

The month of February wore on,—a month
filled with disasters to the Confederate cause.
On the 6th of that month Fort Henry, on the
Tennessee River, was captured ; on the 8th,
Roanoke Island, North Carolina, fell ; on the
12th, the Confederates evacuated Lexington,
Missouri ; and on the 15th, Bowling Green,
Kentucky. Fort Donelson, Tennessee, fell on
the 15th, Nashville on the 26th, and the evacuation of Columbus, Kentucky, was begun on the
27th. It was at this dark hour that Mr. Davis
was inaugurated at Richmond, on February 22,
as first President of the Confederate States.

Meantime, the Federal Administration was
pushing forward its preparations for the campaign against Richmond, and Gen. Johnston
was making his dispositions to meet them.
President Lincoln was anxious to attack Johnston in his position at Manassas, and, as part of
a general advance by all the Federal armies,
which he ordered to take place, on or before
February 22, he directed McClellan to advance
" with all the disposable force of the Army of

the Potomac, after providing safely for the defence of Washington," and seize the Orange
and Alexandria railroad in Johnston's rear.
This plan he abandoned, on the urgent representations of McClellan, and reluctantly adopted
that general's plan of operations, by way of
the lower Chesapeake and the York and James
Rivers.*   But before orders were issued to carry
out this last purpose, it was determined to send
Banks's and Lander's commands forward to
cover the rebuilding of the Baltimore and Ohio
railroad from Harper's Ferry to Hancock, and
to take and hold Winchester and Strasburg.
Measures were taken for this purpose about
February 20.   On the 24th, the advance guard
of Gen. Banks's column † occupied Harper's
Ferry, and a bateau bridge was soon laid across
the Potomac at that point.   Canal boats were
collected for a more permanent bridge, and on
the 26th Gen. McClellan went himself to Harper's Ferry to hasten the forward movement.
He had ordered up two of the brigades of Sedgwick's (late Stone's) division to reinforce Banks.
The first two brigades that arrived at Harper's
Ferry were thrown over on the 26th, and
orders were issued for the others to follow, when
an unforeseen difficulty caused the Federal
commander-in-chief to delay for the time the
contemplated movement.   The canal boats were

* This plan embraced the transfer of the Federal army by
water from the vicinity of Washington and Alexandria to Fort
Monroe, and its advance thence up the peninsula formed by the
York and James Rivers against Richmond.

† Banks had wintered at Frederick, Maryland.

found to be too wide to pass through the lock of the branch canal, which at this point was the only outlet to the river. The permanent bridge could not, therefore, be built at once, and a violent gale threatened the safety of the temporary one, which formed the only means of communication. " It was evident," says Gen. McClellan, " that the troops under orders would only be in the way should they arrive, and that it would not be possible to subsist them for a rapid march on Winchester. It was, therefore, deemed necessary to countermand the order, content ourselves with covering the re-opening of the railroad for the present, and in the meantime use every exertion to establish, as promptly as possible, depots of forage and subsistence on the Virginia side, to supply the troops and enable them to move on to Winchester, independently of the bridge. The next day (Friday, February 28) I sent a strong re-connaissance to Charlestown, and under its protection went there myself. I then determined to hold that place, and to move the troops composing Lander's and Williams's commands at once on Martinsburg and Bunker Hill, thus effectually covering the reconstruction of the railroad."

In accordance with these views Banks advanced slowly. Martinsburg was occupied on March 3, but it was the 6th before all of Lander's division (now under Gen. Shields, who had been sent to it upon Lander's death) were up and the Federals had occupied Bunker Hill and Smithfield [21].

Jackson wrote to Gen. J. E. Johnston on February 24 as follows: " General :—First Lieut. James K. Boswell, of the Provisional Engineers, is directed to report to me for duty. I have plenty of work for him, but if you desire additional fortifications constructed for the defence of Winchester, please state what shall be their character, and I will put him at work immediately after his arrival. The subject of fortifying is of such importance as to induce me to consult you before moving in the matter. If you think that this place will be adequately reinforced if attacked, then it appears to me that it should be strongly fortified. I have reason to believe that the enemy design advancing on this place in large force. The Seventh and Fourteenth Tennessee regiments left, *via* Snicker's Gap, for Manassas on the 22nd. The remaining part of Gen. Loring's command can move at any time, but I deem it prudent to detain them until other troops arrive, or until something further is heard from you respecting their marching. The Third Arkansas regiment left here on the 22nd, for the purpose of taking the cars at 7 A.M. this morning at Strasburg, *en route* for Fredericksburg. Gen. Holmes requested that the Seventh and Fourteenth Tennessee regiments should move to Manassas, where they should halt until they should receive orders to go to Evansport. I am making arrangements to construct, if possible, a raft bridge at Castleman's, so the troops at Leesburg and this place can co-operate with the least loss of time. If the two places were connected by telegraph several hours would be saved " [22].

But the retreat of the main Confederate army from the positions it had held since July, 1861, was about to begin. Gen. Johnston, after conference with President Davis, had begun the removal of stores and baggage on February 22. With the limited railroad facilities possessed by the Confederates, two weeks were not sufficient for the transportation of all the supplies that had been accumulated at and about Manassas, but Gen. Johnston did not think it prudent to delay longer. There were signs of activity among the Federal troops opposite his right, which led him to expect a movement by McClellan in the direction of Fredericksburg. The latter, under urgent pressure from President Lincoln, was really preparing to attack the Confederate batteries which partially blockaded the Potomac on Gen. Johnston's right. Johnston deemed that the time had come to place his army behind the Rappahannock, where he would be in position to meet a direct advance, or to oppose McClellan at Fredericksburg, should the Federal Army choose that route, or to reach Richmond quickly in case of an advance by the York or James Rivers. The movement was begun on the morning of March 7 by the withdrawal of Whiting from the lower Occoquan to Fredericksburg, and of D. H. Hill from Leesburg, by way of Warrenton, to the Rappahannock. The centre fell back from Centreville and Bull Run on the evening of the 9th, and on the 11th all the infantry and artillery were on the south side of Rappahannock.

Jackson, meanwhile, remained at Winchester, watching closely the advance of Banks, and doing what was possible to impede it. Gen. Johnston thus describes the duty assigned to him : " After it had become evident that the Valley was to be invaded by an army too strong to be encountered by Jackson's division, that officer was instructed to endeavour to employ the invaders in the Valley, but without exposing himself to the danger of defeat, by keeping so near the enemy as to prevent him from making any considerable detachment to reinforce McClellan, but not so near that he might be compelled to fight."

Jackson's command at this time consisted of Garnett's brigade (" Stonewall "), containing the Second, Fourth, Fifth, Twenty-seventh, and Thirty-third Virginia regiments ; Burks's brigade, containing the Twenty-first, Forty-second, and Forty-eighth Virginia regiments, and First battalion of regulars (Irish) ; and Fulkerson's brigade, containing the Twenty-third and Thirty-seventh Virginia regiments. These brigades were now numbered in order,—First, Second, and Third brigades of the Army of the Valley. There were five batteries of artillery and Ashby's regiment of cavalry. Jackson's entire force amounted to about four thousand six hundred (4600) effective men, exclusive of some remnants of the militia brigades, distri-

buted at various points in his district [23].
Gen. Banks had his own division, under Williams,
and Shields's (late Lander's) troops now incorporated in his corps, and also the three brigades
of Sedgwick.   On April 1 the strength of Banks's
corps (Fifth), embracing Shields, is given by
Gen. McClellan as twenty-three thousand three
hundred and thirty-nine (23,339), including
three thousand six hundred and fifty-two (3652)
cavalry, and excluding two thousand one hundred (2100) railroad guards.*   Sedgwick's division [24], which was with him in the advance on
Winchester, must have increased his force to
more than thirty thousand (30,000) men.

Jackson sent his stores, baggage, and sick to
the rear, but continued to hold his position at
Winchester to the last moment.   This town lies
in the midst of an open country, and is easily
turned on every side.   Nevertheless, the Confederate commander ordered the fortifications
to be repaired as soon as the movements of the
enemy indicated an advance in his direction.
Banks, as stated, occupied Charlestown on
February 26, and made reconnaissances on the
different roads leading to and around Winchester.   But it was not until March 7 that
his advance reached Stephenson's depot, four
miles from Winchester.   Jackson awaited him,
drawn up in line of battle, on the plain in front
of his fortifications, and between the Berryville
and Martinsburg roads.   The Federals did not

* McClellan's report, in *Rebellion Record*, p. 546, vol. i.,
Supplement.

attack, but withdrew to Charlestown. The
activity of Ashby's cavalry, and the boldness
with which Jackson maintained his position,
impressed his adversary with the conviction
that the Confederate force was much greater
than it was in reality.   No attack was made by
the wary enemy, and no opportunity afforded
of making a dash at some exposed position of
his advance. The Federal left was pushed
gradually forward, as if to envelop Jackson,
and on the 11th occupied Berryville.   Sedgwick's
division was thrown forward to this point.
(Map No. I.)

Excellent roads lead from Berryville to Winchester, and to Newtown and other points in
rear of Winchester. It was no longer safe for
the Confederate leader to hold his position.
The enemy at Berryville was already on his
flank, only ten miles distant, and could easily
reach his rear.   He again drew up his little force,
however, north of the town, to meet the advance of the main body of Banks's force from
the direction of Smithfield and Charlestown,
and remained under arms all day ; but, though
the enemy came on to within four miles of Winchester, they did not attack.   Late in the afternoon Jackson reluctantly withdrew, and after
night followed his trains, which had already been
sent forward to Kernstown and Newtown [25].
The indefatigable Ashby covered the rear, and
Banks occupied the town on the morning of
the 12th.   The same day the main body of the
Confederates reached Strasburg, distant eighteen

miles from Winchester, where they halted until the 15th. Banks sent forward Shields's division, which, on the 19th, entered Strasburg, and Jackson fell back before it to Woodstock and Mount Jackson, the former place being twelve and the latter twenty-four miles south-west of Strasburg. (Map No. I.)

The antagonism between Gen. McClellan and the Federal Administration that ultimately resulted in the removal of the former from command, assumed definite shape soon after the entrance of Mr. Stanton upon his duties as Secretary of War, in January, 1862. As a consequence, there was much vacillation about the movements of the Federal Army of the Potomac. McClellan strongly urged the plan of campaign by way of the Peninsula, with Fortress Monroe as a base. President Lincoln refused to approve, then gave his consent, then half withdrew it by loading down the proposed movement with conditions to be first fulfilled. Gen. Johnston's retirement from Manassas relieved the Federal Administration, in some degree, of its apprehensions in regard to Washington, and induced an acquiescence for the time in McClellan's plans. The following extracts from McClellan's report show the Federal plans at this time : *

" HEADQUARTERS ARMY OF POTOMAC.
" FAIRFAX COURT-HOUSE, *March* 13, 1862.

" A council of the generals commanding army

* McClellan's report, pp. 531, etc., *Rebellion Record*, vol. i., Supplement.

corps, at the headquarters of the Army of the Potomac, were of the opinion—

" I. That the enemy having retreated from Manassas to Gordonsville, behind the Rappahannock and Rapidan, it is the opinion of the generals commanding army corps that the operations to be carried on will be best undertaken from Old Point Comfort, between the York and James Rivers. *Provided :*

" 1st. That the enemy's vessel Merrimac can be neutralized.

" 2nd. That the means of transportation sufficient for an immediate transfer of the force to its new base can be ready at Washington and Alexandria to move down the Potomac ; and

" 3rd. That a naval auxiliary force can be had to silence, or aid in silencing, the enemy's batteries on the York River.

" 4th. That the force to be left to cover Washington shall be such as to give an entire feeling of security for its safety from menace. (Unanimous.)

" II. If the foregoing cannot be, the army should then be moved against the enemy behind the Rappahannock at the earliest possible moment, and the means for reconstructing bridges, repairing railroads, and stocking them with materials sufficient for supplying the army should at once be collected, for both the Orange and Alexandria and the Acquia and Richmond railroads. (Unanimous.)

" N.B.—That with the forts on the right bank of the Potomac fully garrisoned, and those on the left bank occupied, a covering force in front of the Virginia line of twenty-five thousand men would suffice. (Sumner.)

" This was assented to by myself, and immediately communicated to the War Department. The following reply was received the same day :

" ' WAR DEPARTMENT, *March* 13, 1862.

" ' The President having considered the plan of operations agreed upon by yourself and the commanders of army corps, makes no objection to the same, but gives the following directions as to its execution :

" ' 1st. Leave such forces at Manassas Junction as shall make it entirely certain that the enemy shall not repossess himself of that position and line of communication.

" ' 2nd. Leave Washington entirely secure.

" ' 3rd. Move the remainder of the force down the Potomac, choosing a new base at Fortress Monroe, or anywhere between here and there ; or, at all events, move such remainder of the army at once in pursuit of the enemy by some route.

" ' EDWIN M. STANTON, Secretary of War.
" ' MAJ.-GEN. GEORGE B. MCCLELLAN.' "

For the purpose of leaving Washington secure, the defences of that city were well manned, and the command of them given to Gen. Wadsworth, and the following instructions were sent to Gen. Banks :

" Headquarters Army of Potomac,
" *March* 16, 1862.

" Sir :—You will post your command in the vicinity of Manassas, intrench yourself strongly, and throw cavalry pickets out to the front.

" Your first care will be the rebuilding of the railway from Washington to Manassas and to Strasburg, in order to open your communications to the Valley of the Shenandoah. As soon as the Manassas Gap railway is in running order, intrench a brigade of infantry, say four regiments, with two batteries, at or near the point where the railway crosses the Shenandoah. Something like two regiments of cavalry should be left in that vicinity to occupy Winchester, and thoroughly scour the country south of the railway and up the Shenandoah Valley, as well as through Chester Gap, which might, perhaps, be advantageously occupied by a detachment of infantry ; well-intrenched blockhouses should be built at all the railway bridges. Occupy, by grand guards, Warrenton Junction and Warrenton itself, and also some little more advanced point on the Orange and Alexandria railroad, as soon as the railway bridge is repaired.

" Great activity should be observed by the cavalry. Besides the two regiments at Manassas, another regiment of cavalry will be at your disposal to scout towards the Occoquan, and probably a fourth towards Leesburg.

" To recapitulate : the most important points which should engage your attention are as follows :

" 1st. A strong force, well intrenched, in the vicinity of Manassas, perhaps even Centreville, and another force (a brigade), also well intrenched, near Strasburg.

" 2nd. Block-houses at the railway bridges.

" 3rd. Constant employment of the cavalry well to the front.

" 4th. Grand guards at Warrenton Junction, and in advance as far as the Rappahannock, if possible.

" 5th. Great care to be exercised to obtain full and early information as to the enemy.

" 6th. The general object is to cover the line of the Potomac and Washington.

" The above is communicated by command of Maj.-Gen. McClellan.

" S. Williams, A.A.G.

" Maj.-Gen. N. P. Banks, Com. Fifth Corps, Army of Potomac."

In compliance with these instructions, Shields' division was recalled from Strasburg, and Williams's division began its movement towards Manassas on March 20. The Confederate force in front was known to be so small that no difficulty was anticipated in carrying out McClellan's instructions, and no apprehensions were entertained that the force designated by him would not be sufficient to hold the lower Valley and " cover the line of the Potomac."

On the evening of March 21, Col. Ashby, who for several days had been vigorously skirmishing with the enemy between Strasburg and

Woodstock, reported that they had evacuated the former place; and Jackson, apprehensive that this indicated their withdrawal from his military district in the direction of Washington, determined at once to pursue with all his available force. Fulkerson's brigade, which was at Woodstock, marched at dawn on the 22nd, and at the same time Garnett's (" Stonewall ") and Burks's brigades left Mount Jackson. The whole camped at Strasburg on the evening of the 22nd. Ashby had followed the retreating enemy on Friday night, 21st, and on Saturday, 22nd, came up with the Federal pickets about one mile south of Winchester. He attacked about 5 P.M., and drove them in. Gen. Banks was still in Winchester, and, though the last of Williams's division had left early on the morning of the 22nd on the way to Manassas, the Second division, under Shields, was still in the place. This command was ordered under arms, and an infantry brigade and two batteries of artillery and some cavalry were sent out on the Strasburg road to meet Ashby. The latter, who had from two hundred to three hundred cavalry and Chew's battery of three guns, after a brief skirmish, retired to Kernstown, three miles south of Winchester, where he took position for the night. The enemy, having repelled the Confederate cavalry, did not pursue. In the skirmish Gen. Shields was struck by a piece of shell, which fractured his arm and disabled him for a time for service on the field. Gen. Shields says that in this affair he concealed his troops

as much as possible from the Confederates,* and
the impression of the smallness of his force thus
produced was confirmed by the information
obtained within his lines by Col. Ashby. Report was brought to the latter not only that the
mass of the northern troops had left, but that
only four regiments of infantry remained, and
that these were under orders to march to
Harper's Ferry in the morning. This information, transmitted to Gen. Jackson, induced the
latter to hurry forward the next day.

During the night Gen. Shields made his dispositions to resist any further attack, by sending forward Kimball's brigade and Daum's
artillery on the Strasburg road, nearly to Kernstown. Sullivan's brigade was posted in rear of
Kimball's, within supporting distance of it,
covering all the approaches to Winchester by
way of the Cedar Creek, Front Royal, Berryville,
and Romney roads. Tyler's brigade and Broadhead's cavalry were held in reserve. The effective
strength of his whole force Gen. Shields puts
at seven thousand (7000) [26].

But though these precautions were taken, the
Federal commanders did not expect an attack.
The force under Jackson was known to be so
greatly inferior to their own that they did not
think he would risk a battle so far from support
as was Winchester from the position occupied
by Gen. Johnston, behind the Rappahannock
and Rapidan. On the morning of the 23rd a
Federal reconnaissance was made, of which Gen.

* Gen. Shields's report.

Shields says : " Not being able to reconnoitre the front in person, I despatched an experienced officer, Col. J. T. Mason, of the Fourth Ohio Volunteers, about 9 o'clock A.M., to the front to perform that duty, and to report to me as promptly as possible every circumstance that might indicate the presence of the enemy. About an hour after, Col. Mason returned, and reported to me that he had carefully reconnoitred the country in front and on both flanks, and found no indications of any hostile force, except that of Ashby. I communicated this information to Maj.-Gen. Banks, who was then with me, and, after consulting together, we both concluded that Jackson could not be tempted to hazard himself so far away from his main support. Having both come to this conclusion, Gen. Banks took his departure for Washington, being already under orders to that effect. The officers of his staff, however, remained behind, intending to leave for Centreville in the afternoon." *

Jackson, on the other hand, knowing that a large body of Federal troops had left Winchester, and were marching in the direction of Manassas and Centreville, and believing, from the information received through Col. Ashby, that the force remaining in Winchester was much smaller than was actually the case, determined to lose no time in attacking the latter, that he might thereby produce a recall of the troops sent off. At daylight on Sunday morning (23rd) he sent

* Gen. Shields's report, *Rebellion Record*, vol. iv.

forward three companies of the Second Virginia regiment and one of the Twenty-seventh Virginia, under Capt. Nadenbousch, as an infantry support to Col. Ashby, and soon after moved forward with his whole force in the direction of Kernstown. The distance to be marched was fourteen miles, and it was ten o'clock in the forenoon before the advance under Nadenbousch reached Ashby, and 1 P.M. when the main Confederate force reached the vicinity of Kernstown. Col. Mason's report to Gen. Shields of the condition of affairs at 9 A.M. was therefore perfectly correct, for at that time Jackson was still miles away.

When Jackson reached Kernstown his troops were very weary. Three-fourths of them had the day before marched from the neighbourhood of Mount Jackson to Strasburg, a distance of twenty-two miles, to which had been added the march of fourteen miles from the latter place to Kernstown. He therefore gave directions for bivouacking, and says : " Though it was very desirable to prevent the enemy from leaving the Valley, yet I deemed it best not to attack until morning." He continues : " But subsequently, ascertaining that the Federals had a position from which our forces could be seen, I concluded that it would be dangerous to postpone the attack until the next day, as reinforcements might be brought up during the night." *

Meantime, Ashby had been actively skirmish-

* Jackson's report.

ing with the enemy. He had opened on them
near the Strasburg turnpike with Chew's battery, and when Nadenbousch arrived he pushed
forward the infantry companies under the latter
to drive back the Federal skirmishers and
protect the guns. For a little time Ashby advanced, and Nadenbousch drove the enemy's
skirmishers before him. But Col. Kimball, who
commanded the First brigade of Shields's division, and as senior Federal officer commanded
on the field in the absence of Gen. Shields, soon
made his dispositions to counteract this movement of Ashby by sending forward the Eighth
Ohio and two companies of the Sixty-seventh
Ohio as skirmishers, on both sides of the turnpike. He supported them on the right by
Jenks's battery, posted on a hill to the west of
the village of Kernstown and on the left by the
whole of Sullivan's brigade (the second of
Shields's division), with several batteries so
disposed as to protect that flank. Of course
this force soon checked Ashby and compelled
him to retire. When he had fallen back some
four or five hundred yards, he was informed of
the arrival of the main body of the Confederates,
and received orders to prepare for an advance
upon the Federal position, the special duty
assigned him being to " threaten the front and
right " (Federal left). At the same time a part
of his cavalry regiment, under Maj. Funsten,
was detached to operate on the other flank
(left) of the Confederate army. This detachment
was subsequently increased until it amounted

to one hundred and forty men, which left with Ashby only one hundred and fifty cavalry. (Map No. II.)

Jackson's infantry force consisted of the First ("Stonewall") brigade, now under Gen. Garnett, comprising five regiments, and of the Second, now under Col. Burks, comprising three regiments and one battalion, and of the Third brigade, under Col. Fulkerson, comprising only two regiments. The Forty-eighth Virginia regiment, of Burks's brigade, was acting as train-guard, and was not on the field during the battle. All these regiments were much reduced by the absence of re-enlisted men still on furlough, and of those who had fallen out of ranks in the severe two days' march. The number present on the afternoon of the battle was: of infantry, three thousand and eighty-seven (3087), of which two thousand seven hundred and forty-two (2742) were engaged; of artillery, twenty-seven (27) pieces, of which eighteen (18) were engaged; and of cavalry, two hundred and ninety (290) [27]. Gen. Shields, as above, states his force of all arms at seven thousand (7000) [28].

A high ridge lies just beyond the western limits of Winchester, and extends for some miles in both a north-east and a south-west direction from the town. After breaking one mile from the town to let through Abram's Creek, it continues in the south-west direction without serious interruption for six miles, until it is again broken by the valley of the Opequon

Creek, at J. S. McGill's. The Strasburg or
" Valley " turnpike runs not far from the
eastern foot of this ridge to a toll-gate about
two miles south-west of Winchester. At that
point the Cedar Creek turnpike branches off
to the right, and, pursuing a more westerly
direction, soon crosses this ridge at a depression
on J. N. Bell's farm. The main or Strasburg
road, gradually separating from the ridge, continues nearly due south to Kernstown and some
distance beyond, when it again bends to the
south-west. To the west of the last-named
village a considerable elevation, known as Pritchard's Hill, intervenes between the turnpike
and ridge, affording a good position for artillery.
A short distance south of the toll-gate, where
the Cedar Creek road leaves the Valley turnpike, a common dirt road also leaves it, on the
same side but at a less angle. This road,
known as the Middle, or old Cedar Creek road,
runs along the eastern face of the ridge spoken
of, crossing the little spurs that jut out from
it, and passes between Pritchard's Hill and the
ridge, but does not cross the latter. It passes
through the ridge at the gap made by the
Opequon Valley. Several country roads or
lanes connect the " Middle " road with the
Valley turnpike on the one hand, and with the
Cedar Creek turnpike on the other. The most
important of them is one leading from Kernstown over the very crest of the ridge into the
valley beyond, and thence to the Cedar Creek
turnpike. The ridge we speak of commands the

Strasburg road from Kernstown to Winchester.
A level country extends eastward from this last-
named road and gradually falls away towards
the Opequon. (Map No. II.)

Jackson, upon his arrival, found the enemy
in full force of artillery and infantry upon both
sides of the Strasburg road, with guns posted
also above Kernstown, on Pritchard's Hill. The
enemy's position in front was good, and Ashby's
operations had induced him to guard so heavily
his left flank, east of the turnpike, that no
favourable opportunity was there offered for
attack. Jackson therefore determined to seize the
main ridge, turn the enemy's right flank resting
on it, and thus render his whole line untenable.
He left Col. Burks's brigade with Ashby on the
turnpike, to support the latter and to act as
reserve, while he led Fulkerson's brigade and
part of Carpenter's battery towards the left.
When near Opequon Church [29], Carpenter
halted and fired a few rounds at the enemy on
Pritchard's Hill. He then followed the infantry
farther to the left, under a heavy shelling from
the Federal batteries, * until the high ground
was reached. Garnett's brigade was made to
follow. Having found a favourable position for
artillery, Jackson sent for the remainder of
Carpenter's, and also for McLaughlin's and
Waters's batteries, supported by a portion of
Col. Burks's brigade. Jackson directed Ashby

* Col. Fulkerson speaks of this shelling as very heavy. The
remaining infantry were ordered to the ridge by a route more
to the rear and less exposed to the Federal guns. (Map No. II.)

to keep up a continuous demonstration on the turnpike, and now opened vigorously on the left with his batteries. These were located along the ridge, parallel to its general direction, and engaged the Federal batteries to the east and north-east of them, forcing the enemy to withdraw. The Twenty-seventh Virginia (Col. John Echols) and the Twenty-first Virginia (Col. J. M. Patton) were thrown forward as skirmishers in advance of the artillery, and soon became hotly engaged. The Thirty-seventh and Twenty-third Virginia regiments, under Col. Fulkerson, then moved forward on the left of Echols, and, in the face of a heavy musketry fire, occupied a stone fence which ran down the west side of the ridge. This fence ran along the southern edge of a narrow, rocky field, on the northern side of which was a large body of woods. The position of Fulkerson, perpendicular to the direction of the ridge, was nearly at right angles to the line of batteries that constituted the Confederate right wing. Echols and Patton, who were quickly supported by the Thirty-third, Second, and Fourth Virginia regiments, of Garnett's brigade, and the Irish battalion, held the centre, which constituted an angle, since the line did not continue down the east side of the ridge, but having reached the crest was turned back along the top. The Confederate line was thus wedge-shaped : the artillery constituting the right arm, Fulkerson's brigade the left, and four of Garnett's with two of Burks's regiments occupying the centre, to the north-west of the crest of the ridge, and facing, for the most part in the same direction as Fulkerson's. (Map No. II.)

The movements of the Confederates and the fire of their batteries had revealed to Col. Kimball the danger to which his right wing was exposed, and he had taken prompt steps to counteract the threatened onset. Tyler's brigade had reached the toll-gate at the junction of the Cedar Creek and Strasburg roads about 2 P.M., and was waiting there in reserve. This force (composed of the Seventh and Twenty-ninth Ohio, First Virginia, Seventh Indiana, and One Hundred and Tenth Pennsylvania) was ordered to reinforce the Federal right, and to throw itself upon the Confederate left flank. The movement was promptly executed. On its success depended the day, for it was justly feared by Col. Kimball that his right would not be able to sustain the attack of Jackson. Tyler moved out on the Cedar Creek road to the point where that road crosses the ridge, when he left the road and moved rapidly along the crown and both faces of the ridge itself until he reached the battle-field. This he did by 3.30 P.M., which was just when Jackson had sent forward his infantry to flank the Federal right. Tyler at once led his troops to the attack, his right opposite to Fulkerson. A vigorous onset was made against the Confederate line, but it was everywhere repulsed. Fulkerson had just occupied the position behind the stone fence already mentioned. when he was attacked by two Federal regiments attempting to seize the same cover. His fire at close quarters was so severe that the Federal regiments broke, and one of them, the One Hundred and Tenth Pennsylvania, did not recover during the day. The remainder of the Federal line, however, soon rallied and renewed the attack, and a fierce and sanguinary conflict raged, especially along the Confederate centre. A second attempt to turn Fulkerson's left flank was defeated, and the heat of the battle was concentrated on Garnett's part of the line. For two hours the roar of the musketry and artillery was incessant. " Here the struggle became desperate, and for a short time doubtful," says Gen. Shields. Reinforcements drawn from the Federal left, now that it had become evident that the main attack was against the other flank, were rapidly hurried forward to Tyler. The Fifth and Sixty-second Ohio and Thirteenth Indiana, of Sullivan's brigade, Fourteenth Indiana and Eighty-fourth Pennsylvania, and seven companies of the Sixty-seventh Ohio, and three companies of the Eighth Ohio, of Kimball's brigade, went to his assistance, and with these fresh troops a new and more vigorous attack was made on the Confederate position.

Meantime, Jackson was using every effort to make headway against this force, so much larger than he had believed within reach, and so much greater than his own. His thinned and tired regiments were incited to hold on stubbornly to the advantage gained. The places of the fallen were quickly taken by others, and when the ammunition of some was expended they borrowed from those who yet had it. The Fifth Virginia, which had been left in reserve, and the Forty-second Virginia were ordered up, and a messenger was sent back to the train to hurry forward the Forty-eighth, that the last man might be thrown into the wavering scale. But before these slight reserves arrived the onset of Tyler, strengthened as he was by six additional regiments, had staggered the Confederate line and caused it to waver. Gen. Garnett, who was bearing the brunt of the attack, felt that his thinned lines could not longer maintain their position without risk of being overwhelmed. He therefore gave the order to fall back. This order was not known to Jackson, who was at the time on a different part of the field, and he bitterly regretted it, always maintaining that his troops could have held their positions until the reserves had gotten up. The Confederate left wing was easily able from its position behind the stone fence to maintain itself, but the retirement of Garnett involved the retreat of Fulkerson, whose right and rear were thus exposed. The withdrawal had to be effected in the face of a comparatively powerful enemy, and was an operation of difficulty and danger [30]. Gen. Garnett met the Fifth Virginia coming to his assistance, but ordered it back. Jackson, seeing the danger now impending, stopped this regiment as soon as he saw it filing to the rear, and placed it in position in a piece of woods

behind his former position, and ordered the retreating infantry to form upon it. Soon Col.
Burks, with the Forty-second regiment, came up
on the right of Col. William H. Harman, of the
Fifth. In the midst of the fight some guns had
been advanced to assist the infantry ; these
were now placed near the right of the Forty-
second regiment, and these two regiments, with
the artillery, made for a time a vigorous resistance to the advancing enemy, and gave the
retreating troops time to rally and the remainder
of the artillery time to withdraw. Twice were
the attacks on their position repulsed ; but the
advancing Federals, spreading out on both
flanks, pressed back the Fifth and Forty-second
regiments, and finally forced them from the
field [31].

It was now night, and the Federals had full
possession of the field of battle. They picked
up two or three hundred prisoners from the
Confederates as the latter fell back, and also
two guns, both of which had been disabled.
The mass of the Confederates marched by way
of Shady Elm factory to Bartonsville, on the
turnpike. Maj. Funsten checked the Federal
cavalry, and soon all pursuit was abandoned.
Jackson, having reached the Valley turnpike,
fell back five or six miles slowly and sullenly to
his trains, which had been parked a short distance south of Newtown.

The loss of the Confederates in the battle of
Kernstown was eighty killed, three hundred and
forty-two wounded (of whom about seventy

were left on the field), and two hundred and sixty-nine missing ; total, six hundred and, ninety-one (691) [32]. Two pieces of artillery, disabled and left on the field, were captured. In regard to the Federal loss, Gen. Shields says in his report, dated six days after the battle : " The killed and wounded in this engagement cannot even yet be accurately ascertained. Indeed, my command has been so overworked that it has had but little time to ascertain anything. The killed, as reported, are one hundred and three, and among them we have to deplore the loss of the brave Col. Murray, of the Eighty-fourth Pennsylvania Volunteers, who fell at the head of his regiment while gallantly leading it in the face of the enemy. The wounded are four hundred and forty-one, many of them slightly, and the missing are twenty-four."* This gives a total of five hundred and sixty-eight (568).

Next day the citizens of Winchester, headed by Philip Williams, Esq., asked and obtained permission to bury the Confederate dead. The troops from that town were mostly in Jackson's command, and its people began a long series of noble deeds, destined to glorify the great struggle, by tenderly laying to rest, where they fell, the soldiers who at Kernstown had died for their country [33].

Jackson firmly believed that his failure was needlessly brought about by the retirement of Gen. Garnett. The retreat of the latter he

* Shields's report, *Rebellion Record*, vol. iv. p. 330.

considered ill-timed, and a fatal mistake. So strong was his conviction on this point that, notwithstanding the fact that the regimental officers of Garnett's brigade supported their brigade commander, he soon after removed Garnett, and preferred charges against him [34].

Weary and dispirited was the little army which had marched fourteen miles in the morning, had attacked a force more than double its own, and for three hours had wrestled for victory in a most vigorous fashion. Baffled and overpowered, it slowly retraced its path for six miles and sank to rest. In the fence-corners, under the trees, and around the wagons they threw themselves down, many too weary to eat, and forgot, in profound slumber, the trials, dangers, and disappointments of the day. Jackson shared the open-air bivouac with his men, and found the rest that Nature demanded on some fence-rails near the road [35]. Next morning he crossed to the south side of Cedar Creek, and gradually retired before the advancing enemy, once more, to Mount Jackson.

The bold attack of Jackson at Kernstown, though unsuccessful, led to many important results. Its first effect was the accomplishment of one of the principal objects of the Confederates,—the recall of the Federal troops then marching from the Valley towards Manassas. Gen. Shields says: " Though the battle had been won, still I could not have believed that Jackson would have hazarded a decisive engagement, so far from the main body, without expecting reinforcements ; so, to be prepared for such a contingency, I set to work during the night (after the battle) to bring together all the troops within my reach. I sent an express after Williams's division, requesting the rear brigade, about twenty miles distant, to march all night and join me in the morning. I swept the posts and routes in my rear of almost all their guards, hurrying them forward by forced marches, to be with me at daylight. . . . Gen. Banks, hearing of our engagement on his way to Washington, halted at Harper's Ferry, and with remarkable promptitude and sagacity, ordered back Williams's whole division, so that my express found the rear brigade already *en route* to join us. The General himself returned here forthwith, and, after making me a hasty visit, assumed command of the forces in pursuit of the enemy.* This pursuit was kept up with vigour, energy, and activity until they reached Woodstock." Thus the design of McClellan to put Banks's corps at Centreville (see letter of March 16) became impracticable, and that body of twenty thousand troops † was thought necessary to guard against the further movements of Jackson's three thousand and the reinforcements, in large part imaginary, which they attributed to him. This battle, too, no doubt decided the question of the detachment of Blenker's

---

* Gen. Banks, on the 24th, requested Sedgwick, who was leaving the Valley, to remain at Harper's Ferry some hours longer with his troops.

† McClellan's report, p. 546.

division of ten thousand men from McClellan, and its transfer to Fremont, recently placed in command of the Mountain Department [36]. While *en route* from Alexandria to Fremont, Blenker's division was to join Banks, and remain with him as long as he thought any attack from Jackson impending [37]. More important and more fraught with momentous consequences was the next step. For a few days later the sensitiveness of the Federal Government to the danger of Washington, excited by Jackson, led to the detachment of McDowell's corps from McClellan, and its retention in front of the Federal capital in place of that of Banks. When McClellan left, on April 1, for Fortress Monroe, to take command of his army on its advance up the Peninsula towards Richmond, he left for the defence of Washington and its approaches seventy-three thousand four hundred and fifty-six (73,456) men and one hundred and nine (109) field guns.* These were distributed as follows : †

At Warrenton, Virginia .	7,780
At Manassas . . .	10,859
In the Shenandoah Valley (including Blenker) . .	35,467
On the Lower Potomac .	1,350
In Washington and the forts around it . . .	18,000

* To these McClellan adds 4000 new troops organizing in New York, and whom he recommends should be brought to Washington at once.

† McClellan's report, p. 546.

Yet the Federal President, after Kernstown, did
not consider his capital secure, and on April 3
countermanded the order for the embarkation
of McDowell's corps, and detained it in front
of Washington. In a letter to Gen. McClellan
of April 9, President Lincoln says : " Gen.
Banks's corps, once designed for Manassas Junction, was divided and tied up on the line of
Winchester and Strasburg, and could not leave
it without again exposing the Upper Potomac
and the Baltimore and Ohio railroad. This
presented (or would present, when McDowell
and Sumner should be gone, a great temptation
for the enemy to turn back from the Rappahannock and sack Washington. My explicit
directions that Washington should, by the judgment of all the commanders of corps, be left
entirely secure, had been entirely neglected. It
was precisely this that drove me to detain Mc-
Dowell. I do not forget that I was satisfied
with your arrangement to leave Banks at
Manassas Junction, but when that arrangement
was broken up, and nothing was substituted for
it, of course I was not satisfied.; I was constrained to substitute something for it myself " [38].

While these changes were taking place in the
dispositions of the Federal forces, Jackson was
resting and recruiting his little army. He had
fallen back by degrees to Mount Jackson. A
mile to the south of Mount Jackson the north
fork of the Shenandoah River, which drains the
Western Valley from Harrisonburg to Strasburg,

crosses over from the north-west side of the
Valley, along which it at first runs, to the south-
east side, where it continues to keep its course
until it makes its way around the north end of
the Massanutton Mountains, opposite Strasburg,
in order to unite with the main stream near
Front Royal.   At the point where it crosses
the Valley, the meadows which border it are
bounded on the south side by a plateau, the
front of which, on the Valley turnpike, is known
as Rude's Hill.   To this position Jackson finally
(April 2) moved the main body of his forces,
while Ashby and the cavalry were posted in
front to observe the enemy.   The latter advanced to Woodstock on April 1, driving Ashby's
pickets, and finally forcing him back as far as
Edenburg, five miles south of Woodstock.*
Here, however, the line of Stony Creek afforded
Ashby a good defensive position, and Jackson
having reinforced him with a brigade of infantry, he effectually checked the advance of
the Federals.   This support, with the addition
of a section of artillery, was continued to Ashby
for the next two weeks, while he held this line
[39].   The Confederates destroyed the bridges
on the Manassas railroad as they retired.
During the next fortnight no further advances
were made, though frequent skirmishes occurred
along Ashby's line on Stony Creek.   For this
period Jackson remained at Rude's Hill.   At

---

* Jackson made his headquarters at Woodstock on March 24,
at Narrow Passage on the 26th, at Hawkinstown on the 29th,
and at Rev. Mr. Rude's on April 2.

this time his command greatly improved in numbers and spirits. The militia of the Valley had been called out, and the regiments from Augusta county, about five hundred men in all, had reached Mount Jackson before the Confederate advance to Kernstown [40]. A considerable portion of the men enlisted within a few days in the regular army, and the remainder were soon absorbed in the same way, under the operation of the orders of the Governor of Virginia and the stringent measures taken by the Confederate States Congress to fill up the Southern armies. Militia organizations virtually ceased to exist after this time.

The evils growing out of the manner in which the Confederate troops had been everywhere organized, and the short terms for which the greater part had enlisted, had been severely felt. The Confederate regiments were all volunteer organizations which had rushed into service at the beginning of the war, in most cases for twelve months. As the end of this time approached, efforts had been made to induce re-enlistment by appeals to the men and by bounties, and furloughs of thirty or sixty days had been granted to those re-enlisting, the result of which was to deplete to an extreme point all the armies in the field. These efforts were only partially successful, and the uncertainty thus existing, with the fact that all officers were to be elected upon the new organization, rendered discipline lax. The oldest regiments had entered the service in April, 1861, so that their term of service had nearly expired, and a partial disintegration of the army was threatened at the opening of the spring campaign. Fortunately, the Confederate Congress, seeing the impending danger, and stimulated, no doubt, by the misfortunes which had everywhere, in February and March, befallen the Confederate arms, solved the difficulty by passing, on April 16, a general conscription bill, placing all the able-bodied men of the country, between eighteen and thirty-five years of age, in the military service. The discussion of this bill, and the prospect of its passage, had stimulated re-enlistment and volunteering, and the Confederate armies everywhere began to fill up. Jackson found his skeleton regiments much enlarged from these causes, as well as by the return of furloughed men. The cavalry grew rapidly, and Ashby soon found himself at the head of a large regiment. This gallant cavalryman, however, was more at home in leading a dashing charge, or in a hand-to-hand conflict, than in drilling and organizing a mass of raw recruits. As a consequence, while his career was filled with daring and brilliant exploits, the achievements of his cavalry, acting as a mass, did not do justice to the material of which it was composed, nor to his bold leadership.

On April 2, Jackson was informed that a number of disloyal men belonging to the Rockingham militia, and residing in a remote part of the Blue Ridge, had banded together to resist the law calling them into military service. He immediately despatched Lieut.-Col. J. R. Jones, of the Thirty-third Virginia regiment, with four companies of infantry, part of Capt. Harry Gilmor's company of cavalry, and two guns under Capt. Cutshaw, to quell the disturbance. This was soon effected [41], and without blood-shed.

Brig.-Gen. C. S. Winder, having reported to Gen. Jackson, was assigned, April 1, to the command of the " Stonewall " brigade, and Col. W. B. Taliaferro, having been promoted to brigadier-general, was assigned to the command of the brigade consisting of the Thirty-seventh and Twenty-third Virginia regiments [42].

The first half of April was cold and raw, with much snow and rain, and the roads, except the turnpikes, were very deep. But by the middle of the month it had grown milder, and better weather was now to be expected. The Federal commander determined to move forward, and on the 17th his forces were put in motion. A company of Ashby's cavalry, on outpost duty between Mount Jackson and Columbia Furnace, was surprised by the advance and captured.* Shields's division soon pressed back the whole of Ashby's force through Mount Jackson, and the Federal army occupied that place. At the same time Carroll's brigade, of Shields's division, was sent forward on the back road which runs parallel to the main turnpike and west of it,

---

* This was Capt. Harper's company of cavalry. They were captured by four companies of infantry from Donelly's brigade in conjunction with the Ringgold and Washington cavalry.

thus turning the Confederate flank. Ashby destroyed the greater part of the railroad property and bridges as he retired, but failed in his attempt to burn the turnpike bridge over the north fork of the Shenandoah. Here the Federals pressed him closely, seized the bridge and extinguished the fire before it had made any headway. Ashby's horse was badly wounded, but bore him safely from the field before it fell dead. On the same day Jackson broke up his camp at Rude's Hill and retreated before the advancing enemy in the direction of Harrisonburg. This town, which is twenty-five miles south of Mount Jackson, he reached during the morning of the 18th. Here, instead of continuing towards Staunton, he turned off to the left, at right angles, in the direction of the Blue Ridge, and on the night of the 18th camped at Peale's, six miles from Harrisonburg, at the southern end of the Massanutton Mountains [43]. (Map No. I.) Next day, moving by the village of McGaheysville, he crossed the main Shenandoah River at Conrad's Store, and went into camp in Elk Run Valley, between the Shenandoah and Swift Run Gap, in the Blue Ridge.† Over this gap led a good road to Stanardsville and Gordonsville, by means of which he was placed in communication with Gen. Ewell, who then held the line of the Rapidan river.

On the day that Jackson crossed the river he

---

† This "gap" is that by which Governor Spotswood and his Golden Horseshoe Knights obtained, in 1716, the first view had by white men of the Valley of the Shenandoah.

sent some cavalry with Capt. Hotchkiss to burn the bridges on the south fork of the Shenandoah, between Conrad's Store and Luray. The southernmost one was burned, but the enemy had seized the Columbia and White-House bridges near Luray, and they drove off the Confederates, who attempted to retake them. The movements of Jackson led Banks to believe for a time that he had left the Valley [44].

Meantime, the transfer of McClellan's army to the Peninsula had caused the withdrawal of all the Confederate army, except Jackson's and Ewell's divisions, from Northern Virginia, and its concentration in front of the Federal forces. Gen. J. E. Johnston says : " When it was ascertained, about April 5, that the Federal army was marching from Fort Monroe towards Yorktown, D. H. Hill's, D. R. Jones's, and Early's divisions were transferred from the Army of Northern Virginia to that of the Peninsula. The former was thus reduced to four divisions : Jackson's, at Mount Jackson ; Ewell's, on the Rappahannock ; Longstreet's, at Orange Court-House ; and G. W. Smith's, at Fredericksburg.

" Before the 10th, the President was convinced by Maj.-Gen. Magruder's reports that the entire army just brought down the Potomac from Alexandria by Gen. McClellan was then on the Peninsula, to move upon Richmond by that route. He therefore directed me to make such defensive arrangements as might be necessary in the Department of Northern Virginia, and put my remaining troops in march for

Richmond, and then to report to him for further instructions. In obedience to these orders, Maj.-Gen. Ewell was left with his division and a regiment of cavalry in observation on the Upper Rappahannock, and Maj.-Gen. Longstreet was directed to march with his to Richmond. Maj.-Gen. Jackson was left in the Valley to oppose greatly superior Federal forces, and authorized to call Ewell's division to his assistance in case of necessity, and Gen. Ewell was instructed to comply with such a call. Maj.-Gen. G. W. Smith was instructed to leave a mixed force, equal to a brigade, in front of Fredericksburg, and move towards Richmond with all his remaining troops." *   Gen. Johnston was called to Richmond, and on April 17 was placed in command of all the forces opposing McClellan.

Jackson, conscious of his inability with five or six thousand men to resist in the open country the advance of Banks, had availed himself of the nature of the country to take a position where he could be attacked only at great disadvantage, and yet might threaten the flank and rear of the advancing column if it attempted to pass him. Such was his position in Elk Run Valley, at the foot of the Blue Ridge. The main Shenandoah River covered his front,—a stream not easily fordable at any time, and now swollen by the spring rains. The spurs of the Blue Ridge, as they run out towards this river, afford almost impregnable positions for defence ; his

* *Johnston's Narrative,* p. 109.

flanks could only be turned by toilsome and
exposed marches, while good roads led from his
rear over the mountains into the country about
Gordonsville, and placed him within easy reach
of the support he might call for from Gen. Ewell.
Thus secure in his position, Jackson at the same
time more effectually prevented the farther
advance of the Federal column than if he had
remained in its front; for he held the bridge
nearest him over the Shenandoah, and was but
a day's march from Harrisonburg, and should
Banks venture to move forward towards Staunton, he was ready to hurl the Confederate forces
against the enemy's flank and rear [45]. Gen.
Banks, at Harrisonburg, was in the midst of a
hostile country, already one hundred miles from
the Potomac at Harper's Ferry, with which a
long line of wagon communication had to be
maintained. To push on to Staunton, with
Jackson on his flank and rear, was virtually to
sacrifice his present line of communication with
no practicable substitute in view; to attack
the Confederates on the slopes of the mountains,
with even a greatly superior force, was to risk
defeat. He therefore determined to rest satisfied
for the present with the advantages already
gained. The greater part of the Shenandoah
Valley was now in his possession. Jackson had
been " thrown well back," and had been forced
to leave the main highway passing along that
Valley, and to seek refuge in the fastnesses of
the mountains. Staunton was but twenty-five
miles away; another column from the west was

threatening it.   In a short time, by co-operation with this column, the place might be taken ; or, to take a wider view, operations in front of Richmond might soon force Jackson from the Valley altogether.

Jackson rested a few days in Elk Run Valley, at the foot of Swift Run Gap, in the Blue Ridge Mountains.   Here the reorganization of his regiments was completed, and some further additions were made to his numbers by enlistments.   His strength now approached six thousand (6000).*

* The Tenth Virginia regiment of infantry was transferred at this time from Ewell's division to Jackson's. It reached Swift Run Gap on April 21, and was assigned to the Third (Taliaferro's) brigade.

CHAPTER III

McDOWELL

On April 28, Jackson applied to Gen. Lee, then acting as commander-in-chief under President Davis, for a reinforcement of five thousand men, which addition to his and Ewell's forces he deemed necessary to justify him in marching out and attacking Banks, and asked if the troops could not be spared from the force covering Fredericksburg. On the next day Gen. Lee replied as follows :

" Headquarters, Richmond, Virginia, *April* 29, 1862.

" Maj.-Gen. T. J. Jackson, Commanding, etc., Swift Run Gap, Virginia.

" General :—I have had the honour to receive your letter of yesterday's date. From the reports that reach me, that are entitled to credit, the force of the enemy opposite Fredericksburg is represented as too large to admit of any diminution whatever of our army in that vicinity at present, as it might not only invite an attack on Richmond, but jeopard the safety of the army in the Peninsula. I regret, therefore, that your request to have five thousand men sent from that army to reinforce you cannot be complied with. Can you draw enough from the command of Gen. Edward Johnson to warrant you in attacking Banks ? The last return received from that army shows a present force of upwards of three thousand five hundred, which, it is hoped, has been since increased by recruits and returned furloughs. As he does not appear to be pressed, it is suggested that a portion of his force might be temporarily removed from its present position and made available for the movement in question. A decisive and successful blow at Banks's column would be fraught with the happiest results, and I deeply regret my inability to send you the reinforcements you ask. If, however, you think the combined forces of Gens. Ewell and Johnson, with your own, inadequate for the move, Gen. Ewell might, with the assistance of Gen. Anderson's army, near Fredericksburg, strike at McDowell's army, between that city and Aquia, with much promise of success ; provided you feel sufficiently strong alone to hold Banks in check.

" Very truly yours,

" R. E. Lee." *

At this time Gen. Ewell's division was in the vicinity of Stanardsville, and there was no Federal force south of the Rappahannock in his front, McDowell having drawn his forces to the neighbourhood of Fredericksburg. Gen. Edward Johnson,† who had so successfully

* Taylor's *Four Years with General Lee*, p. 38.
† Now placed under Jackson's command.

repulsed the attack made on his camp at
Alleghany,* on December 13, had fallen back
to the Shenandoah Mountain, where it is crossed
by the Staunton and Parkersburg turnpike, to
prevent a flank movement from the direction
of Moorefield. The retreat of Jackson from
Harrisonburg to Swift Run Gap had uncovered
the roads to the rear of this force, and on
April 20 it had fallen back still farther, to West
View, only seven miles west of Staunton. (Map
No. I.) It consisted of six regiments of infantry,
three batteries, and a small force of cavalry,
and numbered, according to the Inspector-
General, Col. A. Smead, at McDowell, a week
after this time, about three thousand (3000)
effective men [46].

The force opposing Johnson consisted of a
brigade under Milroy, supported by another
under Schenck, the two containing some six
thousand (6000) men.† This formed a part of
the command of Gen. Fremont, who was preparing to move forward with other troops to
strengthen it [47]. Schenck was at Franklin,
Pendleton county, while Milroy was at Mc-
Dowell, and had—after the retreat of Gen.
Johnson—pushed his advance over the Shenandoah Mountain to the neighbourhood of the
Harrisonburg and Warm Springs turnpike. This
road would afford an easy and direct means of

* Camp Alleghany is fifteen miles west of Monterey, on the
Staunton and Parkersburg turnpike.

† Fremont puts Schenck's force at " about 3000," and Milroy's
at " 3500 effective men." (Fremont's report.)

communication with Banks at Harrisonburg, and Jackson feared a union of the two armies and a movement on Staunton, which might result in separating him from Edward Johnson and in the capture of that town. Jackson says : " At this time Brig.-Gen. Edward Johnson, with his troops, was near West View, west of Staunton, so that if the enemy was allowed to effect a junction it would probably be followed not only by the seizure of a point so important as Staunton, but must compel Gen. Johnson to abandon his position, and they might succeed in getting between us. To avoid these results I determined, if practicable, after strengthening my own division by a union with Johnson's, first to strike at Milroy, and then to concentrate the forces of Ewell, Johnson and my own against Banks. To carry out my design against Milroy, Gen. Ewell was directed to march his division to the position which I then occupied in Elk Run Valley, with a view to holding Banks in check, whilst I pushed on with my division to Staunton " [48].

Jackson's plans were matured, and the execution of them was begun at once upon the reception of the information that no other troops besides those of Ewell and Johnson could be placed at his disposal at present. This gave him about seventeen thousand (17,000) men, of which about six thousand (6000) were at Swift Run Gap, eight thousand (8000), under Ewell, one day's march in his rear, east of the Blue Ridge, and three thousand (3000) with Edward

Johnson at West View, seven miles west of Staunton, and over forty miles from Swift Run Gap. On the other hand, Banks was at Harrisonburg, twelve or fifteen miles in Jackson's front, with nineteen thousand (19,000) men.* Milroy and Schenck, commanding Fremont's advance of six thousand (6000) men, were in front of Edward Johnson, and Fremont was preparing to join them with a force sufficient to give him a movable column of fifteen thousand (15,000). McDowell, having drawn away from the Upper Rappahannock towards Fredericksburg, was out of the question. It was necessary to strike before Banks and Fremont could unite, and thus oppose Jackson with double numbers. Banks was nearest at hand, but his forces were concentrated, while Fremont's column was yet widely separated. A quick and well-concealed junction of his own division with Edward Johnson's forces might enable Jackson to fall upon Fremont's advance before the main body could join it.

The route for this movement was selected with reference to misleading the enemy, as well as with regard to security from attack. Gen. Jackson determined to march up the east side of the Shenandoah River to Port Republic, a distance of sixteen miles, and then to cross the Blue Ridge Mountains, by way of Brown's Gap, to Mechum's River station, on the Virginia

---

* See Banks's return for May 1. There were about 8000 men for duty in Banks's own division (including cavalry), and 11,000 in Shields's.

Central railroad. (Map No. I.) He designed to reach Staunton from this point by railroad. The first part of his route would be protected by the Shenandoah River, and the crossing of the mountains would leave a doubt as to his destination and suggest the notion that he was *en route* for Richmond. He was never in the habit of informing his subordinates, even those of the highest rank, of his plans, and his staff were more frequently ignorant of them than otherwise. On this occasion only one or two, whose duties made it necessary, knew the General's designs, so that friends as well as foes were mystified.

On April 29, Ashby made demonstrations in force in the direction of Harrisonburg, and this was repeated on the 30th. On the latter day a scouting party was sent to the top of the Peaked Mountain, the south-west end of the Massanutton Mountains, to observe the enemy, who appeared to be quietly camped about Harrisonburg.* In the afternoon of the 30th, Jackson left his camp, which was occupied in a few hours by Ewell's division, and began his march. The route to Port Republic was over an unpaved country road, which runs along the narrow plain that intervenes between the eastern bank of the Shenandoah and the foot of the Blue Ridge. The soil of this plain, formed by the washings from the sandstone foot-hills

* Capt. Hotchkiss, who had charge of this party, says that Ashby drove the enemy's pickets into Peale's, six miles from Harrisonburg.

of the Blue Ridge, was in many places deep
quicksands, and under the excessive rains of
this season had become miry. The past ten
days had been marked by very heavy rains, and
the streams were everywhere swollen. The
Confederates left their camp in the midst of a
rain, and proceeded but a few miles.* Next
day (May 1) was wet, and the miry earth soon
became, under the movement of artillery and
wagons, a perfect quagmire. Men and horses
floundered on through the mud, which was
hourly becoming worse. Those who tried to
find more solid paths through the fields sank
deeper into the mire, and were glad to get back
into the road. The utmost exertions were able
to carry the army forward but five miles more
this day. The troops bivouacked in the woods
along the road, while Gen. Jackson continued
his headquarters at Gen. Lewis's.† The whole
of this day was spent in helping the trains
through the mud. Large details were made to
mend the road and to keep it in a passable condition as train after train moved along. The
General himself took part in the work. He
urged on the labourers, encouraged the soldiers,
and, having dismounted, assisted in carrying
rails and stones. Next day (May 2) the same
struggle with the mud continued, and by night-

* Gen. Jackson made his headquarters on the 30th at Lewiston (Gen. Lewis's home), thirteen miles from Conrad's Store,
but the troops only made five miles, and bivouacked along the
roadside.

† Afterwards the scene of the battle of Port Republic, June 9,
1862.

fall the army had passed Lewiston, and bivouacked, again in the rain, between that place and
the foot of Brown's Gap. The following day
(May 3) the march was resumed by way of
Brown's Gap and Whitehall to Mechum's River
station, on the Virginia Central railroad. On
this morning the clouds broke away and the
sun brought a glorious May day. The hard
mountain road was an infinite relief after the
toil of the past two days. With quick and
cheerful step the army wound its way through
the pass of the Blue Ridge, and poured down
into the beautiful Piedmont country that rolls
away from the eastern base of the mountains.
Saturday night (May 3) found the advance of
the Confederates pleasantly encamped on the
hills and in the meadows about the railroad
station. While struggling forward against the
elements, Jackson had taken precaution to close
his lines, so as to prevent the knowledge of his
movements from reaching the enemy.

Next day, Sunday, May 4, the movement was
continued, the artillery and trains taking the
road to Staunton, and recrossing the mountains
at Rockfish Gap, while the troops were sent by
railroad. Gen. Jackson reached Staunton on
Sunday afternoon, and by the close of the next
day all the troops and trains had arrived at the
same point and were put into camp, the " Stonewall " brigade two miles east of the town, and
the remainder of the division west of it, and
between the town and Gen. Johnson's position
at West View [49].   So secret had been kept his

design that the people of Staunton were taken
entirely by surprise, and when they had convinced themselves that Jackson was on the way
to Richmond were astonished by his appearance
in their midst. A day was spent in resting the
troops, in making the arrangements for the
march, and in getting information ; and early
on the morning of the 7th the army set out
against the enemy. Gen. Edward Johnson's
brigade, which had started the preceding afternoon [50], led the column, followed by Jackson's
three brigades in inverse order, Taliaferro's (the
Third) being next to Johnson, the Second, under
Col. Campbell, coming next, and the First, or
" Stonewall " brigade, under Brig.-Gen. C. S.
Winder, bringing up the rear. " The corps of
cadets of the Virginia Military Institute (where
Jackson had formerly been a professor), under
their superintendent, Gen. F. H. Smith, was also
attached to the expedition. The spruce equipments and exact drill of these youths, as they
stepped out full of enthusiasm to take their
first actual look upon the horrid visage of war,
under their renowned professor, formed a strong
contrast with the war-worn and nonchalant
veterans who composed the army." *

The army moved on the Staunton and
Parkersburg turnpike. Eighteen miles west of
Staunton this road crosses the Big Calf-Pasture
River, and at the same point intersects the Warm
Springs and Harrisonburg turnpike. Soon after
passing this point the Confederate advance

* Dabney's *Life of Jackson*, p. 341.

came up with the first outposts of Gen. Milroy. The Federal picket was dispersed and in part captured, and Gen. Johnson continued his march.

Meantime, Milroy had on this day learned for the first time from his scouts and spies that a junction had been made between the forces of Jackson and Johnson, and that they were advancing to attack him at McDowell. He says : " Having the day previous (May 6) sent out a large portion of the Third Virginia, Seventy-fifth Ohio, and Thirty-second Ohio to * Shaw's Ridge, upon the Shenandoah Mountain, for the purpose of protecting my foraging and reconnoitring parties, I immediately ordered my whole force to concentrate at McDowell, and, expecting reinforcements, prepared for defence there. In the afternoon of the 7th a large force of the rebels was discovered descending the west side of the Shenandoah Mountain, along the Staunton and Parkersburg turnpike. I ordered a section of the Ninth Ohio battery (Capt. Hyman) on Shaw's Ridge to shell them, and endeavour to retard their progress." † The reinforcements he expected consisted of Schenck's brigade, then on the way from Franklin, and which, by a forced march, reached McDowell before midday on the 8th [51].

In consequence of the withdrawal of Milroy's advance on the 7th, Gen. Johnson found only the hastily-evacuated camps of the Federals

---

* This should be " beyond," as Shaw's Ridge is west of the Shenandoah Mountain.

† Milroy's report, *Rebellion Record*, vol. v. p. 34.

in his ascent of Shenandoah Mountain. The greater part of the transportation of this Federal force was not with it at the time, and hence the troops abandoned their stores and camp equipage to the Confederates. Nor was Johnson's descent on the western side obstructed by Capt. Hyman's battery. The latter fired a few shots without effect and then withdrew. Johnson bivouacked for the night on Shaw's Fork,* and the other Confederate brigades at different points in the rear. The mountains of this region afford good camping-grounds only at considerable intervals, and, as the army moved upon a single road, it was eight or ten miles between the front and rear.† (Map No. I.)

" On Thursday morning (May 8) the march was resumed early, with Gen. Johnson's regiments still in advance, and the ascent of the Bull-Pasture Mountain was commenced. This ridge, unlike its neighbours, has a breadth of a couple of miles upon its top, which might be correctly termed a table-land were it not occupied by clusters of precipitous hills which are themselves almost mountainous in their dimensions and ruggedness. The Parkersburg turnpike, proceeding westward, ascends to this table-land, passes across it, and descends to the Bull-Pasture River by a sinuous course along the ravines which seam the sides and top of the

* Twenty-nine miles from Staunton.

† Jackson's headquarters were at Rogers's toll-gate, at the eastern foot of the Shenandoah Mountain, twenty-three miles from Staunton.

mountain alike, so that it is almost everywhere commanded, on one or both sides, by the steep and wooded banks of the valleys which it threads. On the right and left of the road the western portions of the rough plateau which has been described were occupied by pasture-lands, covered with the richest greensward, with here and there the prostrate trunk of a forest-tree long since girdled and killed. The chasm which separates the higher reaches of these lofty pastures is a mile in width, and far down in its bottom the turnpike descends toward the river, until it debouches, through a straight gorge of a few hundred yards in length, upon the bridge. Artillery planted upon a hillock beyond the river commanded this reach of the road with a murderous fire.

" Gens. Jackson and Johnson, having cautiously ascended the mountain, and driven away a picket of the enemy which quartered on its top, proceeded to the western ridge of the pasture-lands on the left of the road and occupied the forenoon in examining the position of the enemy." *

The open ground here is known as Sitlington's Hill, and the high pasture-land on the opposite side of the turnpike, and in a north-easterly direction, is called Hull's Hill. The open field on top of Sitlington's Hill is a mile in length, while the foot of the hill is on all sides steep and heavily wooded. The Confederates reached the open top by way of a ravine which meets

* Dabney's *Life of Jackson*, p. 342.

the turnpike about one and a half miles east of
McDowell, at a point where the turnpike turns
sharply to the north, to find its way around the
base of the hill.   This ravine is narrow and very
steep, and, besides being wooded, is filled with
boulders washed down from above.   From the
open field on top it was easy to look down upon
the village of McDowell and the Federal camps
in the valley of the Bull-Pasture.   The open
ground on the top of Hull's Hill was a mile away.
It was occupied by Federal riflemen, but their
fire was harmless at that distance.   (Map No.
III.)

The small escort accompanying the Confederate generals in their reconnaissance having
attracted his notice, Gen. Milroy sent out parties
of skirmishers through the forest which covered
the western side and base of Sitlington's Hill,
and also opened with a section of artillery from
the farther side of the McDowell Valley.   The
elevation was too great, however, for the guns
to effect anything, and the escort kept the
skirmishers at bay.   The hill would have afforded
the Confederates a plunging fire upon the
Federal camps, but Jackson declined to order
up artillery.   Two reasons prevented him.   The
mode of access to the hill was so rugged and
difficult as to forbid the use of horses, and the
guns could only have been gotten up by hand
with great exertion.   In case of a successful
advance by the enemy, there would have been
no possibility of withdrawing them.   Another
and a controlling motive was found in his

determination not to attack the enemy at once from the commanding position of Sitlington's Hill, but merely to occupy him until a flanking column could find its way, by a considerable detour, to a point beyond McDowell, seize the turnpike between that village and Monterey, and thus block Milroy's direct line of retreat. The Confederate engineers had discovered that a route practicable for artillery passed to the right of Hull's Hill, and, making a circuit, re-entered the turnpike five miles west of Mc-Dowell. Jackson decided to move a consider-able force of artillery, with adequate infantry supports, by this road during the night, with the hope of crushing his foe when hemmed in on the morrow. Gen. Johnson's brigade, though out of sight, was close at hand, in case the enemy should make any effort in force to occupy Sitlington's Hill, and Taliaferro's and Campbell's were within supporting distance, while the " Stonewall " brigade was ordered to encamp some distance in the rear.

While the Confederates were thus employed, Milroy had been reinforced by the arrival of Schenck's brigade, which, omitting " several companies then on detached and other duty, brought into the field an aggregate of only about thirteen hundred (1300) infantry, besides De Beck's battery of the First Ohio artillery, and about two hundred and fifty (250) cavalry." * His skirmishers had reported that the Con-federate force was increasing, and that there

* Gen. Schenck's report.

were indications of the planting of artillery on Sitlington's Hill. In such an event the Federal position at McDowell was entirely untenable. Gen. Milroy, therefore, with the approval of Gen. Schenck, who, as senior, now commanded, moved forward with portions of his own brigade and one regiment of Schenck's brigade to seize the hill. Milroy's brigade consisted of the Twenty-fifth, Seventy-fifth, and Thirty-second Ohio, and Third Virginia regiments. Numerous detachments of these regiments were absent on other duty, and several companies were already engaged as skirmishers, and Gen. Milroy reports that the force he carried forward to this main attack, including the Eighty-second Ohio, of Schenck's brigade, was between two thousand two hundred (2200) and two thousand three hundred (2300) men. It was now after three o'clock in the afternoon. As soon as Jackson perceived the advance of the Federals in force, he ordered up four regiments of Johnson's brigade. The Fifty-second Virginia came first, and was placed on the left. It was deployed as skirmishers, and sent forward to engage the enemy. The Twelfth Georgia was posted in the centre of the Confederate position, on the crest of the hill, and the Forty-fourth Virginia on the right, near a ravine. The Fifty-eighth Virginia was sent to the left to support the Fifty-second. The Confederate line was a curve, with the convexity towards the enemy, so that the right of it was in a direction nearly perpendicular to the left. The advance of the Federals was protected for some distance by the convexity of the hill, and in part by the wood that covered its base and lower sides.   As the Federals emerged from the wood and attained the face of the hill they became engaged with the skirmishers of the Fifty-second Virginia, Col. M. G. Harman. It was the Twenty-fifth and Seventy-fifth Ohio, under Col. McLean, of the Seventy-fifth, that led the attack on the Confederate left.   Resolutely climbing the hill, they pushed back the skirmish line opposed to them, until they came upon the Confederate line of battle on the brow of the hill.   Here the struggle became fierce and sanguinary.   Meantime, Milroy had sent the Thirty-second and Eighty-second Ohio and Third Virginia (Federal) farther to his left, that they might attack the right of the Confederates, and, if possible, turn it.   The two Ohio regiments pressed up the face of the hill, and vigorously attacked Johnson's right, while the Third Virginia (Federal) pushed along the turnpike and threatened to turn his flank.   Anticipating the latter movement, Jackson had placed the Thirty-first Virginia to hold the turnpike in advance of the point at which the Confederates had diverged from it to ascend the hill.   The attack which was made on Johnson's right, on the hill where only the Forty-fourth Virginia was posted, caused Jackson to withdraw the Thirty-first from the turnpike, and to send it and the Twenty-fifth Virginia to Gen. Johnson, who placed them in support of the Forty-fourth. The guarding of the turnpike was then committed to the Twenty-first Virginia (Col. Cunningham), of Campbell's brigade, which was directed to hold it at all hazards. But the Federals did not press in this direction, and Col. Cunningham was not seriously attacked. Gen. Milroy states that he ordered two twelve-pounders to be placed on the turnpike, but did not get them into position "until after twilight." The attack upon the Confederate right was vigorous and well sustained, and now, by the junction of the two attacking Federal columns, the battle became general. Repeated efforts were made to carry the crest of the hill, but these were repulsed. The firing was incessant and at close quarters. The Confederates had the advantage of position, and in some parts the undulations of the ground gave them some cover; but, for the most part, their line, showing plainly against the evening sky, afforded an excellent mark for the Federal soldiers. On the other hand, though the Federal troops had to push up the steep acclivity of the hill, they reaped the usual advantage in such cases, resulting from the high firing of the Confederates. The most advanced portion of the Confederate line was the centre, where, without any protection from the nature of the ground, the Twelfth Georgia regiment bore the brunt of numerous attacks and gallantly held its position. It was suffering heavily, but refused to yield, or even to take advantage of such cover as the place afforded.

Gen. Jackson says: "The engagement had

now not only become general along the whole
line, but so intense that I ordered Gen. Taliaferro to the support of Gen. Johnson.*   Accordingly, the Twenty-third and Thirty-seventh
Virginia regiments were advanced to the centre
of the line, which was then held by the Twelfth
Georgia with heroic gallantry. . . . At this
time the Federals were pressing forward on our
right, with a view of flanking that position.
This movement of the enemy was speedily de-
tected, and met by Gen. Taliaferro's brigade and
the Twelfth Georgia with great promptitude.
Further to check it, portions of the Twenty-
fifth and Thirty-first Virginia regiments were
sent to occupy an elevated piece of woodland
on our right and rear, so situated as to fully
command the position of the enemy.   The
brigade commanded by Col. Campbell coming
up about this time, was, together with the Tenth
Virginia (the rear regiment of Taliaferro's brigade), ordered down the ridge into the woods,
to guard against movements against our right
flank, which they, in connection with the other
force, effectually prevented.   The battle lasted
four hours,—from half-past four in the afternoon
until half-past eight.   Every attempt, by front
or flank movement, to attain the crest of the
hill, where our line was formed, was signally
and effectually repulsed.   Finally, after dark,
their force ceased firing, and the enemy retreated.
The enemy's artillery, posted on a hill in our

* To Gen. Johnson had been intrusted the command of the
troops engaged.

front, was active in throwing shot and shell up to the period when the infantry fight commenced ; but, in consequence of the great angle of elevation at which they fired and our sheltered position, inflicted no loss upon our troops." * This artillery consisted of a section which had been firing all the day from the western side of the McDowell Valley. There was also a gun in action from the Twelfth Ohio battery, which, Gen. Milroy says, "was placed in position on the mountain on the left of the turnpike (Hull's Hill) with the greatest difficulty," whilst his troops were advancing against the Confederate right.

The Confederate forces actually in the battle consisted of Johnson's brigade (six regiments) and of Taliaferro's brigade (three regiments) ; Col. Campbell's brigade arrived in time to be used in protecting the right flank, but was not engaged, and the " Stonewall " brigade was some miles in the rear. The nine regiments engaged numbered about four thousand five hundred (4500) men, and Col. Campbell's brigade contained about fifteen hundred (1500) more. The Federal strength, under Schenck and Milroy, was over six thousand (6000) men [52], but, according to the reports of those officers, not more than two thousand five hundred (2500) of these were in the battle. The Confederate official report gives Jackson's loss as seventy-one killed and three hundred and ninety wounded,—total, four hundred and sixty-

* Jackson's report of the battle of McDowell.

one (461). Among the Confederate killed was
Col. Gibbons, of the Tenth Virginia, who fell
while gallantly leading his regiment. Gen.
Edward Johnson, who commanded the troops
engaged, was seriously wounded in the foot
near the close of the fight. Col. M. G. Harman,
of the Fifty-second Virginia, Col. Smith and
Maj. Higginbotham, of the Twenty-fifth Virginia, and Maj. Campbell, of the Forty-second
Virginia, were also wounded. Gen. Schenck
reports twenty-eight killed, and two hundred
and twenty-five wounded, and three missing,—
total, two hundred and fifty-six (256), as the
Federal loss [53].

Though Gen. Milroy failed altogether to obtain possession of Sitlington's Hill, or to effect
any lodgment from which he might renew the
attack on the morrow, he maintained the fight
in the most spirited manner until dark, and in
this way saved himself from disaster ; for, under
cover of the darkness and fog, he quietly withdrew from the field, unmolested by the Confederates, the country being too broken and
difficult to admit of pursuit at night. McDowell
was entirely untenable with the Confederates
holding Sitlington's Hill, and so Gen. Schenck,
as soon as the Federal troops had been safely
withdrawn from the battle-field, having lighted
his camp-fires, evacuated the place, and fell
back during the night in the direction of
Franklin. He says : " The withdrawal was
effected without the loss of a man, and without
loss or destruction of any article of public

property, except of some stores for which Gen. Milroy was entirely without the means of transportation."*

Meanwhile, the Confederates, having collected the wounded and left a guard on the field, sought needed rest in their bivouac. This rest was short, for it was late in the night before all was quiet, and with the early morning the army was astir. At dawn Jackson was in the saddle, but when he had ascended again to the battle-field, it was only to look down on the deserted camps and smouldering camp-fires of the foe. He occupied McDowell without delay, and, having provided for the captured stores, prepared to follow the retreating army.

The following was Jackson's laconic despatch announcing his victory to the Adjutant-General:

"VALLEY DISTRICT, *May* 9, 1862.

" To GEN. S. COOPER :

" God blessed our arms with victory at Mc-Dowell yesterday.

"T. J. JACKSON, Major-General."

Gen. Schenck fell back by gradual stages to Franklin, taking advantage of the rugged country to hold the pursuers in check. On Friday (9th) he halted for some hours at the intersection of the Monterey and Franklin roads, but, before any considerable portion of Jackson's force was

* Schenck's report. A considerable quantity of camp equipage was left, and many tents, the latter standing.

up, he moved on.*   Next day the Confederates pursued closely, but were easily prevented in these mountains from doing any serious damage.

The plan of the Confederate leader was to beat the armies opposed to him in detail.   The force under Gen. Schenck had been repulsed, but it was still formidable.   If reinforced from Gen. Banks, the strengthened force might be able in this mountainous country to withstand him.†   He therefore took steps to prevent reinforcements from being sent from Banks to Schenck, or a union of the two commands. For this purpose he sent a party of cavalry, under Capt. Hotchkiss, topographical engineer, to blockade the roads leading from the direction of McDowell and Franklin through North River and Dry River Gaps.   These roads lead to Harrisonburg, and at the points named pass through narrow defiles, where, by felling trees, they could be made impassable long enough to give time for the making of dispositions to defeat the movement.   Another party was sent to do the same on the road leading through Brock's Gap, directly west of Harrisonburg, and the citizens were requested to aid by obstructing every available point.‡   These detachments

---

* Jackson was compelled to spend some hours at McDowell, in order that his troops might be fed.

† He was not aware how large a portion of Banks's troops were about to go to reinforce Gen. McDowell at Fredericksburg.

‡ The blockading of these roads was one of the causes which subsequently prevented Fremont from marching on Harrisonburg when ordered to go to the relief of Banks, and induced him to go by a circuit to Strasburg.

having been sent off, the army continued its
march in the wake of the retreating Federals.

On the succeeding day (11th), as Jackson
again closed up to the rear of the Federal army,
the latter adopted the expedient of setting fire
to the forests along the road. " Soon the sky
was overcast with volumes of smoke which
almost hid the scene, and wrapped every distant
object in a veil impenetrable to the eyes and
the telescopes of the officers alike. Through
this sultry fog the pursuing army felt its way
very cautiously along, cannonaded by the enemy
from every advantageous position, while it was
protected from ambuscades only by detachments of skirmishers who scoured the burning
woods on each side of the highway. As fast as
these could scramble over the precipitous hills
and the blazing thickets, the great column crept
along the main road like a lazy serpent, the
General often far in advance of its head, in his
eagerness to overtake the foe. He declared
that this smoke was the most adroit expedient to
which a retreating army could resort to em-
barrass pursuit, and that it entailed upon him
all the disadvantages of a night attack. By
slow approaches and constant skirmishing the
enemy were driven to the village of Franklin,
when the double darkness of the night and the
fog again arrested his progress." * Gen. Schenck
says : " From McDowell I fell back by easy
marches on the 9th, 10th, and 11th to this place
(Franklin), the enemy cautiously pursuing. . . .

* Dabney's *Life of Jackson*, p. 351.

While awaiting the arrival of the general commanding (Fremont), with reinforcements at this point, on the 11th, 12th, and 13th, the rebel army having advanced within two miles of our position, we were kept constantly engaged in watchful preparations for an expected attack." *

On Monday morning, May 12, Jackson, finding Schenck strongly posted, and knowing that affairs in the east would not admit of his protracted stay in the mountains, determined to withdraw from the Federal front without further battle. He had found it impossible to do any considerable injury to an army retreating in such a country. Now the Federals were within reach of Fremont's main body, and having taken a stand at Franklin in a strong position, might either hold him in check until the reinforcements arrived or continue their retreat until a junction with Fremont was effected. Such a junction once made, the Confederate general might be forced to fight a superior force † without the aid of Ewell's division, which had been left in Elk Run Valley to watch Banks. Again, time was all-important. The enemy could make a campaign in the mountains tedious. An emergency at Fredericksburg or Richmond might cause the recall of Ewell's division, which had been ordered to co-operate with Jackson for making some movement against Banks which would relieve

---

* Schenck's report.
† Jackson had with him near 9000 men ; Fremont 15,000.

Fredericksburg and prevent troops from that point or the Valley going to reinforce McClellan. He decided to unite his whole force without more delay and strike at Banks, who in the open country of the Valley could be more readily assailed. Milroy and Schenck had been driven away from the position that enabled them to threaten Staunton; had been pushed away, too, from Banks, so that there was no longer any danger of a junction of the two commands. Jackson believed that by a prompt movement against the latter officer, he might defeat him before Fremont would sufficiently recover from the disarrangement of his plans, produced by the defeat and retreat of Schenck, to interfere actively with the operations of the Confederates.

Having so decided, Jackson sent a courier to Gen. Ewell to announce his coming, and prepared for the return. He granted the soldiers the half of Monday (12th) as a season of rest in lieu of the Sabbath which had been devoted to warfare, and issued the following order to them:

" SOLDIERS OF THE ARMY OF THE VALLEY AND
    NORTH-WEST:
    " I congratulate you on your recent victory at McDowell. I request you to unite with me this morning in thanksgiving to Almighty God for thus having crowned your arms with success, and in praying that He will continue to lead you on from victory to victory until our

independence shall be established, and make us that people whose God is the Lord. The chaplains will hold Divine Service at 10 o'clock A.M. this day, in their respective regiments." *

* Dabney's *Life of Jackson,* p. 353.

CHAPTER IV

WINCHESTER

In the afternoon of May 12 the Confederate army began to return, and on the evening of Wednesday, 14th, reached McDowell. On the latter day, Fremont arrived at Franklin with the troops he was bringing to the assistance of Schenck. Here he remained quietly for the following ten days repairing his losses, and, as Jackson had anticipated, made no attempt to interfere with his operations [54]. Jackson continued his march in the direction of Staunton. On the night of the 15th he camped at Lebanon Springs, where the road forks, the one branch leading to Staunton and the other to Harrisonburg. The next day was spent in camp, in deference to the proclamation of the Confederate President appointing May 16 as a day of fasting and prayer. On Saturday, 17th, the troops turned towards Harrisonburg, and moved on over roads made heavy by the rain of the preceding day. They camped for the night at Mossy Creek and Bridgewater, and here they rested during Sunday, the 18th.

We must now glance at affairs in the Valley. During the nineteen days that had elapsed since Jackson left his camp at Elk Run, important changes had taken place in the disposition of the Federal troops in Northern Virginia. President Lincoln, as heretofore stated, had given a reluctant assent to Gen. McClellan's plan of campaign, which involved the transfer of the main Federal army to the peninsula between the York and James Rivers, and the movement by that route upon Richmond. To the apprehensions of the Federal President and his Cabinet this movement seemed to uncover Washington. They feared an irruption of the Confederates, which might place the Federal capital in hostile hands before an adequate force could be recalled for its defence. Hence the most stringent orders were given McClellan to leave a force so disposed as to cover Washington, and amply sufficient to protect it in any emergency. The latter officer thought he had complied fully with this order when he left over sixty-three thousand (63,000) men and eighty-five (85) pieces of artillery in the various commands that were located in the Shenandoah Valley, at Warrenton, at Manassas, and in and around Washington [55]. In addition to this force, ten thousand (10,000) men and twenty-four (24) guns, under Blenker, had been detached and ordered to Fremont, whose movable column was thus increased to twelve or fifteen thousand (12,000 or 15,000) men, even after deducting Blenker's mass of stragglers. This aggregate of over seventy-five thousand (75,000) men was really equal to the entire Confederate strength available for offence in Virginia at this time.

But with fears greatly aroused by Jackson's attack at Kernstown, and no doubt stimulated by want of confidence in Gen. McClellan, the Washington authorities deemed it inadequate, and so the Federal commander had hardly reached Fortress Monroe (April 2), to assume the personal direction of the operations there, before the President ordered (April 3) McDowell's corps to remain in front of Washington.* On April 4, Gen. McDowell was detached altogether from McClellan's command and placed in charge of the Department of the Rappahannock, and Gen. Banks was given independent command of the Department of the Shenandoah.† To McDowell was assigned the duty of protecting the capital, by the following order :

"WAR DEPARTMENT, *April* 11, 1862.

" SIR :—For the present, and until further orders from this Department, you will consider the national capital as especially under your protection, and make no movement throwing your force out of position for the discharge of this primary duty.

" E. M. STANTON, Secretary of War.
" MAJ.-GEN. MCDOWELL."

McDowell at first moved out towards Catlett's station, rebuilding the Orange and Alexandria railroad, and pushed his advance in the direction of the Rappahannock and Culpeper. Subsequently he asked and obtained permission to move down to Fredericksburg, but was pro-

* See page 64, *ante,* † See page 65 and note 38, page 236.

hibited from crossing the river there, or making any advance beyond occupying the town with a small force. The early days of May found him opposite Fredericksburg, where he remained inactive for three weeks. When McDowell's corps had been detached from McClellan's army, one division (Franklin's) had been allowed to go to the Peninsula, and this deficiency was to be made up from the commands about Washington and in Northern Virginia. Thus a new division was organized under Gen. Ord, partly of troops drawn from Banks's and Abercrombie's* commands, and partly of troops from Washington. This new division, added to those left with him (McCall's and King's), gave McDowell a force of thirty thousand (30,000) men.† To increase his strength still further, with reference to operations against Richmond, President Lincoln ordered Shields's division to be detached from Banks's corps and sent to McDowell.‡

When Gen. Banks learned, on May 1, that Ewell's division had entered the Valley, and that Jackson was moving, fearing an attack from their combined forces, he evacuated Harrisonburg and gradually withdrew to New Market, and thence, after the detachment of Shields's division, to Strasburg. He thus drew nearer to his base and the forces on which he

* Abercrombie was in command at Warrenton.

† McDowell's " return " for May 17 (excluding Shields) shows his strength, officers and men present for duty, to have been 29,652.

‡ See McDowell's testimony before the Committee on the Conduct of the War, Part I., 1863.

might call for succour in case of need. Ashby followed the retreating army with his cavalry, and frequent skirmishes occurred between his forces and the Federal rear guard.

On May 7 an affair of outposts occurred between the Seventh Louisiana infantry and a part of the Sixth Virginia cavalry, of Ewell's division, and a company of Federal cavalry, supported by the Thirteenth Indiana regiment, at a little place called Summersville, on the eastern side of the main Shenandoah River, in the Luray Valley. The Federal cavalry were partly surrounded, and compelled to swim the river for safety, while the infantry was driven from the field.* A few days after, Shields's division left the Valley by way of Luray and Front Royal, and thence over the Blue Ridge towards Fredericksburg.† This transfer deprived Banks of more than one-half his forces, for Shields took with him eleven thousand (11,000) men, and left about eight thousand (8000) [56]. Gen. Banks now retired from the Upper Valley entirely, posting the main body of his forces at Strasburg ‡ and sending Col. Kenly, with the First Maryland regiment and some cavalry and artillery,—in all about one thousand (1000) men,—to Front Royal (May 16) to protect the railroad and the bridges at that place over the north and south forks of the Shenandoah.

* See report of Col. Foster, of Thirteenth Indiana, *Rebellion Record*, vol. v. p. 27.

† Shields left New Market May 12.

‡ Here he constructed earthworks, and prepared to hold his position.

Thus it was that the middle of May found Fremont, who had hurried forward with Blenker's division to the assistance of Schenck, resting from the fatigues of the march at Franklin, while Shields was in full march to join McDowell at Fredericksburg, and Banks had assumed a strictly defensive attitude at Strasburg to hold the lower valley of the Shenandoah, and especially to cover the Baltimore and Ohio railroad.

McClellan's urgent and repeated calls for reinforcements and earnest representations that the holding of such a mass of troops idle in front of Washington was endangering his success, had at last induced the Federal Administration to agree to an advance on the part of McDowell from Fredericksburg. The quiet which had existed for some weeks in the Shenandoah Valley and on the line of the Rappahannock, and the absence of Jackson in the mountains of Western Virginia, where he was still supposed to be, seem to have reassured the Federal Cabinet [57]. On May 17 the following order was sent to McDowell :

" GENERAL :—Upon being joined by Shields's division you will move upon Richmond by the general route of the Richmond and Fredericksburg railroad, co-operating with the forces under Gen. McClellan, now threatening Richmond from the line of the Pamunkey and York Rivers. While seeking to establish as soon as possible a communication between your left wing and the right wing of Gen. McClellan, you will hold yourself always in such a position as to cover the capital of the nation against a sudden dash by any large body of the rebel forces" [58].

The transfer of Shields's forces from Banks to McDowell at Fredericksburg, and the indications of an advance on Richmond from that direction, convinced the Confederate authorities that no time was to be lost in meeting this new danger. For weeks they had watched with anxiety the army gathering at Fredericksburg, as well as the movements of Gen. Banks. The forces of McDowell, moving down from the north on Richmond, cutting the railroads that united that city with the great Valley and Western Virginia, and joining the splendid army under McClellan, which was advancing from the east upon it, threatened the most serious consequences, and was to be prevented if possible. The burden of Gen. Lee's * despatches to Gens. Jackson and Ewell for some time past had been to strike Banks, and thus prevent his reinforcing McDowell or McClellan, and possibly cause the recall of troops to his aid. If no chance offered for this, and he moved towards Fredericksburg, Ewell was to go to the assistance of the Confederate troops before that town. Thus, on May 8, while Jackson was fighting at McDowell, Gen. Lee writes Ewell that there is no necessity for his remaining at Swift Run Gap

* Gen. Lee was acting as commander-in-chief under President Davis at this time.

if Banks is retreating, and if the latter is making towards Fredericksburg, Ewell is to try to strike him while *en route*. On the 12th, Gen. Lee approves of Ewell remaining at Swift Run Gap "so long as the enemy remains stationary in the Valley, or while it is necessary to the movements of Gen. Jackson." On the 14th, Gen. Lee's assistant adjutant-general, Col. Taylor, writes to Jackson congratulating him on his victory (at McDowell), and says Lee is "of opinion that Banks cannot be as strong as he has been represented; if so, his course is inexplicable. He thinks that if you can form a junction with Gen. Ewell, that with your combined forces you would be able to drive Banks from the Valley." On the 14th, Gen. Lee was informed by Ewell of the movement of Shields's division towards Front Royal, and on the 16th writes to Jackson: "Whatever may be Banks's intention, it is very desirable to prevent him from going either to Fredericksburg or to the Peninsula, and also to destroy the Manassas road. A successful blow struck at him would delay, if it did not prevent, his moving to either place, and might also lead to the recall of the reinforcements sent to Fremont (Blenker's division) from Winchester, as reported by you. Gen. Ewell telegraphed yesterday that in pursuance of instructions from you he was moving down the Valley. . . . But you will not, in any demonstration you may make in that direction, lose sight of the fact that it may become necessary for you to come to the support

of Gen. Johnston. . . . Whatever movement
you make against Banks do it speedily, and if
successful, drive him back towards the Potomac,
and create the impression, as far as practicable,
that you design threatening that line."

Gen. Ewell rode across the Valley to confer
in person with Gen. Jackson. He reached Mount
Solon, where Jackson was encamped, on Sunday
morning, May 18, and these two officers decided
upon the plan for a most energetic pursuit of
Banks. It was agreed that one of Ewell's
brigades (Taylor's Louisianians), which constituted, too, the bulk of his command, should
march from Elk Run Valley, by way of Keezletown, and unite with Jackson on the Valley
turnpike at Sparta, a few miles south of New
Market, while the remainder of his force followed
the course of the south fork of the Shenandoah
to Luray. Ewell returned on the afternoon
of the 18th to direct the movement of his
troops [59].

That portion of the great Valley of Virginia,
called the Valley of the Shenandoah, extends
in a south-westerly direction from Harper's
Ferry, where the Shenandoah empties into the
Potomac, to the head-waters of the former, a
distance of about one hundred and forty miles.
It is bounded on the east by the Blue Ridge
Mountains, to the base of which finally gather
all the waters of the Valley, and on the west by
the North Mountain and other ridges which
run parallel to the principal range of the Alleghanies. The width varies from twelve to twenty-

four miles. An important subdivision of this valley exists for a part of its length. Near Front Royal, thirty-six air-line miles from its mouth, the Shenandoah divides into two branches or " forks." A mountain chain called the Massanutton rises abruptly between these two branches, and runs in a direction parallel to the Blue Ridge for fifty miles to the south-west, when it sinks, as suddenly, into the general level at a point a few miles east of Harrisonburg. This chain, being much nearer to the Blue Ridge than to the North Mountain, divides the Valley very unequally. The western side, or main Valley, is known as the " Valley " simply, while the narrow portion, between the Massanuttons and the Blue Ridge, is called the Page * or Luray Valley. The north fork, which is the smaller branch of the Shenandoah, rising in the North Mountain, west of Harrisonburg, drains the main Valley between the North and Massa-nutton ranges. It runs for some distance on the north-western side, but at Mount Jackson crosses to the base of the Massanutton Moun-tains, which it follows with a tortuous course to Strasburg, where it finds its way around the north end of that chain, and finally joins the south fork near Front Royal. The south fork, which is the principal river, waters the narrow Luray Valley. Ascending this stream beyond the south end of the Massanutton Mountains, we find that it again branches at and near Port

* " Page " is the name of the county comprising the greater part of this valley, and Luray is the county-seat of Page.

Republic. Three streams—the North, Middle,
and South *Rivers*—constitute the head-waters
of the principal fork of the Shenandoah, and,
spreading over the whole width of the Valley
from the Blue Ridge to the North Mountain,
drain the upper part of Rockingham and nearly
the whole of Augusta county. The two first
named unite three or four miles south-west of
Port Republic, and the South River, having
found its way along the base of the Blue Ridge,
joins the others at that village.

The principal means of communication between Staunton and Winchester was, then, the
Valley turnpike, an excellent macadamized road,
which passes through Harrisonburg, New Market, Mount Jackson, and Strasburg. Leaving
Staunton, it crosses, by wooden bridges, the
Middle and North *Rivers* before reaching Harrisonburg, and the north *fork* of the Shenandoah
at Mount Jackson. Common dirt roads run
parallel to it for the greater part of its length.
From New Market a turnpike leads at right
angles over the Massanutton Mountains, crosses
the south or main *fork* of the Shenandoah at
White-House Bridge, passes Luray, and crosses
the Blue Ridge by Thornton's Gap, to Sperryville and Culpeper. An unpaved road runs
down the Luray Valley from Port Republic to
Front Royal, and from the latter point a good
turnpike leads to Winchester, and ungraded
country roads to Strasburg, Middletown, and
other places on the Valley turnpike. From
Winchester excellent macadamized roads lead

to Harper's Ferry, and through Martinsburg to Williamsport, on the Potomac. (Maps Nos. I. and V.)

At Strasburg, going northward, just before the principal and Luray valleys unite, the principal valley contracts in width, in consequence of the approach of the North and Massanutton Mountains. The latter is here three parallel ranges, containing between them two small valleys known as Powell's Big Fort Valley and Powell's Little Fort Valley. At this part of the principal valley the country is broken and cut up by deep ravines, and the heights around afford good defensive positions. Here it was that Gen. Banks had taken position, his pickets being thrown out a few miles towards Woodstock. He deemed his force sufficient to resist any attack in front that was likely to be made, and, besides, believed Jackson to be fully occupied with Fremont, whose forces were now concentrated in the mountains about Franklin. He had sent Col. Kenly with about a thousand men to hold Front Royal, but this was not so much to guard against a flank attack as to protect the stores at that point, and the railroad and the bridges over the Shenandoah, from a dash of cavalry or the depredations of guerrillas. He saw no indications of a serious attack upon his position.

Jackson left Mossy Creek on Monday morning, the 19th, and moved forward rapidly towards New Market. He reached this point next day, having been joined *en route* by Taylor's brigade

of Ewell's division.   Ashby had already occupied
the Valley below this point upon the withdrawal
of Shields and the retreat of Banks to Strasburg.
Gen. Jackson says : " To conceal my movements
as far as possible from the enemy, Brig.-Gen.
Ashby, who had remained in front of Banks
during the march against Milroy, was directed
to continue to hold that position until the
following day, when he was to join the main
body, leaving, however, a covering force sufficient to prevent information of our movements
crossing our lines."   Having taken these steps
to keep the enemy in ignorance, Jackson, on the
21st, turned off at New Market to the right, on
the way to Luray.   He crossed the Massanutton
Mountains, and the south fork of the Shenandoah
at White-House Bridge.   Here he met Gen. Ewell
with the other brigades of his division, which
had marched down the Luray Valley, and
encamped at the eastern entrance of the New
Market gap of the Massanuttons.   (Map No. IV.)

Ewell's division consisted of the brigades of
Taylor (Sixth, Seventh, Eighth, and Ninth
Louisiana regiments, and Wheat's battalion),
Trimble (Twenty-first North Carolina, Twenty-
first Georgia, Fifteenth Alabama, and Sixteenth
Mississippi), and Elzey (Thirteenth Virginia and
First Maryland) [60], of Courtenay's (six-gun)
and Brockenbrough's (four-gun) batteries, and
of the Second and Sixth Virginia cavalry,
under Cols. Munford and Flournoy.   This division numbered, including the cavalry, about
eight thousand (8000), and increased Jackson's

effective force to some sixteen or seventeen thousand (16,000 or 17,000) men, with eleven batteries, containing forty-eight (48) guns [61].

On Thursday, the 22nd, the Confederates moved quietly down the Luray Valley in the direction of Front Royal, and Ewell's division, which was in advance, bivouacked at night ten miles from the latter place. Next morning Jackson made his dispositions to attack and capture the force stationed at Front Royal. In order to get as close as possible without being discovered, he diverted the head of his column from the main road [62] to the right until it reached the Gooney Manor road, at Mrs. King's, by which he approached the town from the south instead of the south-west, and was in a better position to prevent the enemy's retreat by way of Manassas Gap. At the same time the cavalry under Ashby and Flournoy, leaving the main column at Spangler's cross-roads, were sent across the south fork of the Shenandoah, at McCoy's Ford, to destroy railroad and telegraphic communication between Front Royal and Strasburg, and to prevent reinforcements being sent from the latter place. This done, Flournoy, with the Second and Sixth regiments of Virginia cavalry, was to move down between the rivers to take the enemy in flank and rear if they should retreat towards Winchester or Strasburg [63].

The First Maryland regiment, Col. Bradley T. Johnson, and Wheat's Louisiana battalion of five companies, were thrown forward as the advance of the infantry, and they were supported by the remainder of Taylor's brigade. No opposition was met with, and no pickets found, until about 2 P.M., when the Confederates, under Johnson and Wheat, had reached the immediate vicinity of the town. Here, about one and a half miles from the village, Col. Kenly's infantry pickets were placed. They were driven in and rapidly followed up. Two companies of Kenly's regiment were supporting the pickets, and one company occupied the town. Another company was on detached service, guarding the Manassas railroad at Linden station, some distance off. The remaining six were in camp on a hill on the Front Royal side of the river, near the bridge. Col. Kenly had also a section of Knapp's battery—two ten-pounder Parrotts—in camp, while two companies of the Twenty-ninth Pennsylvania infantry were stationed between the rivers to protect the railroad bridges. The two companies supporting the picket and the one in the town were soon driven back, and a charge by the Confederates sent them through the town in haste to join their main body. This they did, with the loss of eighteen or twenty killed, wounded and captured.

Col. Kenly quickly posted his guns and the main body of his regiment on a " commanding height " * to the right of the turnpike which

---

* Jackson's report. This is a cherty ridge, some one hundred and fifty feet above the river, that extends to the north-east of the turnpike. It lies between the south fork of the Shenandoah and Happy Creek.

leads from Front Royal to Winchester, and near his camp, and disposed a portion of his force to protect his flanks. During the continuance of the fight at this point he was joined by two companies of the Fifth New York cavalry, which had just arrived from Strasburg. Here he made a spirited resistance for a time. His artillery was well served, and his infantry kept up a steady fire. The Confederates had in the advance no rifled artillery, and it was some time before an effective fire could be made upon the Federal position. At length Col. Crutchfield, chief of artillery for Jackson, got three guns— one of them rifled—into position, and replied to the Federal battery. But the Confederate infantry had not waited for this. The Sixth Louisiana was sent to the Confederate left, through some woods, to flank the enemy's battery, while Maj. Wheat and Col. Johnson (the latter's troops all excitement when they found their opponents to be from the same State) pressed forward in front with the greatest ardour. Meantime, Col. Flournoy, with his cavalry, was moving down between the rivers and threatening the Federal rear. Col. Kenly, seeing himself about to be surrounded, did not await the infantry attacks in front, but retreated rapidly across the two rivers, having set fire to his camp and attempted to burn the bridges. Though he failed in this last attempt, he succeeded in doing sufficient damage to the bridge over the North Fork to impede the Confederates. The Federal commander made a further attempt to check his pursuers on the hill—known as Guard Hill—overlooking the North Fork, but a few shells from Lusk's battery, and the approach of the forces in pursuit, caused him speedily to retreat.*   Leaving the two New York cavalry companies to cover the rear, he hurried the artillery and infantry forward on the Winchester road.   The damage to the bridge detained the Confederates for a little while, but Col. Flournoy at last succeeded in getting four companies of his cavalry regiment over, and Gen. Jackson, without waiting for more, dashed with this force up the turnpike after the retreating enemy. They were soon overtaken.   Flournoy was at once ordered to charge the New York cavalry, which constituted the rear guard.   These last make but a feeble resistance, are soon thrown into confusion and routed, and now demoralized, take to flight.   Col. Kenly, learning that the cavalry are being hard pressed, has meantime halted his infantry and artillery, ordering the latter to hold the road, and forming his infantry in the fields on each side.   But the Confederates, under Jackson's own guidance, and inspired by his enthusiasm, do not stop.   Company B, Capt. Grimsby, charges directly up the turnpike, supported by Company E, Capt. Flournoy, on the left and Companies A and K, Capts. Dulaney and Baxter, on the right.   The Federal lines do not stand the charge.   They are broken and

* Mr. Kirkley says that "the river below was alive with (Confederate) horsemen crossing in two different places by fording." (*History of First Maryland Infantry, Federal.*)

thrown into confusion. Col. Kenly makes another gallant effort to stay the disaster. He reforms a portion of his command a little to the rear, in an orchard, on the east side of the turnpike, and makes a last desperate struggle to check defeat. But it is in vain. His troops are thoroughly demoralized by the events of the day. The cavalry is flying in confusion to the rear,—the artillery is trying to get away. The panic-struck Federal soldiers magnify Col. Flournoy's four companies of cavalry into an army. The latter dash among them with the boldness of assured victory. Col. Kenly's personal efforts to restore order only result in his falling desperately wounded. The rout quickly becomes hopeless and complete. The Confederates ride around the broken infantry on every side. The mass, seeing no chance of escape, throw down their arms and surrender. By this time two more of Flournoy's companies (D and I) have reached the field, and they join in pursuit of the Federal cavalry, wagons, and artillery. One gun is overhauled near the field. The wagon-train soon falls into the hands of the victors. Scattered cavalrymen are picked up along the road. The Confederates continue to chase the fugitives until within four miles of Winchester. There they find the other Parrott gun abandoned in the road and two of the Confederates take some plough-horses from a field and bring it back with them.

The victory is complete. The Federal loss is thirty-two (32) killed, one hundred and twenty-two (122) wounded, and seven hundred and fifty (750) prisoners; total, nine hundred and four (904), by the report of the Federal surgeon-general. The historians of the First Maryland regiment * (Federal) make it nineteen (19) killed, sixty-three (63) wounded, and six hundred and ninety-one (691) prisoners; total, seven hundred and seventy-three (773). The Confederate loss is thirty-six (36) killed and wounded.† Gen. Banks reports Kenly's force present for duty as about nine hundred (900) men, though Capt. Smith and other officers present of the First Maryland regiment (Federal) put the force at one thousand and sixty-three (1063) [64]. Not over one hundred and thirty (130) have escaped under cover of the woods, for on the 28th, Capt. Smith reports but eight (8) officers and one hundred and twenty (120) men present. The scene of this engagement is near Cedarville, a small village about five miles from Front Royal, where an ungraded road leaves the Winchester turnpike and leads to Middletown on the Valley turnpike. (Map No. V.) The credit of the final overthrow of Col. Kenly's command lies entirely with Flournoy's cavalry. The advance of the Confederate infantry and artillery, jaded by the day's long march, was not able to come up with the enemy until the fight was over, while the mass of the Con-

---

* *Historical Record of First Maryland Regiment of Infantry*, Camper and Kirkley. Some of the wounded are included also among the prisoners.

† Jackson's report.

federate forces only reached Front Royal at nightfall [65].

" While these occurrences were in progress, Gen. Ashby, who, after crossing at McCoy's Ford, had moved with his command farther to the west, so as to skirt the base of the Massanutton Mountains, came suddenly upon the infantry guard, consisting of two companies (Davis's, of the Twenty-seventh Indiana, and Hubbard's, of the Third Wisconsin) that had been posted at and near Buckton for the protection of the railroad. This force, however, quickly threw themselves into the depot building and Mr. Jenkins's house and stable, and from this cover maintained a very spirited contest with the Confederate cavalry, in which fell Capts. Sheets and Fletcher, two of the best of Ashby's officers. The Federals were finally overpowered and dispersed, and the railroad track was torn up.*

" The result of this first day's operations was the capture of about seven hundred (700) prisoners, among them about twenty officers, a complete section of rifled artillery (ten-pounder Parrotts), and a very large amount of quartermaster and commissary stores [66]. The fruits of the movement were not restricted to the stores and prisoners captured : the enemy's flank was turned, and the road opened to Winchester." †

Jackson's movements took Gen. Banks, who

* See Gordon's *History of the Second Massachusetts Regiment*, Third Paper, pp. 79-81.
† Jackson's report.

was at Strasburg, entirely by surprise. The first information he received of the appearance of this strong force on his flank was from Col. Kenly, who, finding the telegraph cut, had sent a courier in the earlier stages of the fight, before he had fallen back over the Shenandoah, to report to Banks the overwhelming attack that was being made upon him [67]. Gen. Banks says : " Information was received on the evening of May 23 that the enemy in very large force had descended on the guard at Front Royal (Col. Kenly, First Maryland regiment, commanding), burning the bridges and driving our troops towards Strasburg with great loss. Owing to what was deemed an extravagant statement of the enemy's strength, these reports were received with some distrust ; but a regiment of infantry, with a strong detachment of cavalry and a section of artillery, were immediately sent to reinforce Col. Kenly." *

The statement that a large force was at Front Royal evidently seemed incredible to the Federal commander, who took steps to reinforce Col. Kenly as if against a dash of cavalry or a raid of guerrillas.

Gen. Banks continues : " Later in the evening despatches from fugitives who had escaped to Winchester informed us that Col. Kenly's force had been destroyed, with but few exceptions, and the enemy, fifteen or twenty thousand

---

* Gen. Gordon says he was instructed to send the Third Wisconsin regiment and a section of his battery to Kenly's assistance.

(15,000 or 20,000) strong, were advancing by rapid marches on Winchester.

" Orders were immediately given to halt the reinforcements sent to Front Royal, which had moved by different routes, and detachments of troops under experienced officers were sent in every direction to explore the roads leading from Front Royal to Strasburg, Middletown, Newtown, and Winchester, and ascertain the force, position, and purpose of this sudden movement of the enemy. It was soon found that his pickets were in possession of every road, and rumours from every quarter represented him in movement in rear of his pickets in the direction of our camp.

" The extraordinary force of the enemy could no longer be doubted. It was apparent also that they had a more extended purpose than the capture of the brave little band at Front Royal.

" This purpose could be nothing less than the defeat of my own command or its possible capture, by occupying Winchester, and by this movement intercepting supplies and reinforcements, and cutting off all possibility of retreat. . . .

" Under this interpretation of the enemy's plans, our position demanded instant decision and action. Three courses were open to us: first, a retreat across Little North Mountain to the Potomac River on the west ; second, an attack on the enemy's flank on the Front Royal road ; third, a rapid movement direct upon Winchester, with a view to anticipate his occupation of the town by seizing it ourselves, and thus placing my command in communication with its original base of operations, and in the line of reinforcements by Harper's Ferry and Martinsburg, and securing a safe retreat in case of disaster. To remain at Strasburg was to be surrounded; to move over the mountain was to abandon our train at the outset, and to subject my command to flank attacks without possibility of succour; and to attack, the enemy being in such overwhelming force, could only result in certain destruction. It was therefore determined to enter the lists with the enemy in a race or a battle, as he should choose, for the possession of Winchester, the key of the Valley, and for us the position of safety.

" At three o'clock A.M., May 24, the reinforcements—infantry, artillery, and cavalry—sent to Col. Kenly were recalled; the advance guard, Col. Donelly's brigade, were ordered to return to Strasburg; several hundred disabled men, left in our charge by Shields's division, were put upon the march, and our wagon-trains ordered forward to Winchester, under escort of cavalry and infantry. Gen. Hatch, with nearly our whole force of cavalry and six pieces of artillery, was charged with the protection of the rear of the column and the destruction of army stores for which transportation was not provided, with instructions to remain in front * of the town as long as possible, and hold the enemy in check, our expectations of attack

* That is, on the south or Staunton side.

being in that direction. All these orders were executed with incredible alacrity, and soon after nine o'clock the column was on the march, Col. Donelly in front, Col. Gordon in the centre, and Gen. Hatch in the rear " [68].

Thus Banks, having partly realized his danger, was taking steps to avert it. He did not yet realize, however, that Jackson's whole force was on his flank at Front Royal, but expected the principal attack to be made from the direction of Woodstock. Gen. Hatch, with a considerable cavalry force, was sent to reconnoitre in that direction, but, finding no enemy, he returned to follow the main column, which meantime had moved out from Strasburg towards Winchester [69].

Jackson's conception of the situation and his plan of operations for Saturday, May 24, are given in his report as follows : " In the event of Banks leaving Strasburg, he might escape toward the Potomac ; or if we moved directly to Winchester, he might move *via* Front Royal towards Washington city. In order to watch both directions, and at the same time advance upon him if he remained at Strasburg, I determined, with the main body of the army, to strike the Valley turnpike near Middletown, a village five miles north of Strasburg, and thirteen south of Winchester. Accordingly, the following morning, Gen. Ashby advanced from Cedarville towards Middletown, supported by skirmishers from Taylor's brigade, with Chew's battery and two Parrott guns from the Rockbridge artillery

(Capt. Poague), followed by the whole command, except the troops left under command of Gen. Ewell near Cedarville. Gen. Ewell, with Trimble's brigade, the First Maryland regiment, and the batteries of Brockenbrough and Courtenay, had instructions to move towards Winchester. Ashby was directed to keep scouts on his left, to prevent Banks from passing unobserved to Front Royal. Brig.-Gen. George H. Steuart, who was now temporarily in command of the Second and Sixth Virginia cavalry, had been previously despatched to Newtown, a point farther north than Middletown, and eight miles from Winchester, with instructions to observe the movements of the enemy at that point. He there succeeded in capturing some prisoners, and several wagons and ambulances with arms and medical stores. He also advised me of movements which indicated that Banks was preparing to leave Strasburg."

Jackson moved towards Middletown as fast as his troops, weary from severe marches, could go. The cavalry, under Steuart, was in advance, and struck the Valley turnpike near Newtown, while the main body was still some distance in the rear. They found the Federal wagon-train passing, and, dashing into it and up the road towards Middletown, with a few shots threw everything into confusion. A part of Broadhead's First Michigan cavalry, supported by the Twenty-ninth Pennsylvania regiment, had been reconnoitring from Middletown towards Front Royal, and having discovered Jackson's advance, was at this moment returning to the former place. The head of the main Federal infantry column (Donelly's brigade) had just crossed Cedar Creek, and was also approaching the town. Information soon reached Gen. Banks "that the enemy had attacked the train, and was in full possession of the road at Middletown." This report was confirmed by the return of fugitives, refugees, and wagons, which came tumbling to the rear in fearful confusion.* The train was halted, and Donelly's infantry ordered to the front to clear the way, while orders were sent to Gen. Hatch to follow from Strasburg "with all his available cavalry, leaving Col. De Forrest to cover the rear and destroy stores not provided with transportation." At the same time a company of infantry was stationed at the Cedar Creek bridge, to prepare it for the flames in case Banks should be forced to recross it and return to Strasburg.

Broadhead and Donelly hastened forward through Middletown, and speedily drove back the Confederate cavalry which had caused such a commotion. The Michigan cavalry went on to Newtown and held the road, while the Forty-sixth Pennsylvania infantry and a section of artillery pushed back the Confederate cavalry on the right of the turnpike for some distance. When this had been done, the Federals turned back to the main road, and their column resumed its march, after only an hour's loss of time. Col. Broadhead, with the First Michigan cavalry,

* Banks's report.

was ordered " to advance, if possible, cut his way through, and occupy Winchester. It was the report of this energetic officer that gave us the first assurance that our course was yet clear, and he was the first of our column to enter the town." * No time was lost by the Federal commander in hurrying forward his column. The knapsacks of the soldiers were left where they had been put, along the roadside, when Donelly's brigade had gone forward to clear the turnpike. There was no time to return or send for them. The Confederate cavalry, under Gen. Steuart, at Newtown, was not strong enough to impede the march seriously, so that the Federal advance reached Winchester without further molestation.

So rapid was his enemy's progress, that when Jackson reached the vicinity of Middletown, two or three hours afterwards, with his main body, the whole of the Federal infantry had already passed that point, and the cavalry, under Gen. Hatch, were beginning to go through. Driving back the cavalry guard sent to observe his movements [70], by a few shots from Poague's battery, Jackson pressed eagerly forward. " When the little village of Middletown came in view, across the broad and level fields, the highway, passing through it at right angles to the direction of Gen. Jackson's approach, was seen, canopied with a vast cloud of grey dust, and crowded beneath, so far as the eye could reach, with a column of troops. At the sight

* Banks's report.

the artillery dashed forward in a gallop for a rising ground, whence to tear their ranks with shell ; Ashby swooped down on their right like an eagle, cut through their path, and arrested their escape on that side ; while Gen. Taylor, throwing his front regiment into line, advanced at a double-quick to the centre of the village, his men cheering, and pouring a terrific volley into the confused mass which filled the street." *

Gen. Jackson says : " The road was literally obstructed with the mingled and confused mass of struggling and dying horses and riders. The Federal column was pierced, but what proportion of its strength had passed north towards Winchester I had then no means of knowing. Among the surviving cavalry the wildest confusion ensued, and they scattered in disorder in various directions, leaving, however, some two hundred prisoners with their equipments in our hands. A train of wagons was seen disappearing in the distance towards Winchester; and Ashby, with his cavalry, some artillery, and a supporting infantry force from Taylor's brigade, was sent in pursuit." †

The Confederates had struck the head of Banks's cavalry under Hatch. When these last had recovered a little from the confusion and disorder into which they were thrown, Hatch, with the main body,‡ turned to his left and

---

* Dabney, p. 371.   † Jackson's report.

‡ Maj. Collins, with three companies, blinded by the dust, charged, unknowingly, into the Confederate lines, and his command was nearly all killed or captured.

attempted, by a circuit through roads north-west of the turnpike and in its general direction, to rejoin the main body of the Federal army. So hurried was the march of the latter that for a time his efforts were unavailing. Several times he tried to regain the turnpike, hoping to find the rear of the Federal infantry, but was driven off. Finally, at Newtown, five miles north of Middletown, he came up with Gordon's brigade, which had there made a stand to check the pursuit and save the trains and artillery.

While Gen. Hatch, with the advance of the Federal cavalry, was making efforts to pass round the Confederates and rejoin Banks, the rear of his command was attempting to open the way along the turnpike. "But a few moments elapsed before the Federal artillery,* which had been cut off with the rear of the column, opened upon us, with the evident intention to cut its way through to Winchester. Our batteries were soon placed in position to return the fire, and Gen. Taylor was ordered with his command to the attack. After a spirited resistance this fragment of the Federal army retreated to Strasburg." † Gen. Banks says : " Six companies of the Fifth New York, Col. De Forrest, and six companies of the First Vermont cavalry, Col. Tompkins, after repeated and desperate efforts to form a junction with the main body,—the road being now filled with (Confederate) infantry, artillery, and cavalry,—

* This was Hampton's battery and a howitzer of Best's.
† Jackson's report.

fell back to Strasburg, where they found the
Zouaves d'Afrique.* The Fifth New York, fail-
ing to effect a junction at Winchester, and also
at Martinsburg, came in at Clear Spring † with
a train of thirty-two wagons and many stragglers.
The First Vermont, Col. Tompkins, joined us at
Winchester with six pieces of artillery, and
participated in the fight of the next morning " [71].
The latter body took a country road leading from
Strasburg to Winchester, considerably west of
the turnpike. The other, having followed the
same road for a time, bore still more to the west,
leaving Winchester and Martinsburg some distance to the right.

While Jackson was engaged in disposing of the
Federal rear guard, Ashby had been sent forward, as above stated, towards Winchester.
The main body of the Confederates had been
halted at Middletown until the Confederate
commander could ascertain whether or not the
whole of Banks's infantry had passed him.
The overthrow of the Federal cavalry soon
satisfied him that the main body was already
between him and Winchester, and without further
delay Jackson, with the mass of his forces,
followed Ashby in that direction. In regard to
this pursuit, Jackson says : " The large number
of wagons loaded with stores and abandoned by
the enemy between Middletown and Newtown
plainly indicated his hurried retreat [72]. From

* These had been stationed at Cedar Creek bridge early in
the day.

† In Maryland, north of the Potomac.

the attack upon Front Royal up to the present moment every opposition had been borne down, and there was reason to believe if Banks reached Winchester it would be without a train, if not without an army; but in the midst of these hopes I was pained to see, as I am now to record, the fact that so many of Ashby's command, both cavalry and infantry, forgetful of their high trust as the advance of a pursuing army, deserted their colours and abandoned themselves to pillage to such an extent as to make it necessary for that gallant officer to discontinue further pursuit.* The artillery, which had pushed on with energy to the vicinity of Newtown, found itself, from this discreditable conduct, without a proper support from either infantry or cavalry. This relaxation of the pursuit was unfortunate, as the enemy was encouraged by it to bring up, about two hours later, four pieces of artillery, which were planted upon the northern skirt of Newtown, and opened upon our batteries. This fire was replied to by Capt. Poague's two rifled guns with skill and accuracy. When I overtook the advance it was thus held in check by the enemy's artillery."†

Banks had hurried on to Newtown and beyond. Here the train was threatened by the cavalry under Gen. Steuart, which had been watching the passing army all day, and harassing

---

* Among the abandoned wagons that lined the road were many loaded with sutler stores. These were especially attractive to the Confederate troops.

† Jackson's report.

it as opportunity offered on the march. Some confusion was produced by this force in the train following the Federal infantry, and the Twenty-seventh Indiana and a section of artillery were ordered to remain and do what was possible to protect the rear. This was sufficient for a time to check Steuart's cavalry, while Ashby's pursuit, as above stated, was not pressed with vigour. As the Confederates continued to push forward, this rear guard was strengthened, and a strong effort made to save the trains from further loss. The head of Gordon's brigade was already beyond Bartonsville, and only five miles from Winchester. Col. Gordon was ordered to take two regiments (Twenty-eighth New York and Second Massachusetts) and two sections of artillery, and return to Newtown, there to hold the Confederates in check. He countermarched as rapidly as possible, and joined the regiment already there. He checked the confusion into which the rear was being thrown, and boldly drove the Confederate advance back through the town. Gen. Hatch soon joined him with the cavalry he had succeeded in bringing round the Confederate flank, and this united force prevented the farther advance of the Confederates, until Jackson's infantry had in part closed up. The display of increasing force, the advance of Ewell along the Front Royal road on his flank as well as the information brought by Gen. Hatch of the dispersion of all the Federal troops in the rear, induced Col. Gordon to retreat at dusk. His skill and determination had effected the object in view. The trains and artillery that had passed Newtown were enabled to reach Winchester. A number of wagons, in the haste and confusion that existed before Gordon's stand, had been overturned, or had been left without horses in the road. These, including a pontoon-train, he fired. Leaving the Second Massachusetts (Lieut.-Col. Andrews) and a section of artillery to cover the rear, he retreated with great expedition to Winchester, which he reached at midnight.

It was now dark, but Jackson continued to press forward after the retreating enemy. His march was skilfully impeded by Lieut-Col. Andrews, who, taking advantage of the darkness, contested stubbornly the Confederate advance at every favourable point. The ability and courage with which Col. Andrews managed his regiment (Second Massachusetts) on this night march were admirable. Jackson, with various regiments in turn of the " Stonewall " brigade, which was in front, drove back this rear guard from point to point; but all the impatient energy of the Confederate leader could not make his progress other than slow. Anxious to occupy the heights overlooking Winchester before dawn, he continued the pursuit all night. The troops in advance (Fifth Virginia regiment, Col. Baylor) were not allowed to lie down at all; to the others was given only an hour's rest.

Meantime, Gen. Ewell had advanced during the day with Trimble's brigade, the First

Maryland regiment, and Brockenbrough's and Courtenay's batteries, on the direct road from Front Royal to Winchester. After halting, when eight miles from Front Royal, for some hours, to await the results of Gen. Jackson's attack, he moved on late in the afternoon, when it became apparent that the enemy were retreating towards Winchester. As he approached the latter town he was joined by Steuart's cavalry from Newtown. When between two and three miles from Winchester, Col. Kirkland, with the Twenty-first North Carolina regiment, drove in the enemy's pickets. He held the position thus gained during the night. The remainder of this command "slept on their arms" one mile in the rear [73].

The results of the day's operations were altogether favourable to the Confederates. Forced to a precipitate evacuation of his position at Strasburg, the Federal commander had made a retreat of eighteen miles upon Winchester, so hurried, and marked by so considerable a loss of stores and wagons, as to give it the aspect of a flight. His cavalry had been attacked, and for the time dispersed, the fragments of it rejoining him at intervals afterwards. Many prisoners had been taken from him, and only the prompt haste of his movement, the fatigue of the march-worn Confederates, and the inefficiency of Ashby's command at a critical moment, had saved his whole army from a complete rout. At best, it was but a broken and dispirited force which rested at Winchester during the night, and prepared to resist the advance of the Confederates on the morrow.

The movement of Jackson had been so sudden and unexpected that Gen. Banks was slow in realizing the true state of the case. The latter says : " The strength and purpose of the enemy were to us unknown when we reached Winchester except upon surmise and vague rumours from Front Royal. These rumours were strengthened by the vigour with which the enemy had pressed our main column, and defeated at every point the efforts of detachments to effect a junction with the main column. At Winchester, however, all suspicion was relieved on that subject. All classes—secessionists, unionists, refugees, fugitives, and prisoners—agreed that the enemy's force at or near Winchester was overwhelming, ranging from twenty-five to thirty thousand. . . . I determined to test the substance and strength of the enemy by actual collision, and measures were promptly taken to prepare our troops to meet them " [74].

For this purpose Gordon's (Federal) brigade was stationed south of the town, on the Valley turnpike. The right of his command was posted on the ridge running south-west from the town and west of the turnpike, about half a mile from the suburbs.* The left rested on the turnpike itself, to which the line was perpendicular. Pickets were thrown out on the hills

---

* This is the same ridge which two miles farther to the southwest was the scene of the battle of Kernstown.

that continue the ridge in front. The Second Massachusetts regiment was on Gordon's right, the Third Wisconsin on his left, near the turnpike, and the Twenty-seventh Indiana and Twenty-ninth Pennsylvania were in reserve, ready to take position wherever needed. Six guns, placed on the crest of the ridge, strengthened Gordon's right, beyond which, under cover of the hill, was Broadhead's cavalry. Near the turnpike, and constituting the centre of the line, were two guns, supported by Hatch's cavalry. On the left was Donelly's brigade, extending across the Front Royal and Millwood roads, thus covering the approaches to the town from the south-east. Here, too, in commanding positions, were placed eight pieces of artillery. The two last-mentioned roads, as they approach Winchester, unite about a mile from the town. In front of this junction a short distance, on a ridge running in the direction of the Front Royal road, was Donelly's crescent-shaped line. Here the battle opened. Gen. Ewell had bivouacked not far in front of the Federal line, and, moving his troops at dawn, he soon came up to the enemy, drove in his outposts, and attacked him. The Twenty-first North Carolina regiment, Col. Kirkland, was in advance, and at 5 A.M. boldly made a dash at the position held by Donelly across the road. The North Carolinians met with a bloody reception. The Federals, taking advantage of the stone fences with which that country is everywhere intersected, had posted their line behind some of these fences, and poured a well-directed front and flank fire into the Confederates as they advanced across the open field. In a few moments the Twenty-first North Carolina, having lost both the field officers present, and a large number of men killed and wounded, fell back [75]. This check was, however, but brief in its duration. When Kirkland advanced in the centre, Col. Johnson, with the First Maryland regiment, moved forward on his left, nearer the Valley turnpike, and, meeting with little opposition, reached the suburbs of the town. On the right of the Twenty-first North Carolina, Col. Mercer, with the Twenty-first Georgia, advanced, turned the flank of the enemy on that side, and, by means of an enfilading fire, quickly drove them from the position unsuccessfully attacked by Col. Kirkland. Latimer (in command of Courtenay's guns) and Brockenbrough contributed to this result with their batteries. The Federals took a new position nearer the town. The remainder of Trimble's brigade (Sixteenth Mississippi and Fifteenth Alabama regiments) now joined the Twenty-first Georgia; but instead of attacking in front again, Gen. Ewell adopted the suggestion of Trimble, and moved farther to the right, so as to threaten the Federal flank and rear. This manœuvre, combined with Jackson's success on the other flank, caused the whole to give way.

It is time to return to the main Confederate attack. All night had Jackson pressed onward at the head of the " Stonewall " brigade. Soon after dawn, as he approached Winchester, he saw the Federal skirmishers on a hill belonging to the ridge on his left, and ordered Gen. Winder to " seize the hill as speedily as possible. The Fifth Virginia regiment, Col. Baylor, was accordingly thrown out in advance as skirmishers, and the Second, Fourth, Twenty-seventh, and Thirty-third Virginia regiments being placed in order of battle, the whole line was ordered to advance, which was done in handsome style, and the position on the crest secured, although the enemy made a resolute but unsuccessful effort to dislodge our troops from so commanding a position. Two Parrott guns from the Rockbridge artillery, and the batteries of Carpenter and Cutshaw, were promptly posted on the height to dislodge a battery of the enemy, which was playing from the front with great animation and effect upon the hill." *   The Second Brigade, Col. Campbell, was sent to support the batteries, while Taliaferro's brigade, under Col. Fulkerson, was placed on the left in support of Winder, and to extend his line.

It was at this time that Gordon moved the Second Massachusetts farther up on the ridge, where he already had the six guns that had opened upon Winder when the latter was driving back the Federal outposts. As the regiment moved to the Federal right it had to bear a heavy fire from the Confederate batteries already in position, but the movement was completed in good order.   Some of the Federal guns were

* Jackson's report.

now moved more to the right, and took a position which enabled them to enfilade the section of Poague's (Rockbridge) battery. A company of the Second Massachusetts was thrown out before these guns as sharpshooters, and, sheltering themselves behind a stone fence, they poured a destructive fire into the midst of Poague's horses and men. Turning his guns, Poague directs his fire upon these assailants; but the fire of artillery is not effective against sharpshooters. Another company of the Second Massachusetts reinforces the first behind the stone wall, and Poague sees his men and horses falling fast. Withdrawing and placing his guns to the left and rear, he opens vigorously from the new position upon the battery that has enfiladed and the sharpshooters that have so seriously annoyed him. At this point he is joined by the remaining four guns of his battery. He disconcerts the Federal sharpshooters by firing solid shot at the stone fence which protects them. Meantime, Cutshaw and Carpenter hold their positions to the right of Poague, and pour an effective artillery fire upon the enemy. The Federal commander now moves up the Twenty-seventh Indiana and Twenty-ninth Pennsylvania regiments from the turnpike, and places them on the right of the Second Massachusetts, with the design of holding the crest of the ridge, and, if possible, turning the Confederate left. Jackson, seeing this strengthening and extending of his enemy's right, orders up Taylor's Louisianians, who, passing behind Winder, form on his left and overlap the Federal flank. The Tenth and Twenty-third Virginia, of Taliaferro's brigade, extend Taylor's line, the former regiment on his left, and the other on his right. Regardless of the artillery fire and the musketry of the sharp-shooters, this strong body formed in line, and, moving to the crest of the hill, " swept magnificently down the declivity and across the field, driving back the Federal troops and bearing down all opposition before it. In this gallant advance all the troops of Gen. Winder joined except those left as supports to the batteries." *

Col. Gordon says of this charge of the Confederates : " They were received with a destructive fire of musketry poured in from all parts of my brigade that could reach them. Confident in their numbers, and relying upon large sustaining bodies, . . . the enemy's lines moved on but little shaken by our fire. At the same time in our front a long line of infantry showed themselves, rising the crest of the hills just beyond our position. My little brigade, numbering in all two thousand one hundred and two (2102), in another moment would have been overwhelmed. On the right, left, and centre immensely superior columns were pressing ; not another man was available,—not a support to be found in the remnant of the army corps left Gen. Banks. To withdraw was now possible ; in another moment it would have been too late. At this moment I should have assumed the responsibility of requesting permission to

* Jackson's report.

withdraw, but the right fell back under great pressure, and compelled the line to yield."*

Jackson now ordered Elzey's brigade forward on the Valley turnpike, while Taylor and Winder swept back the enemy rapidly over the hills into the town. It was at the time of Taylor's successful charge, between 8 and 9 A.M., that Ewell, having pushed back Donelly on the Front Royal road into the suburbs of the town, was moving to the Confederate right and threatening the Federal rear. Ashby took possession of the Berryville road, which leaves Winchester on the east side, and thus cut off a retreat by that route to Harper's Ferry. Finding himself beaten on both flanks and his line of retreat endangered, Banks made no further attempt to hold the town or check the progress of the Confederates. Passing quickly through Winchester, and in such order as was possible, he fled northward with great haste by the Martinsburg road, leaving many prisoners in the hands of his antagonist.

Jackson followed through the town, and without delay continued the pursuit. He says: "Notwithstanding the fatiguing marches and almost sleepless night to which the mass of our troops had been subjected, they continued to press forward with alacrity. The Federal forces, upon falling back into the town, preserved their organization remarkably well. In passing through its streets they were thrown into confusion, and shortly after debouching upon the plain and turnpike to Martinsburg, and after

* Gordon's report.

being fired upon by our artillery, they presented the aspect of a mass of disordered fugitives. Never have I seen an opportunity when it was in the power of cavalry to reap a richer harvest of the fruits of victory. Hoping that the cavalry would soon come up, the artillery, followed by infantry, was pressed forward for about two hours for the purpose of preventing, by artillery fire, a re-forming of the enemy ; but as nothing was heard of the cavalry, and as but little or nothing could be accomplished without it in the exhausted condition of our infantry, between whom and the enemy the distance was continually increasing, I ordered a halt and issued orders for going into camp and refreshing the men." *

Two causes prevented an efficient pursuit by the Confederate cavalry. Ashby's command had become scattered in the pillage of the day before, and during the night march and fight of the morning he had had but little opportunity to collect them. With such as were at hand he had moved to the enemy's left to prevent a retreat by way of Berryville to Harper's Ferry, and with the hope of " cutting off a portion of his force." From this cause he only entered the Martinsburg road and joined the cavalry under Steuart some ten or twelve miles from Winchester, and after Banks had passed. Gen. George H. Steuart, of the Maryland line, now in command of the Second and Sixth Virginia cavalry regiments, was with Ewell during the

* Jackson's report.

morning, and when Lieut. Pendleton, of Jackson's staff, found him, with an urgent order to follow the enemy, he wasted valuable time on a point of military etiquette,* and consequently did not overtake the advance of the Confederate infantry until an hour after it had halted.   Gen. Steuart then pushed on with vigour and picked up a good many prisoners, but the delay had enabled the Federal army to make such headway that it was " beyond the reach of successful pursuit." †   Banks halted in his rapid course at Martinsburg for an hour or two, and then continued his retreat to Williamsport, which he reached at sundown. Here, during the night and next morning, he crossed to the north side of the river. The Federal army, after the defeat of the morning, thus marched the distance from Winchester to the Potomac (thirty-four miles) in one day. Steuart with his cavalry followed it to Martinsburg, where he captured a large amount of stores. " There is good reason for believing that, had the cavalry played its part in this pursuit as well as the four companies had done under Col. Flournoy two days before, in the pursuit from Front Royal, but a small portion of Banks's army would have made its escape to the Potomac." ‡

But the victory was complete and glorious, even if Jackson's weary and march-worn command had not achieved all that their tireless and

---

* He declined to obey the order until it came through Gen. Ewell.

† Jackson's report.   ‡ Jackson's report.

indomitable leader thought possible. In forty-eight hours the enemy had been driven between fifty and sixty miles from Front Royal and Strasburg to the Potomac, with the loss of more than one-third of his entire strength. His army had crossed the latter river a disorganized mass. Hundreds of wagons had been abandoned or burnt. Two pieces of artillery and an immense quantity of quartermaster, commissary, medical, and ordnance stores had fallen into the hands of the victor [76]. " Some two thousand three hundred (2300) prisoners " were taken to the rear when Jackson fell back, besides seven hundred and fifty (750) wounded and sick paroled and left in the hospitals at Winchester and Strasburg, making a total of about three thousand and fifty (3050) [77]. The Federal surgeons captured in attendance at their hospitals were at first paroled, but next day, at the suggestion of Medical Director Hunter McGuire, of Jackson's staff, they were unconditionally released.* Jackson's loss during the entire expedition was four hundred (400) men [78].

But the most important result of Jackson's victory did not consist in the overthrow of the small army under Gen. Banks and the capture of the large stores accumulated in the Lower Valley. It disorganized the plan of campaign against Richmond, and, for a time, paralyzed McClellan's movements. President Lincoln had yielded, as heretofore stated, to Gen. McClellan's

---

* For the terms of this parole, see Appendix to *Medical and Surgical History of the War*, p. 118.

urgent appeal for reinforcements, so far as to order McDowell, on May 17, to prepare to move down the Fredericksburg and Richmond railroad, in order to unite with the main Federal army in front of Richmond. Shields's division was sent from the Valley to swell his force to forty thousand (40,000) men for this purpose. On Friday, May 23, President Lincoln and Secretary Stanton went to Fredericksburg to confer with Gen. McDowell, found that Shields had already reached that point, and determined, after consultation, that the advance should begin on the following Monday, May 26. McClellan was informed of the contemplated movement and instructed to assume command of McDowell's corps when it joined him [79]. This fine body of troops, moving from the north against the Confederate capital, would have seized all the roads entering the city from that direction, and would have increased McClellan's available force by forty or fifty per cent. There was strong reason to expect that this combined movement would effect the downfall of Richmond.

The Federal President returned to Washington on the night of the 23rd, to await the result. He there received the first news of Jackson's operation at Front Royal on that same afternoon. The first despatches indicated only an unimportant raid, and McDowell was directed to leave his " least effective " brigade at Fredericksburg, in addition to the force agreed upon for the occupation of that town [80]. Later, on the 24th, the news from Banks became more alarming, and Gen. McDowell was telegraphed that "Gen. Fremont has been ordered by telegraph to move from Franklin on Harrisonburg, to relieve Gen. Banks and capture or destroy Jackson's and Ewell's forces. You are instructed, laying aside for the present the movement on Richmond, to put twenty thousand (20,000) men in motion at once for the Shenandoah, moving on the line, or in advance of the line of the Manassas Gap railroad. Your object will be to capture the forces of Jackson and Ewell, either in co-operation with Gen. Fremont, or, in case want of supplies or of transportation interferes with his movement, it is believed that the force with which you move will be sufficient to accomplish the object alone.* . . ." The following was sent to McClellan :

> " WASHINGTON CITY, *May* 24, 1862,
> " 4 P.M.

" In consequence of Gen. Banks's critical position, I have been compelled to suspend Gen. McDowell's movement to join you. The enemy are making a desperate push on Harper's Ferry, and we are trying to throw Fremont's force and part of McDowell's in their rear.
> " A. LINCOLN."

Next day the news from Banks seems to have

---

* Report on Conduct of the War, Part I. p. 274. (McDowell's testimony.)

greatly increased the excitement in Washington. The following telegrams were sent to Gen. McClellan:

"U. S. MILITARY TELEGRAPH.
"WAR DEPARTMENT, WASHINGTON, D. C., *May* 25, 1862.

"The enemy is moving north in sufficient force to drive Banks before him, in precisely what force we cannot tell. He is also threatening Leesburg, and Geary * on the Manassas Gap railroad, from both north and south, in precisely what force we cannot tell [81]. I think the movement is a general and concerted one, such as could not be if he was acting upon the purpose of a very desperate defence of Richmond. I think the time is near when you must either attack Richmond or give up the job and come to the defence of Washington. Let me hear from you instantly.

"A. LINCOLN.
"GEN. McCLELLAN."

"U. S. MILITARY TELEGRAPH.
"WAR DEPARTMENT, WASHINGTON, D. C., *May* 25, 1862.

"Your despatch received. Banks was at Strasburg with about six thousand (6000) men,† Shields having been taken from him to swell a column for McDowell to aid you at Richmond, and the rest of his force scattered at various places. On the 23rd a rebel force of seven to ten thousand (7000 to 10,000) men fell upon one

* Gen. Geary commanded a force guarding this railroad. His strength present for duty May 17 was about 1900.
† See statement of Banks's forces in note 74, page 254.

regiment and two companies, guarding the bridge at Front Royal, destroying it entirely; crossed the Shenandoah, and on the 24th (yesterday) pushed to get north of Banks on the road to Winchester. Banks ran a race with them, beating them into Winchester yesterday evening. This morning a battle ensued between the two forces, in which Banks was beaten back into full retreat towards Martinsburg, and probably is broken up into a total rout. Geary, on the Manassas Gap railroad, just now reports that Jackson is now near Front Royal with ten thousand (10,000), following up and supporting, as I understand, the force now pursuing Banks; also that another force of ten thousand (10,000) is near Orleans, following on in the same direction.* Stripped bare, as we are here, it will be all we can do to prevent them crossing the Potomac at Harper's Ferry, or above. We have about twenty thousand (20,000) of McDowell's force moving back to the vicinity of Front Royal, and Fremont, who was at Franklin, is moving to Harrisonburg. Both of these movements are intended to get in the enemy's rear. One more of McDowell's brigades is ordered through here to Harper's Ferry. The rest of his forces remain for the present at Fredericksburg. We are sending such regiments and dribs from here and Baltimore as we can spare to Harper's Ferry, supplying their place

* These were of course entirely imaginary creations of Gen. Geary's informant, and show the consternation that Jackson's movement had inspired.

in some sort by calling in militia from the adjacent States. We also have eighteen cannon on the road to Harper's Ferry, of which arm there is not a single one yet at that point. This is now our situation. If McDowell's force was now beyond our reach we should be utterly helpless. Apprehensions of something like this, and no unwillingness to sustain you, has always been my reason for withholding McDowell's forces from you. Please understand this, and do the best you can with the forces you have.

" A. LINCOLN [82].

" GEN. MCCLELLAN."

The operations of Jackson thus not only occupied all the troops in and around Washington, together with Fremont's forces, but for the time completely neutralized the forty thousand men under McDowell, and disconcerted McClellan's plans. It is true that both McDowell and McClellan, deeming the fears of the Federal Administration exaggerated, deprecated the interference with McDowell's advance on Richmond, but in vain. McDowell says, May 24, in reply to the order sending half his corps after Jackson: " I beg to say that co-operation between Gen. Fremont and myself, to cut off Jackson and Ewell, is not to be counted upon, even if it is not a practical impossibility; next, that I am entirely beyond helping distance of Gen. Banks, and no celerity or vigour will avail, so far as he is concerned; next, that by a glance at the map it will be seen that the line of retreat of the enemy's forces up the Valley is shorter than mine to go against him. It will take a week or ten days for the force to get to the Valley by the route which will give it food and forage, and by that time the enemy will have retired.* I shall gain nothing for you there, and shall lose much for you here. It is therefore not only on personal grounds that I have a heavy heart in the matter, but that I feel it throws us all back; and from Richmond north we shall have all our large masses paralyzed, and shall have to repeat what we have just accomplished." † McClellan says: " It will be remembered that the order for the co-operation of Gen. McDowell was simply suspended, not revoked, and therefore I was not at liberty to abandon the northern approach to Richmond." ‡ This fact, together with the necessity of protecting his communications with the York River, caused him to retain a part of his army on the north side of the Chickahominy, while the remainder was separated from him by that troublesome stream,—a circumstance that contributed not a little to his subsequent defeat.

The Federal Administration, however, adhered to its plans, and hastened McDowell's movement to the Valley. The moral effect of a Confederate advance to the neighbourhood of Washington was dreaded, and still more, perhaps, the irrup-

---

* He little appreciated Jackson's boldness, who remained at Harper's Ferry until McDowell's advance had occupied Front Royal.

† McDowell's testimony.   ‡ McClellan's report.

tion of a victorious Southern force into the
State of Maryland. The mass of the people of
this State sympathized with the South. They
were kept down only by the presence of Federal
troops. It was a matter of grave consequence
that Jackson should not be able to maintain
himself north of the Potomac, even for a short
time. Such considerations outweighed even the
prospect of taking Richmond.

While President Lincoln was thus " taking
counsel of his fears," * and promptly ordering
troops from all directions to overwhelm Jackson,
the latter was resting from the fatigues of his
forced marches. Having turned over the pursuit
of the enemy to the cavalry at midday on Sunday
(25th), he placed his army in camp at Stephenson's, five miles north of Winchester, and,
returning himself to the town, took up his
headquarters there. This historic town and its
beautiful environs represented on that glorious
May afternoon an aspect of quiet and repose
strangely in contrast with the stormy scenes of
the morning. Several warehouses filled with
stores had been fired by the flying Federals, and
this involved the burning of a considerable
number of other buildings. But now the fire
was over ; the citizens were busy looking after
the wounded, or paying the last sad rites to the
dead. Universal joy, even when mingled with
sorrow at the loss of loved ones, was manifested
at Gen. Jackson's return.

* A favourite aphorism of Jackson's was : " Never take
counsel of your fears."

Next morning Jackson issued an order in the following terms : " Within four weeks this army has made long and rapid marches ; fought six combats and two battles, signally defeating the enemy in each one ; captured several stands of colours and pieces of artillery, with numerous prisoners, and vast medical, ordnance, and army stores ; and finally driven the boastful host, which was ravaging our beautiful country, into utter rout. The General commanding would warmly express to the officers and men under his command his joy in their achievements, and his thanks for their brilliant gallantry in action and their patient obedience under the hardships of forced marches, often more painful to the brave soldier than the dangers of battle. The explanation of the severe exertions to which the commanding General called the army, which were endured by them with such cheerful confidence in him, is now given in the victory of yesterday. He receives this proof of their confidence in the past with pride and gratitude, and asks only a similar confidence in the future.

" But his chief duty to-day, and that of the army, is to recognize devoutly the hand of a protecting Providence in the brilliant successes of the last three days (which have given us the results of a great victory without great losses), and to make the oblation of our thanks to God for His mercies to us and our country in heartfelt acts of religious worship. For this purpose the troops will remain in camp to-day, sus-pending, as far as possible, all military exercises ;

and the chaplains of regiments will hold divine service in their several charges at 4 o'clock P.M." *

Another day was spent in resting, and then the Confederate leader was ready for action. " Immediately after the battle of Winchester he had sent a trusty officer to the capital with despatches explaining his views. The decision of the government was that he should press the enemy at Harper's Ferry, threaten an invasion of Maryland and an assault upon the Federal capital, and thus make the most energetic diversion possible to draw a portion of the forces of McDowell and McClellan from Richmond." † Early on the 28th, Gen. Winder, with four regiments and two batteries of his brigade, was sent forward towards Charlestown by way of Summit Point. He picked up a few cavalry scouts on the way, through whom he learned, when within five miles of Charlestown, that the enemy occupied it in force. He communicated this information to Jackson, who then ordered Ewell to move in the same direction.

The troops in front of Winder were part of a force that had been rapidly concentrated at Harper's Ferry. Col. Miles had held that post for some time with a small force, but with no artillery.‡ Upon the reception of the news of Banks's defeat, Gen. R. Saxton had been sent to take command, and troops and artillery were hurried forward. Saxton arrived on the 26th, and by the evening of the 27th a force of some

* Dabney, p. 384.   † Dabney, p. 386.
‡ See President Lincoln's despatch, p. 119.

seven thousand (7000) men * and eighteen (18) pieces of artillery † had been gathered there. He at once occupied Bolivar Heights, the high plateau in the fork of the Shenandoah and the Potomac, with his troops, and placed a naval battery of Dahlgren guns on the point of the mountain north of the Potomac, known as " Maryland Heights." This last position completely commands the town and the Bolivar Heights. He attempted, on the evening of the 27th, to take possession of the point of the mountain opposite the Maryland Heights, on the Virginia side, and known as the Loudoun Heights, but the two companies sent for this purpose were driven off by some guerrillas. Next day a " reconnaissance in force was made towards Charlestown by the One Hundred and Eleventh Pennsylvania regiment, the First Maryland cavalry, and a section of Reynolds's battery." ‡ This force drove the Confederate cavalry scouts out of the town, and took up a position near its southern limits. It was soon after that Gen. Winder reached the vicinity of the town ; and, forcing back the Federal cavalry pickets through a piece of woodland, he found the main body drawn up in line of battle beyond. Seeing that the Federal force was far less than had been reported, he made arrangements to attack at once. To reply to the two Federal guns that had opened on him, he placed Car-

* Saxton's report, *Rebellion Record*, vol. v. p. 159.
† President Lincoln's despatch, above referred to.
‡ Saxton's report.

penter's four pieces in position, and supported
them by the Thirty-third Virginia regiment.
" This battery was admirably worked, and in
twenty minutes the enemy retired in great
disorder, throwing away arms, blankets, haver-
sacks, etc. The pursuit was continued rapidly
with artillery and infantry. Capt. Poague was
ordered up with a gun and howitzer. These,
with Carpenter's guns, were placed in position
wherever practicable." * Saxton, hearing of the
repulse of his advance, sent forward the Seventy-
eighth New York and the remainder of Reynolds's
battery to cover the retreat. The Federals
reached Bolivar Heights with the loss of nine
prisoners, and Saxton formed his main body
" in line of battle extending along the crest
of Bolivar Heights across the peninsula from
the Potomac to the Shenandoah." † The Confederates continued the pursuit to Halltown,
when, finding the enemy in position at Bolivar,
and tired from a march of over twenty-one miles,
they were content to return and go into camp
in the vicinity of Charlestown. Gen. Ewell
arrived at nightfall. (Map No. V.)

Next day (29th) the main body of the Confederate army " took position near Halltown,
and the Second regiment of Virginia infantry was
sent to the Loudoun Heights, with the hope of
being able to drive the enemy from Harper's
Ferry across the Potomac." ‡

These movements consumed the greater part

* Winder's report.   † Saxton's report.
‡ Jackson's report.

of the day, which was not marked otherwise on the Confederate side, save by the driving in of the Federal pickets and the repulse of the reconnoitring parties sent out by Gen. Saxton.

The latter continued throughout the day to hold the Federal forces in order of battle on Bolivar Heights. In the afternoon, the fact that no attack had been made in front, the appearance of a Confederate force on Loudoun Heights, and a report that Jackson was crossing one division over the Potomac, above Harper's Ferry, caused him to fear an attack on Maryland Heights in his rear. He therefore determined to move part of his infantry to the north side of the Potomac, and place it on those heights, so as to secure his battery, already there, and to withdraw the remainder from Bolivar to the hill immediately above Harper's Ferry, where his line would be shorter and his troops more completely protected by the guns on the Maryland Heights. These changes he effected during the night of the 29th.

These precautions, however, were unnecessary. Jackson had no time at his disposal for crossing the Potomac and investing the enemy on all sides. He had already carried his instructions, to threaten an invasion of Maryland and a movement upon Washington, to the extreme point consistent with safety. The movements of the large bodies of troops which the Federal President had been for some days urging with such haste towards his rear, now imperatively demanded his attention. Jackson's strength was

not over fifteen thousand (15,000) men.* All
the energy of a great government was now
being expended in gathering about him a force
of between fifty-five and sixty thousand (55,000
and 60,000) men [83].

The despatch of President Lincoln to Gen.
McDowell, already given, required him to send
half his corps after Jackson. Subsequent orders
directed him to increase still further this force.
McDowell moved King's division after those of
Shields and Ord. The front division (Shields's)
was pushed forward as rapidly as possible, and
by the evening of the 29th was so far advanced as
to be within striking distance of Front Royal the
next day. Gen. McDowell was himself directing
the march of the other divisions towards the same
point, and reached Rectortown on the 30th [84].

On the other hand, Gen. Fremont, who had
been quietly resting at Franklin for ten days,
while Jackson was making forced marches after
Banks, was startled by the news from the latter
on the 24th, and next day (Sunday, 25th) took
up his march, under President Lincoln's orders,
for Strasburg [85]. The route he chose was by way
of Petersburg (where he left all surplus baggage
and tents) and Moorefield. His progress was
delayed by rain and bad roads, so that it was
Friday night (30th) when he reached Wardensville.

NOTE.—Some interesting reminiscences of the battle of
Winchester were received from Gen. Trimble after the fore-

* Dabney. Jackson's force has been greatly exaggerated in
many of the accounts of this campaign.

going chapter was in print. It seems that Ewell's division moved forward early on the morning of May 24 towards Winchester, Trimble's brigade in front. At eight o'clock the troops halted to rest, when Gen. Trimble descried the smoke of burning stores in the direction of Strasburg, and suggested a march directly to Newtown to cut the main road from Strasburg to Winchester. Jackson, however, thinking it more probable that Banks was retreating from Strasburg westwards towards the Potomac, left Ewell with Trimble's brigade and some other troops at this point, and, taking Taylor's brigade with the remainder of the army, moved towards Middletown that he might the sooner strike Banks if he had taken the route supposed. Ewell remained at Nineveh the greater part of the day waiting for orders. These orders, by the failure of the courier to find him, instead of being delivered by mid-day, did not reach him until 3.30 p.m. They directed him to move on Newtown, but when received, the artillery fire indicated that Jackson, with the main body, in following up Banks, had already advanced to that point. Hence, after consultation, Gens. Ewell and Trimble marched towards Winchester, the vicinity of which they reached at dusk.

Next morning the artillery fire on Jackson's wing was heard by seven o'clock. Trimble's brigade was then moving forward on the other flank. " Gen. Ewell in person directed the Twenty-first North Carolina regiment to enter the suburbs at a mill on the south-east part of the town, directing the other regiments of Trimble's brigade and the artillery to ascend the high grounds and take a position on the east of Winchester, a half-mile or so distant from that place.

" As soon as the North Carolina regiment passed the mill-stream they were met by a destructive fire from behind stone fences, and could not advance. Col. Mercer, of the Twenty-first Georgia, skilfully moved farther to the right, charged the enemy in flank and drove them off. Gen. Ewell relinquished the attack at that point, and marched his whole command to the high ground before named, ordering his artillery to open fire on the enemy's batteries, which could be discovered on the south edge of the town. After a cannonade of fifteen minutes, a dense fog obscured the Valley completely and laid over the town for perhaps half an hour, during which the firing ceased on both sides entirely. It was about nine o'clock. After this, the fog was lifted as a curtain, displaying everything, houses and the enemy's troops, in full view. Then a fierce artillery fire at once opened, displaying in the bright sunshine as inspiring a battle-scene as was ever witnessed. . . .

" A half-hour after the fog rose, the southern yell of Taylor's brigade was heard far off on the opposite heights, as they charged down on the flank of the enemy's position. Gen. Jackson had ordered Taylor to pass in the rear, out of view, gain the enemy's right flank and charge down on him."

Gen. Trimble now desired to move to the north end of the town and seize the Martinsburg road. Gen. Ewell, after some delay, directed the movement to be made, but when Gen. Trimble reached the Martinsburg road the mass of the Federal troops had already passed the point, and their rapid flight soon placed them out of reach of the Confederate infantry. The severity of the service undergone by Jackson's troops in this expedition may be gathered from the fact, stated by Gen. Trimble, that at Winchester 20 per cent. of his brigade were barefooted. The abundant stores captured were a God-send to the ill-provided Confederates.

CHAPTER V

CROSS KEYS AND PORT REPUBLIC

JACKSON had been watching the approach of his enemies, and concluded, on Friday morning (30th), that it was time for him to withdraw if he would pass between the converging armies of Fremont and McDowell [86]. Accordingly, " orders were issued for all the Confederate troops, except Winder's brigade, the First Maryland regiment, and the cavalry, to return to Winchester on the 30th. Directions were given to Gen. Winder to recall the Second Virginia regiment from Loudoun Heights, and, so soon as it should return to its brigade, to move with his command, including the cavalry, and rejoin the main body of the army." *

While Jackson, with the main body of his forces, was thus returning to Winchester from the vicinity of Harper's Ferry, Shields, with a small body of cavalry and the advance infantry brigade of his division, was already crossing the Blue Ridge, and pouring down from the mountain-pass upon Front Royal. The Twelfth Georgia regiment, Col. Conner, and a section of Rice's battery, had been left by the Confederate commander to hold this post and cover the

* Jackson's report.

removal of the very large amount of stores there captured. These last were being removed as fast as Maj. John A. Harman, chief quarter-master, could effect it. All the captured wagons, and those that could be spared from the army, as well as all that could be hired or impressed in the vicinity, had been for some days engaged in taking the stores from Winchester and Front Royal to the rear. Trains of wagons were loading, under the direction of Capt. Cole, assistant quartermaster, Thirty-seventh Virginia regiment, at the time of Shields's approach. Col. Conner seems not to have been aware of the vicinity of the enemy until they were almost upon him. He then hastily abandoned the town, and with his small force fell back over the Shenandoah on the road to Winchester. Capt. Cole was with difficulty able to send his wagons beyond the reach of pursuit, and had barely time to fire the depot and buildings containing the remainder of the Federal stores. The recapture of them by Shields was thus prevented. The latter officer pursued the re-treating Confederates some distance on the road to Winchester, Col. Conner making but a feeble resistance, and losing in the retreat six Federal prisoners that were in his hands, as well as a considerable number of his own men, and one piece of artillery [87].

The condition of affairs when Jackson reached Winchester on the evening of that day (the 30th) was as follows : McDowell was in possession of Front Royal, which is but twelve miles from

Strasburg, while Winchester is eighteen. Fremont was at Wardensville, distant twenty miles from Strasburg, and had telegraphed the Federal President that he would enter the latter place by 5 P.M. on the next day [88]. The mass of Jackson's forces had marched twenty-five miles to reach Winchester, and his rear guard, under Winder, after skirmishing with the enemy at Harper's Ferry for the greater part of the day, had, upon the reunion of the Second Virginia regiment with it, camped in the vicinity of Halltown, which is about forty-three miles distant from Strasburg. Thus, while the head of Jackson's column was still eighteen miles from Strasburg, and the rear forty miles distant, the head of McDowell's army was but twelve miles from the same point, and Fremont's forces were but twenty miles away. The combined forces of McDowell and Fremont were nearly triple the Confederate strength. They were hastening from opposite directions to cut off Jackson's retreat, and once at Strasburg the way would be barred. From the Potomac side the combined forces of Banks and Saxton amounted to fourteen thousand (14,000) men, and were ready to close in on the rear of the retreating Confederates. In this perilous situation the Confederate leader decided to occupy Strasburg in advance of his enemies, and to pass swiftly between the two principal armies gathering for his destruction. It was a case in which supreme audacity was the most consummate skill.

No time was to be lost if the Confederates

were to escape from the dangers that threatened them, and Jackson lost none. Orders were issued for everything at Winchester to move early the next morning (May 31). The two thousand three hundred (2300) Federal prisoners were first sent forward, guarded by the Twenty-first Virginia regiment ; next, the long trains, including many loaded with captured stores ; then followed the whole of the army except the rear guard under Winder. Capt. Hotchkiss was sent with orders to Winder to hasten on to Winchester and not to camp until he had made some part of the distance between that place and Strasburg [89].

The march was made without molestation, and during the afternoon the main body of the Confederates reached Strasburg, and camped there for the night. Gen. Winder, late in the day, passed through Winchester to the neighbourhood of Newtown, where he went into camp, some parts of his command having marched thirty-five, and all of it twenty-eight, miles !

Jackson thus in a single day put thirty miles between himself and the tardy columns of Saxton and Banks, and took position directly between the two armies of Fremont and McDowell, which had been sent to crush him. But the latter were moving with too great caution for their purpose towards the appointed rendezvous. Gen. Shields consumed the day in getting the whole of his division into Front Royal, and in posting it out on the various roads leading from that village. He had exaggerated ideas of Jackson's strength, and was also imposed upon by a report that a force under Longstreet was approaching to the relief of Jackson by the Luray Valley. When Gen. McDowell, therefore, who had during the day urged forward Ord's (now Rickett's) division towards Front Royal, came up with Shields at nightfall, he found that one of the latter's brigades had been posted with reference to a force approaching from Luray, while another was at the fords of the Shenandoah, a third in the direction of Strasburg, and the fourth in Front Royal itself.* Shields had not ventured, however, to push out to any considerable distance from the latter place. He made no attempt to occupy Strasburg, or to impede and harass Jackson's retreat by striking the Valley turnpike, on which the latter was moving. He awaited the arrival of McDowell and the remaining divisions.

Fremont, on the other hand, left Wardensville on Saturday morning. He was to have entered Strasburg on that afternoon, according to his despatches to Mr. Lincoln, but he stopped several miles short of the town, at Cedar Creek. The heavy roads and a violent rain-storm in the afternoon may have induced him to cut short his march before he reached the Confederate outposts; but, whatever the cause, the result was the loss of all opportunity to seriously hinder the retreat of Jackson.

Saxton, at Harper's Ferry, had moved out,

* McDowell's testimony.

and, finding that Winder was gone, advanced as far as Charlestown, but there went into camp, and made no further effort to follow. He reports his men as having been " completely worn out by fatigue and exposure " consequent upon the skirmishes and movements of the preceding days.

Next morning (Sunday, June 1) the clouds broke away, and a bright day succeeded the rain-storm of the preceding afternoon and night, —a welcome change to the weary soldiers of both armies as they rose from their wet bivouac.

Jackson, during the morning, continued the movement of his prisoners and all surplus trains to the rear, while he retained the bulk of his force at Strasburg to keep possession of the road until Winder should arrive. Finding that Fremont was preparing to force in his cavalry outposts, under Ashby, on the Wardensville road, he ordered Gen. Ewell, with his division, to support them, and subsequently strengthened Ewell by other troops, so as to make a display of force. Fremont's effort to advance was, however, very feeble. Cluscret's brigade was in the front of his command, and engaged the Confederate advance, but, after a spirited skirmish, the brigade was withdrawn, because of the advantageous position of the Confederate artillery, and Fremont took position a short distance to the rear. Here he remained the greater part of the day,* making no further

---

* On the water-shed between Cedar Creek and the Shenandoah, about three miles from Strasburg.

attack on the Confederate lines, evidently hesi-
tating to bring down the whole of Jackson's
force on himself, while uncertain that McDowell
was within supporting distance.

Meantime, Jackson's rapid movements seem
to have completely bewildered McDowell and
Shields. The former gives the following account
of the day's operations : " The next morning
(June 1) I endeavoured to get in the division of
Gen. Ord, then Gen. Rickett's division. They
were wet, had no tents, and were very much
exposed, but they got along the best way they
could. They kept coming in in driblets, sometimes in considerable bodies. We heard firing,
and that animated them somewhat, and they
began to come in pretty fast. The firing seemed
to be in the direction of Winchester. I saw
Gen. Shields, and it was arranged that he should
take the road at once with his division, as he
knew the country and we did not. He said if
he could only get his troops in from the different
places where they had been posted, he could
accomplish the movement. I told him that he
could give orders that they should take up
their march, and I would see that those positions
they then occupied were cared for. He was to
go on the direct road to Strasburg, and not
cross the North Fork of the Shenandoah until
near Strasburg, and that if he should interpose
between Jackson's advance, Ord's division should
throw itself upon his flank.

" After some time in getting Ord's, or rather
Rickett's, division together, I started out to

the front. I met one of Gen. Shields's aides-de-camp coming in from (to ?) Front Royal, and asked him how far out he had met Gen. Shields. He said he had not met him at all. I told him he had started to go out, and he said he must have lost his way. Without stopping to see what had become of him, I took Bayard's cavalry brigade, the only one ready to move, and sent it forward by the direct road to Strasburg.* I then went to see where Gen. Shields was, and found him over on the road towards Winchester. He had sent his troops on that road, instead of on the one I had ordered him to send them on. He said that he had received information from his aide-de-camp that Jackson had fallen back, and he had sent his troops this way. When I got up there they were coming in.

" Well, it was too late to get ahead of Jackson then. The only way then was this : I expected Gen. Fremont would be coming into Strasburg, and to come in from the south, instead of the north. But we heard the firing in another direction, showing that the force was not coming the way we expected. So Gen. Shields went off with my consent to Luray, as giving the only chance to effect anything. He knew the country, the roads, bridges, etc., better than I did, and I sent forward this cavalry brigade of Bayard's to hang upon the rear of the enemy." †

* Lieut. Boswell, of Gen. Jackson's staff, scouting with five men, found the Federal cavalry on the road from Strasburg to Front Royal. Jackson sent some cavalry to stop their advance, but no serious effort was made to force a way.

† Report of Committee on Conduct of the War, Part I. p. 265.

Thus Shields's division was sent forward first on the Strasburg road [90]; then had its line of march changed, under information entirely worthless, to the Winchester road; * and lastly, in despair of overhauling Jackson by moving directly on his line of retreat, it was moved over to the Luray road. The day was thus wasted, and Shields was finally sent in pursuit by a longer and rougher route, with the sanguine expectation of " heading off " Jackson, who had gained a day's start, and was moving by the shorter and better road.

Winder reached Strasburg about noon. Jackson in the afternoon withdrew the troops that had been holding Fremont in check, and his whole force, now reunited, continued to retreat in the direction of Harrisonburg. The rear of the Confederates was covered by the cavalry. The latter camped some four miles south of Strasburg, while Jackson, with the mass of his army, rested for the night at Woodstock.

On Friday morning Jackson was in front of Harper's Ferry, which place is fifty miles from Strasburg; Fremont was at Moorefield, thirty-eight miles from Strasburg, with his advance ten miles on the way to the latter place; Shields was not more than twenty miles from Strasburg, for his advance entered Front Royal, which is but twelve miles distant, before mid-day on Friday; while McDowell was following with

* The roads to Strasburg and Winchester from Front Royal are the same for two miles out from the latter village, and separate in the fork of the rivers.

two divisions within supporting distance. Yet by Sunday night Jackson had marched a distance of between fifty and sixty miles, though encumbered with prisoners and captured stores ; had reached Strasburg before either of his adversaries, and had passed safely between their armies, while he held Fremont at bay by a show of force, and blinded and bewildered McDowell by the rapidity of his movements.

As the Confederates withdrew from Strasburg, Cluseret's brigade, of Fremont's forces, followed them and occupied the town. A force, sent forward to reconnoitre the Confederates, came up with the rear, consisting of the Second and Sixth Virginia cavalry regiments, some four or five miles south of Strasburg. In the darkness of the night a small party of Federal cavalry, being mistaken for some of Ashby's men, passed the Confederate picket and produced some confusion in the Sixth regiment. They were soon repulsed, however, and thus ended the operations of the day. The main body of Fremont's army bivouacked for the night in the position it had occupied during the day. It was only next morning that this general entered Strasburg with the mass of his troops, at about the same time as Bayard's cavalry brigade, which had been sent forward by McDowell the day before. Ordering Bayard to take the advance, Fremont now pressed forward in pursuit with a vigour which might have been more effective if it had been manifested two or three days sooner.

Simultaneously, Shields was advancing from

Front Royal towards Luray. McDowell turned over to this officer the further pursuit of Jackson by that route, and held Ord's division for the time at Front Royal. McDowell says : " Just as Gen. Shields left, he seemed to be disturbed about the question of supplies. He had been in that country before, and his command had suffered somewhat. He wrote me a letter stating his apprehensions, saying that if troops instead of supplies kept coming over, the troops would starve, and asking why I should bring so many there ; that he had enough men to clear the Valley out, and for God's sake not to send him any more men, but to send him supplies. I wrote back to him that the road * had been finished, and that there were supplies in abundance at Front Royal, and he could supply himself at that place with the trains that he had, and that I was willing he should follow up Jackson as far as his better knowledge of the roads of that country would, in his judgment, render it profitable and advisable, with the single direction that when he moved he should move with his whole division together, so that the different parts of it should be in supporting distance of each other." †

The fact that though McDowell's advance had entered Front Royal on Friday morning, it had not appeared near Strasburg as late as Sunday afternoon, caused Jackson to suspect the move-

* Manassas Gap railroad.

† McDowell's testimony, Report of Committee on Conduct of the War, Part I. p. 266,

ment by the Luray valley.* The graded road up this valley runs on the east side of the main or South Fork of the Shenandoah, a river in ordinary stages fordable at but few points, and now swollen so as to be impassable except at the bridges. It was now crossed by but three bridges in the whole distance of over fifty miles from Front Royal to Conrad's Store, where the Luray Valley merges into the Great Valley by the sinking of the Massanutton Mountains into the general level.† One of these, the most southerly, was at Conrad's Store; two were on the road that leads from New Market across the Massanutton Mountains. This road divides at the eastern base of the Massanuttons, the one branch going north-east *via* Luray and Thornton's Gap in the Blue Ridge to Culpeper, the other east by Alma and Fischer's ‡ Gap to Madison Court-House. The first of these roads crosses the Shenandoah by the White-House, the other by the Columbia Bridge. It was by the former that Jackson had crossed, when ten days before he had moved down to turn Banks's flank at Front Royal. To prevent Shields from crossing at these two bridges was to prevent his junction with Fremont, and to keep him from making any effort to " head off " Jackson short of Harrisonburg, as well as to condemn him to a

* See Jackson's report, Confederate Official Reports, vol. i., 1862.

† The Red Bridge, the first one north of Conrad's Store, had been destroyed in April.

‡ Sometimes erroneously called Milam's. The latter is farther south-west.

march of sixty miles over muddy roads to reach a point not over fifty miles distant now from the Confederates, and which they were approaching by a good macadam road. The Confederate commander despatched a detachment of cavalry to burn the bridges, which was effected without opposition [91].

Having taken this measure to free himself for the time from one of his pursuers, Jackson fell back more leisurely before the other. On Monday (June 2) he retreated to Mount Jackson. All day his rear was closely followed by Fremont's advance. Ashby, who had received his commission as brigadier-general at Winchester a few days before, was now placed in command of all the cavalry, and to him was committed the duty of protecting the rear. He skirmished constantly with the enemy, checking them whenever they advanced too close. At one time the enemy, securing a favourable position for artillery, shelled the rear guard so as to throw it into confusion. Bayard threw his cavalry quickly forward to take advantage of this. Ashby sees the coming charge and the Confederate cavalry retreating in confusion. He dismounts, and gathering a few stragglers of the infantry, who, too foot-sore and tired to keep up, are at hand, posts them in a wood near the roadside, and pours a volley at close quarters into the charging column. The column is checked and partly thrown into disorder. The advance, however, keep on, and ride through the rear of the nearest infantry regiment. The brigade commander, Col. J. M. Patton, files another regiment to the roadside, and a volley from this sends all who are not killed or wounded back in confusion.*

Jackson moved his trains over the North Fork of the Shenandoah, near Mount Jackson, on the afternoon of the 2nd, and on the 3rd fell back to New Market. Ashby again covered his rear, burning the bridge over the Shenandoah as he retired, notwithstanding the enemy's efforts to prevent it. Here this gallant officer had his horse killed, and narrowly escaped with his life. The destruction of the bridge checked Fremont's advance for a day [92].

Next day Jackson continued his retreat, and on the 5th reached Harrisonburg, which he entered before mid-day. Here he changed his line of march, and leaving the Valley turnpike, moved in the direction of Port Republic and Brown's Gap.

When he retired before Banks, six weeks before, he had gone to Elk Run Valley, at the foot of Swift Run Gap. His special object in selecting that route had been that it placed him most readily in communication with Ewell at Madison Court-House.

Now in retiring towards Port Republic Jackson secured a better and shorter route to the Virginia Central railroad, if it should become necessary to leave the Valley, while the configuration of the mountains at Brown's Gap gave him an almost impregnable position, should

* Jackson's report, Dabney, p. 397.

he desire to hold it [93]. At Port Republic there was no danger that Fremont would attempt to pass him towards Staunton.

To leave Harrisonburg, however, by this route was to leave open a means of communication between Fremont and Shields over the road Jackson had himself formerly used from Harrisonburg to Conrad's Store. His first care was to prevent a union of these forces by this means in his front. The only bridge over the Shenandoah between Port Republic and those he had destroyed was at Conrad's Store. A detachment of cavalry was sent to destroy it. Shields had not yet advanced to this point, but had sent some cavalry to learn the condition of the bridge and to guard it. While this party was absent on a scout after some stores reported to be in the hands of a small Confederate guard a few miles off, the cavalry sent by Jackson reached the place and burnt the bridge. Jackson now held the only ready means of communication between his enemies,—the bridge at Port Republic. By destroying the other bridges he had placed a very troublesome barrier between his two pursuers, and now he occupied the point where their two routes converged. No farther to the rear would the Shenandoah serve as a barrier to their junction, for south of Port Republic its head-waters are easily fordable.

On the 5th, Jackson sent the sick and wounded to Staunton, crossing them over North River at Mount Crawford by means of a ferry. The bridge at this place had been destroyed when

Banks advanced some weeks before, and the river was now so much swollen as to make fording and even ferrying apparently impossible. But Jackson would not be baulked by this difficulty. From midnight of the 4th he continued to send officers and messengers to hurry forward the preparations. Early in the day on the 5th, Capt. C. R. Mason, in charge of pioneers, succeeded, after much labour and some risk, in constructing a ferry which carried over the ambulances and sick, and thus saved them the long and muddy detour by Port Republic. By means of the signal station established by Capt. Hotchkiss a day or two before on the end of the Massanutton chain, Jackson kept himself informed of the movements of Shields. He continued to occupy Harrisonburg with his rear guard until Fremont's advance once more came up. This was about mid-day on the 6th. Ashby allowed the enemy to occupy Harrisonburg without opposition, and retired to a position about two miles south, on the Port Republic road. Here he was attacked an hour later by a body of Fremont's cavalry under Col. Sir Percy Wyndham.* This cavalry fight is vividly described by a Federal officer engaged in it, in a letter to the *New York Tribune*, dated Fremont's headquarters, June 7. He says: " When all the cavalry had come up, a force, consisting of the First New Jersey, First Penn-

---

* This was an English officer who had taken service in the Federal cause, and was now commander of the First Jersey cavalry.

sylvania, two companies of the Fourth New York, and two companies of Connecticut cavalry, in all about eight hundred (800), under command of Col. Wyndham, of the First New Jersey regiment, was ordered forward by Gen. Fremont to take possession of the town and reconnoitre a short distance beyond. Before this column moved, a report was brought by a scout that there were three hundred rebel cavalry within a mile of the town, who were prevented from retreating by the destruction of a bridge a short distance in advance, and that they were rapidly rebuilding the bridge, and would be able to advance in an hour. This information was communicated to Col. Wyndham.*

" About half-past one o'clock Col. Wyndham moved his force, and went through the long main street of the town at a rapid trot. Arriving on the other side, the column turned to the left and advanced through two or three fields to the summit of a hill overlooking an open valley, from which rose another hill beyond, covered with woods. No enemy was in sight. The cavalry were halted, and skirmishers sent ahead and on the flanks. They were gone some time, and returned with no satisfactory report. Nevertheless, Col. Wyndham, though he had reached the point beyond which he was ordered not to push his reconnaissance, decided to advance. With full knowledge that the enemy was somewhere in front of him, whom he might

* This information was unreliable.

have to charge at any moment, he nevertheless hurried on his tired horses, advancing for more than two * miles at an unbroken trot. The enemy's cavalry were suddenly discovered in front, drawn up, as usual, across the road, and extending into the woods on either side. It was impossible to determine their force, and there was no support within three or four miles. But Col. Wyndham determined to attack, and, without any attempt to discover by skirmishing the strength or position of his enemy, or whether any infantry were opposed to him, ordered a charge, and rashly led his own regiment, the First New Jersey cavalry, straight up the hill.

" On the left of the road was nothing but woods. On the right, for some distance before the rebel line was reached, was a field of wheat. In this field was concealed a strong body, not less than a regiment, of rebel infantry.† They were not completely screened from view by the tall grain, but were visible at least to the officers and men of the second squadron. Utterly un-suspicious of such a force on his flank, Col. Wyndham charged with speed up the hill. When the first squadron was fairly within the line of flanking fire the rebels poured in a volley, which, coming so close at hand and on the flank, threw the whole squadron into confusion. Col. Wyndham's horse was shot under him, and he was taken prisoner. Capt. Shellmere, Com-

* Really one mile.

† A mistake. The troops referred to were some of Ashby's dismounted cavalry.

pany A, bravely striving to rally his men, was killed by a rifle-shot. All the officers bravely but vainly endeavoured to rally their men, and after one or two feeble efforts to hold their ground the first battalion was driven down the hill. Capt. Janeway, Company L, who was leading the second squadron, perceiving as he advanced up the hill that the wheat-field covered a force of infantry, as soon as the first squadron was thrown into disorder by the unexpected fire on the flank, endeavoured to lead his men through the woods on the left of the road, in order both to shelter them from the infantry fire and to flank the cavalry on the hill. This movement was skilfully planned, but before it could be wholly executed part of the squadron was thrown into confusion by the retreat of the advance, which came down the hill in disorderly flight, and nothing was left but to retire. . . . The regiment lost thirty-six killed and wounded."*

Besides Col. Wyndham, sixty-three of his men were taken prisoners.† The Confederate loss was Maj. Green, of the Sixth Virginia cavalry, severely wounded.‡

Gen. Ewell, whose division was nearest Ashby, now coming on the field, the latter asked for an infantry support, anticipating confidently a renewal of the attack in stronger force. Gen. Ewell sent him the First Maryland regiment, Col. B. T. Johnson, and the Fifty-eighth Virginia, Col. Letcher.

* *Rebellion Record,* vol. v. p. 185.　　† Jackson's report.
‡ Col. Munford's report.

" As soon as news of the repulse of Wyndham's attack was received at Fremont's headquarters, Gen. Bayard, with the Bucktail rifles, four companies, and the First Pennsylvania cavalry ; and Col. Cluseret, with his brigade, comprising the Sixtieth Ohio and Eighth Virginia (Federal) infantry, were ordered forward to hold the farther end of the town and the approaches on that side." * When this force reached the vicinity of the Confederates, Col. Cluseret, with one regiment, advanced on the left, while Kane's Bucktails, supported by the Eighth Virginia, moved forward on the right.

Maj. Dabney, Gen. Jackson's chief of staff, thus describes the combat that followed : " Ashby disposed the Marylanders in the woods so as to take the Federal advance in flank while he met them in front at the head of the Fifty-eighth. Indicating to Gen. Ewell the dispositions of the enemy, which he had exactly anticipated, and his own arrangements to meet them, he seemed to the spectators to be instinct with unwonted animation and genius. At this moment the enemy's infantry advanced, and a fierce combat began. They, approaching through the open fields, had reached a heavy fence of timber, whence, under the partial cover, they poured destructive volleys into the ranks of the Fifty-eighth Virginia regiment. Ashby, seeing at a glance their disadvantage, galloped to the front and ordered them to charge and drive the Federals from their vantage-ground.

* *New York Tribune.* Letter above quoted.

At this moment his horse fell, but extricating himself from the dying animal, and leaping to his feet, he saw his men wavering. He shouted, ' Charge, men ! For God's sake charge ! ' and waved his sword, when a bullet pierced him full in the breast and he fell dead. The regiment took up the command of their dying general and rushed upon the enemy, while the Marylanders dashed upon their flank. Thus pressed, the Federals gave way ; the Confederates occupied the fence, and poured successive volleys into the fleeing mass until they passed out of musket range." *

While this was going on, the Federal left had driven in the Confederate skirmishers, over ground that had been recently occupied as a camp, but without loss to either side ; and the defeat of the Federal right involved the retreat of the whole. In this attack the Bucktails, on whom fell the greatest part of the loss, left their commander, Lieut.-Col. Kane, a prisoner, and had fifty-five (55) killed, wounded, and missing out of the one hundred and twenty-five (125) carried into the battle.† The Confederate loss, besides Gen. Ashby, was seventeen (17) killed, fifty (50) wounded, and three (3) missing.‡ When the dead and wounded, as far as possible, had been cared for, the Confederate rear guard followed the army towards Port Republic.

The interest attaching to this fight between

---

* Dabney's *Life of Jackson*, pp. 399, 400.
† Letter in *New York Tribune*.
‡ Jackson's report.

Jackson's rear guard and Fremont's advance
does not grow mainly out of the engagement
itself, which was comparatively unimportant,
but out of the fact that it was the occasion of
the fall of Gen. Turner Ashby.* This gallant
soldier had led the life of a Virginia country
gentleman on his property in Fauquier county,
Virginia, until the outbreak of the war. He
at once took up arms, and entered the service
at the head of a company of horsemen (known
as the Mountain Rangers) composed of his
friends and neighbours. He soon became pre-
eminent for dash and courage. Nor for these
alone. In him the qualities that most excite
admiration in a soldier were happily united to
those that most excite enthusiastic affection
and devotion. Insensible to danger, or oblivious
of it, the more daring an enterprise the greater
was its attractiveness for him. Of great energy
and ceaseless activity, he was ever on the alert,
and his name had become a dreaded one by the
foe. With such qualities were united the utmost
generosity and unselfishness, a delicacy of senti-
ment and feeling equal to a woman's, and a
respect for the rights of others which permitted,
within the limits of his authority, no outrage
on friend or foe. Says Jackson in his official
report : " An official report is not an appro-
priate place for more than a passing notice of
the distinguished dead ; but the close relation
which Gen. Ashby bore to my command for
most of the previous twelve months will justify

* Ashby was killed on the farm of Mr. Joseph Good.

me in saying that as a partisan officer I never knew his superior. His daring was proverbial, his powers of endurance almost incredible, his tone of character heroic, and his sagacity almost intuitive in divining the purposes and movements of the enemy."

The remains of Ashby were removed to Port Republic and prepared for burial [94]. His home in Fauquier county being within the Federal lines, it was resolved to bury him at the State University at Charlottesville, Virginia. On Saturday the corpse was sent under military escort to Waynesboro', whence it was carried by railroad to the University. The day was one of the most beautiful that can be conceived. Summer covered with glory the mountains and valleys of this beautiful region. The bright green fields and darker woodlands, the rolling hills, intersected everywhere by the valleys of the streams, the bold mountains towering above the Shenandoah and showing in the distance the softest and most delicate of outlines against the June sky, presented a picture to charm the dullest imagination. The storm of battle, even, seemed to have ceased out of respect for the dead. No gun was to be heard in the distance. Both armies were resting, taking breath, as it were, for the morrow's struggle. Along the base of the mountains, up the valley of South River, winds the road to Waynesboro'. Slowly and sadly the funeral cortège passed on its way. An escort of the brave comrades of Ashby, with bowed heads and sad mien, their arms reversed, accompanied the hearse. Behind it came the chieftain's horse and trappings, led by his negro servant, whose grief was more demonstrative. His personal staff next followed. The whole, as it wound along the quiet country road in the broad sunlight, seemed to recall some rite of ancient chivalry; and surely no nobler, braver, truer knight was ever borne by more devoted hearts to a glorious tomb.

The infantry of Jackson's army enjoyed a sorely-needed rest on the 6th and 7th. In the twenty-four days that had intervened between the time that Jackson had withdrawn from Fremont's front at Franklin and his arrival at Port Republic his army had marched three hundred miles, besides driving Banks over the Potomac. Lying on the north side of the Shenandoah, along Mill Creek, a few miles in front of Port Republic, these exhausted and march-worn men refreshed themselves, and at the end of two days were as ready as ever for battle.

Meantime, Jackson, having prevented the junction of his two opponents by burning the bridges across the South Fork of the Shenandoah, below Port Republic, was preparing to take advantage of their enforced separation. He adapted his strategy to the character of the country and the rivers. About four miles south-west of Port Republic the North and Middle Rivers, the principal tributaries that go to form the Main or South Fork of the Shenandoah, unite, and flow thence in a north-east direction to this village. At this place the third tributary, South

River, coming from the south-west along the base
of the Blue Ridge, joins the stream. It is
smaller than either of the other two, and is
fordable. Port Republic lies in the angle formed
by South River and the main stream. (Map
No. VI.) The bridge over North River, on the
Valley turnpike, was destroyed, and that river
was past fording in its swollen state. Just
above the junction of the main stream with
South River was the bridge, now held by Jackson,
which carried the road from Harrisonburg to
Brown's Gap into Port Republic. The latter
village is but twelve miles from Harrisonburg,
and the intervening country is high and rolling.
This country terminates along the river in an
abrupt, bluff-like terrace, which continues for
some miles below. This bluff completely commands the bridge, the village, and the eastern
bank below the village. For many miles the
country on the eastern side consists of a plain
from one to two miles broad, sloping in successive terraces from the foot of the Blue Ridge
to the river's brink. Beyond this a densely-
wooded tract ascends gradually to the mountain-
side. The low grounds were covered with cultivated fields or meadows. Through them, and
for the most part not over half a mile from the
river, runs the road to Conrad's Store and Luray,
the road Jackson had himself used when on
April 30 he had left his camp in Elk Run Valley
for Port Republic, and the road by which
Shields must now approach. The road from
Harrisonburg, after crossing the bridge into

Port Republic, divides, and while one branch leads to Staunton, the other, crossing the South River by a ford, leads through the wooded plain on the east side to Brown's Gap, five miles distant.* (Map No. VI.)

Fremont was equal to Jackson in force, Shields was inferior [95]. Together they largely outnumbered him. Jackson determined to retreat no farther, but to fight them in detail, while separated. To retire towards Brown's Gap was to allow his enemies to unite. To concentrate on the east side at once against Shields as the weaker, and burn the bridge to keep Fremont back, was to run the risk of having the battle-field in the plain on the eastern side commanded by Fremont's guns, which would then crown the heights on the left bank. While it might not thus entirely paralyse Fremont in the struggle with Shields, it would certainly prevent Jackson from returning in case of success to attack Fremont. The Confederate commander, therefore, took the other plan remaining to him, and, having sent off his prisoners to the railroad at Waynesboro' and removed his trains to Port Republic, placed his army in position on the north side of the river; Gen. Ewell's division [96] at Cross Keys, halfway on the road to Harrisonburg, and Gen. Winder's † division on the heights above the

* The road leads up Madison Run, a stream so named from the ancestors of President and of Bishop Madison.

† Winder now commanded Jackson's old division as senior brigadier.

bridge along the river. Here artillery was at hand to command the town and bridge and plain by which Shields must approach. Fremont was well closed up, and his vigorous pursuit of the last few days indicated a prompt attack without waiting for the co-operation of Shields. The latter was not so well up as Fremont, but his advance under Col. Carroll came within six miles of Port Republic on Saturday evening, June 7.

Jackson thus took a position where he might receive the attack of Fremont, while it was in the power of a small part of his force to hold Shields in check. His position, if the latter attempted to attack in aid of Fremont, was impregnable. Gen. Tyler thought it " one to defy an army of fifty thousand (50,000) men." * Defeat by Fremont would have rendered Jackson's condition precarious, but this contingency he did not anticipate.

His sagacity was made manifest, and his strategy approved by the movements of his adversaries. Fremont had failed to seize the Confederate line of retreat at Strasburg when it was possible, and had permitted Jackson, encumbered with prisoners and captures, to pass by him unmolested. His pursuit of the retreating Confederates had emboldened him, and now, having followed them over fifty miles farther, he was ready to attack, in a chosen position, the army he had hesitated to fight when hampered by its trains and captures. Then

* Tyler's report.

McDowell was within reach to aid, now an impassable river prevented all co-operation. Shields, on the other hand, condemned by the burning of the bridges to make his toilsome way along the muddy roads of the Luray Valley, had halted at Columbia, and sent forward his advance brigades to harass Jackson's flank, with orders to go as far as Waynesboro' and break the railroad. The movements of Carroll's brigade are thus described by a Northern writer :*

" On the 4th instant, while at Conrad's Store, Col. Carroll received orders to go forward at once, with cavalry and guns, to save the bridge at Port Republic. At that time it was impossible for him to move. The heavy rains which had prevailed for some days had so swollen the streams that Col. Carroll was entirely separated from his command, having with him only his staff, fifteen cavalry, and two pieces of artillery. His infantry was five miles in his rear, and compelled to remain there, by the impassable creeks, between two and three days.

" On Saturday, the 7th, Col. Carroll received orders to move forward to Waynesboro', distant some thirty-five or thirty-seven miles, by the way of Port Republic, for the purpose of destroying the railroad depot, track, bridge, etc., at that place, and to seize Jackson's train and throw his force upon Jackson's flank. Col. Carroll marched, in obedience to these orders, on Saturday afternoon. His infantry, cavalry, and artillery had in the meantime come up, and he

* *National Intelligencer.* See *Rebellion Record*, vol. v. p. 113.

started from Conrad's Store with less than a thousand of the former, with one hundred and fifty cavalry, and with a single battery of six guns.

"Halting in the night, six miles before reaching Port Republic, Col. Carroll sent forward a party of scouts, who returned with the information that Jackson's train was parked near Port Republic, with a drove of beef cattle herded near by, and the whole guarded by about two or three hundred cavalry."

On the same day (7th) Gen. Tyler, with his brigade, was ordered forward from Columbia Bridge to co-operate with Carroll. He reached the neighbourhood of Port Republic at 2 P.M. on the 8th.

Jackson had placed his headquarters on the south-western outskirts of the village,* and his trains had been parked in the adjoining fields. Carrington's battery, which had just joined his command, was also camped here; but with this exception, and that of a few troopers and train-guards, there was no force on the Port Republic side of the river. Two companies of cavalry had been sent across South River in the direction from which Gen. Shields must approach, the one to reconnoitre and the other to do picket duty. The mass of Shields's forces were known to be miles away, and the cavalry scouts were expected to give timely warning of his approach.

---

* Jackson's headquarters at Mr. Kemper's were near the site of an old fort (built as a protection against Indians in early times), and the first clerk's office of Augusta county.

Sunday morning, June 8, was bright with all the glory of summer in the Valley of the Shenandoah. Quiet reigned throughout the Confederate camp, and men and animals alike seemed to enjoy the rest which for a day or two had succeeded to the excessive toils and marches of the campaign. Jackson was just mounting his horse to ride to the front, when a bold and unexpected dash by Col. Carroll opened the fight at Port Republic itself and for a few moments threatened serious damage.

Col. Carroll, having learned the evening before, through renegades familiar with the country, the location of Jackson's trains and the smallness of the guard, pushed on early in the morning. Confirming his previous information by a new reconnaissance when within two miles of the town, he dashed forward with his cavalry and two pieces of artillery, leaving the remainder of his command to follow. The Confederate cavalry pickets are quickly driven in and their supports put to flight. Carroll dashes on without halting, and reaches the bank of South River, opposite the village, almost as soon as the flying Confederates. Jackson, informed of the attack, and followed by his staff, rides rapidly through the town towards the bridge and the troops stationed a few hundred yards from it on the north side hills. Carroll, stopping but a moment at the South River, boldly crosses it, and rides into the middle of the town so quickly as to intercept the two hindmost of Jackson's staff and make them prisoners [97]. One piece of artillery he promptly places at the south end of the bridge, so as to command the approaches to it from the north side, the other he prepares to use in attacking the train lying just outside the town to the south-west, and towards which he moves. His unexpected approach has thrown teamsters and camp-followers into great confusion. The trains are moving out from their park and taking the Staunton road. A few minutes more of unimpeded advance, and the Federal cavalry would have produced a general stampede of the trains. But this was not to be. A small company of disabled soldiers acted as guard at headquarters. Some fifteen or twenty of them are at hand, and are quickly placed at the angle where the road emerges from the village into the fields containing the trains. A piece of Carrington's battery is brought a few yards and placed so as to rake the main street of the village. Some of the Federal troopers reach the angle of the road, and a volley from the guard checks them. Before they have time to recover a charge from Carrington's gun is poured into the rear of the column along the main street. The movement is checked ; the Federal cavalry seek the middle of the village. Meantime, Jackson has reached the troops nearest the bridge on the north side. Three batteries are instantly ordered to the brow of the terrace overlooking the river. Taliaferro's brigade, of Winder's division, is the nearest infantry ; Gen. Taliaferro has them drawn up for inspection. Ordering them forward, Jackson places himself at the head of the leading regiment (Thirty-seventh Virginia, Col. Fulkerson) and the first of Poague's guns that is ready, and rushes at a double-quick towards the bridge. Poague is directed to engage with his piece the enemy's gun near the south end of the bridge. To avoid the line of artillery fire the Thirty-seventh regiment is directed to the north side of the road, and descends obliquely against the upper side of the bridge. At the word from Jackson, Poague fires a charge, which disconcerts the enemy; then follows a volley from the infantry and an immediate charge with the bayonet [98]. In a moment the Federal gunners are down, their gun is captured, and the bridge is again in Jackson's possession. The Confederates have lost two men wounded, and the Federals their chance of destroying the bridge. Carroll, seeing himself attacked from both ends of the village, rides out of it as rapidly as he had entered it. He re-fords South River, abandons another piece of artillery to the Confederates, and soon meets his infantry advancing to his support.* But the Confederate batteries (Wooding's, Poague's, Carpenter's) are now in position on the bluff on the north side, and they rain fire so on all the approaches to the town and bridge from the south and east side that any further attempt is futile, and Carroll's whole force is obliged to retreat. To avoid the galling fire, they move out some distance towards the mountain before turning down

---

* Col. Carroll reports his loss on this occasion as 40 men, 2 guns and limbers, and 14 horses.

the river.   As Carroll moves towards Lewiston *
the Confederate batteries follow, on the bluff,
and continue to shell him until he is entirely
out of range, some two and a half miles below.
The whole affair has only occupied about an
hour, and quiet once more replaces the noise of
battle.   To provide against any repetition of
this attack, Jackson now stations Taliaferro's
brigade in the village to hold the fords of South
River, and places the " Stonewall " brigade on the
north side of the main river, opposite Lewiston,
to observe the enemy and impede by artillery
any renewed advance.   The remainder of Winder's
division is held in reserve to assist Ewell if
need be [99].

While these arrangements are being made the
battle opens along Ewell's front.   On Saturday
evening Fremont had made a reconnaissance,
and, having found the Confederates in force
near Cross Keys, gave orders for a general
advance the next morning [100].   Gen. Ewell
has selected for his position one of the ridges with
which the country is filled, a short distance south
of the Keezletown road.   In front the ground
declined rapidly to a small rivulet, and then rose
into a lower parallel ridge, which was occupied
by the Federals.   The ridge held by Ewell was
wooded, with cleared fields in front, especially
opposite his centre [101].   It was crossed on his
left by the Keezletown road, with the direction
of which it makes nearly a right angle.   The
road from Harrisonburg to Port Republic crosses

* The country-seat of the Lewis family.

the ridge through the centre of the position held by Gen. Ewell. The Fifteenth Alabama infantry, Col. Canty, had been thrown out on picket, and, while they were stubbornly resisting Fremont's advance, Ewell carefully disposed his troops along the ridge, placing the four batteries of Courtenay, Lusk, Brockenbrough, and Raines in the centre, near the Harrisonburg road, and near Mill Creek Dunkard Church, and throwing Trimble's brigade to the right and Steuart's to the left, while Elzey was retained in rear of the centre as a reserve ready to reinforce either wing. The ridge at the point to which Gen. Trimble was ordered was heavily wooded, descended very abruptly to the creek, and was easily turned. Not deeming this position eligible, and seeing one half a mile to the right front which appeared better, Gen Trimble was permitted to occupy it. The Twenty-first North Carolina regiment had been left to support Courtenay's guns, and the Sixteenth Mississippi, Col. Posey, and the Twenty-first Georgia, Col. Mercer, were now quickly transferred to the new position in advance, where they were soon joined by the remaining regiment of the brigade, —the Fifteenth Alabama, Col. Canty. The latter regiment was placed on the extreme right of Trimble's line. This new position of Gen. Trimble was on a flat ridge, flanked on the right by a stream, while in front lay a narrow valley, from which, on the opposite side, rose a similar height occupied by the Federals. While these dispositions were being made on the right, Gen. George

H. Steuart was posted on the Confederate left wing [102], following the direction of the ridge from the batteries towards the west. His left flank approached the Keezletown road where it crosses the ridge, and was protected by heavy timber.

Fremont disposed his forces for attack as follows : Stahl's brigade (five regiments), of Blenker's division, was assigned to his left, opposite Trimble. Bohlen's brigade, of the same division, supported Stahl, while the remainder of Blenker's troops were held in reserve. Milroy, with five regiments, and Cluseret, with three, were sent against the Confederate centre, while Schenck, with five regiments, constituted Fremont's right, and was to operate against the Confederate left wing and flank. Batteries were placed on the spurs of the ridge in front of and parallel to that occupied by Gen. Ewell. For some time a spirited artillery fire was maintained between the opposing batteries, when, though Schenck was not yet in position, Fremont's left wing moved forward to the attack. Stahl's brigade advanced boldly across the open space that separated them from Trimble, driving in his skirmishers. Trimble ordered the three regiments with him to " rest quietly in the edge of the open wood " until the enemy, after having crossed " the field and hollow, should come within fifty steps " of his line. Stahl continued to advance until he had come near enough to receive Trimble's fire. Then deadly volleys are poured in the faces of the Germans ; their advance is at once checked, and in a few moments they waver and break. Their supports fail to come forward. Trimble orders an advance, and Stahl's troops are quickly driven down the hill, across the meadow, and into the woods from which they had advanced.* Here are the reserves on which they reform. The Confederates do not advance beyond the crest of the hill on which they are stationed, but, having driven the enemy out of the open space, remain in their position on the hill to await another attack. But the repulse has been too bloody to invite a speedy renewal. Trimble waits a short time, and, perceiving no indications of a new advance, determines to move against the enemy. On the extreme left of Fremont, and half a mile in front of the Confederates, is a battery which plays on them. Trimble moves out to his right, and, under cover of a ravine and the woods, approaches Blenker's flank. He is joined *en route* by Col. Walker, of Elzey's brigade, with two regiments (Thirteenth and Twenty-fifth Virginia). Walker moves on Trimble's right and tries to turn the Federal flank. Meanwhile, Trimble presses forward, In a few minutes the Federals retreat, taking off the battery which Trimble had hoped to capture. While this is doing, Walker, who has moved too far to the right, is met and staggered for the moment by a fierce fire of musketry and canister.† The con-

---

* One of Stahl's regiments (Eighth New York) lost 65 in killed alone in this attack. (Fremont's report.)

† Gen. Walker says this was in moving to the right of Ever's house and barn. (See Map No. VII.)

fusion produced is, however, soon remedied. Walker presses forward, and Trimble throws his regiments once more on the Federal lines. The struggle is short and sharp, the Federals are forced to yield, the artillery limbers up and retires, and in a few minutes the whole Federal left wing is retreating towards the position near Union Church, on the Keezletown road, which it had held before the opening of the battle [103].

Meantime, Milroy has advanced against the Confederate centre. A fierce artillery duel is here the principal feature of the contest. The Confederate batteries are well located, and, in spite of loss of horses and men in some of them, keep up so spirited a fire that no serious attempt is made on this part of the line. The Federals drive in the Confederate skirmishers and feel the lines behind them, but there is no real attack. Thus, at the centre of the contending armies, the hours pass in which the fate of the day is being decided on Blenker's front.

Schenck is last to take his post in the Federal line. He arrives on the field at 1 P.M., and moves in rear and to the right of Milroy, to take position to attack the Confederate left. Unacquainted with the ground, he proceeds cautiously, and it is some time before he secures an eligible position for his troops. This movement is marked by artillery firing and some skirmishing, the Federals driving back a part of the Forty-fourth Virginia regiment of Steuart's brigade, and being in turn checked by its supports. Gen. Ewell, seeing the movement of troops towards his left, strengthens his line there with the part of Elzey's brigade * yet in reserve, and subsequently sends Patton's brigade and two regiments of Taylor's [104] to extend his line on the same flank. This delays Schenck's aggressive movements, and before he is ready to attack in earnest the battle has been decided by the defeat of Blenker ; and Fremont, alarmed by the disaster on his left wing, orders both centre and right to withdraw. Ewell, conscious of his inferiority of force [105], and anticipating an attack from Schenck on his left, has been content with the advantages already gained until his enemy's purposes are developed. As the Federal right and centre withdraw he follows, pushing forward his skirmishers and occupying the ground in front of the field. Night is at hand, however, and Gen. Ewell decides to bivouac in the position he holds rather than risk a night attack on the enemy [106].

Thus ends the battle of " Cross Keys." Ewell has repulsed Fremont so decisively on one wing as to paralyse his army and to secure all the advantages of victory. This has been done too with but a small part of the total force at command. The losses are greatly disproportioned. Ewell's total loss is two hundred and eighty-seven (287).† That of Fremont is six hundred and sixty-four (664), of which four hundred and twenty-seven (427) are in Stahl's brigade, by

* Twelfth Georgia and Thirty-first Virginia.
† Ewell's report.

letter dated June 9, from his headquarters, to the Cincinnati " Commercial " [107].

During this engagement the advance force of Gen. Shields continued quiet on the east side of the river. Col. Carroll remained in the position beyond Lewiston to which he had retired in the morning, and from which he could observe, but not attack, the Confederate batteries on the north-west bank of the river. Here he was joined by Gen. Tyler with his brigade about 2 P.M.* The latter deemed the combined force still too small and the Confederate position too strong to admit of an aggressive movement.† Hence no diversion in favour of Fremont was made.

Jackson, emboldened by the inactivity of Shields's advance, and the easy repulse of Fremont, conceived the audacious design of attacking his two opponents in succession the next day, with the hope of overwhelming them separately. For this purpose he directed that during the night a temporary bridge, composed simply of planks laid upon the running-gear of wagons, should be constructed over the South River at Port Republic, and ordered Winder to move his brigade at dawn across both rivers and against Shields. Ewell was directed to leave Trimble's brigade and part of Patton's to hold Fremont in check, and to move at an early hour to Port Republic to follow Winder. Taliaferro's brigade was left in charge of the batteries along

---

* Gen. Tyler says he had about 3000 infantry and 16 guns. Gen. Shields puts this brigade at 2500.

† Tyler's report. *Rebellion Record*, vol. v.

the river, and to protect Trimble's retreat if necessary. The force left in Fremont's front was directed to make all the show possible, and to delay the Federal advance to the extent of its power. The Confederate commander proposed, in case of an easy victory over Shields in the morning, to return to the Harrisonburg side of the river and attack Fremont in the afternoon [108]. In case, however, of delay, and a vigorous advance on Fremont's part, Trimble was to retire by the bridge into Port Republic, and burn it to prevent his antagonist from following.

Jackson superintended in person the construction of the foot-bridge over South River, and before five o'clock in the morning Winder was already crossing. Next followed Taylor, and with these two brigades, separated as they were by a considerable interval, Jackson moved at once against the Federal troops at Lewiston, leaving orders for the remaining troops to follow as rapidly as possible. The foot-bridge was defective, and a good deal of time was lost in getting the troops over. Jackson, impatient of delay, without waiting for the remainder of his forces, ordered an attack upon Tyler as soon as Winder had reached the vicinity of the Federals.

The position occupied by Gen. Tyler was an admirable one, on the second terrace from the Shenandoah. His centre was near Gen. Lewis's house, his right extending through the open fields towards the river, while his left rested in the dense wood east of the main road, at the site of an old coal-pit. The ground held by the left and centre was elevated, and commanded all the available approaches from Port Republic. Especially was this the case on his left, which was the key to the whole position. Here he had six guns planted.* A dense and almost impenetrable forest protected this flank, and made all direct approach to it difficult, while the batteries there placed covered a large part of the front, and enfiladed Winder's advance. In this position Gen. Tyler disposed his force. He seems, though on the alert, not to have been aware [109] of Jackson's rapid approach until the latter was deploying in his front, but he was altogether ready to meet the attack.

Winder deployed his skirmishers, and advancing on both sides of the road, drove in the outposts. He soon found that the Federal batteries commanded the road and its vicinity completely. Jackson then directed him to send a force to his right through the woods to turn the Federal left flank. Two regiments under Col. J. W. Allen (Second and Fourth Virginia) † were detached for this purpose with two guns of Carpenter's. At the same time he placed two guns of Poague's battery on the west of the road, supporting them by the Twenty-seventh Virginia (Col. Grigsby) and the Fifth Virginia

* Three guns of Clark's and three of Huntington's batteries. One of Robinson's was near. (Daum's report. Col. Daum was chief of artillery for Gen. Shields.)

† The Fourth numbered 317, and the Second 224, rank and file, by the regimental reports.

(Col. Funk), the remainder of his brigade present.*
Allen made his way with great difficulty through
the dense thickets opposite the Federal left
until he reached the vicinity of the hostile battery.
Here he found two regiments of infantry sent
by Tyler to support the guns, and in a short
time two more regiments reinforced them. Carpenter was unable to get his guns through the
brush, and Allen's infantry, unable of itself to
make headway against the foe, and subjected to
a heavy fire of musketry and canister, was soon
thrown into confusion and forced to retire.
Meantime, Poague's guns on the west of the road
had drawn on them a heavy fire. Gen. Winder
finds it necessary to separate them. One is sent
some distance to the left, into the low grounds,
and Funk's regiment (Fifth Virginia) goes to
support it. The enemy soon make dispositions
to meet this movement.† Two guns of Clark's
and two of Huntington's battery (Federal) are
placed in position to reply to Poague. The
Seventh Indiana and the Twenty-ninth and
Seventh Ohio are sent to check the attack on
the Federal right wing. Poague has tried in
vain to find a good position for his guns; there
is nothing to be done unless the enemy are
driven from theirs. Winder, with less than
twelve hundred (1200) men [110], finds himself
unable to cope with the force before him and,

* The Thirty-third Virginia, under Col. Neff, having been on
picket duty the night before, did not rejoin the brigade until
the battle was virtually over.
† Tyler's report.

seeing signs of an aggressive movement against his left near the river, sends to Jackson for reinforcements. The latter is hurrying them forward as fast as possible. Hays's Seventh regiment is sent to the left, and placed between Funk (Fifth Virginia) and Grigsby (Twenty-seventh Virginia), while the whole of Poague's and the section of Carpenter's battery that had returned from its fruitless attempt with Allen are placed to aid a forward movement by the Confederate left. At the same time that Hays is sent to reinforce the left, Jackson sends the mass of Taylor's brigade to make a detour through the woods on the Confederate right, and renew the attack in which Allen had failed. It requires some time for Taylor to get through the thicket into position, and while he is moving, Winder has ordered the Confederate left wing to advance and carry the enemy's position with the bayonet. The three regiments (Funk's, Hays's, and Grigsby's) move forward in fine style, and the artillery follows closely. The Seventh Indiana regiment, which is on the extreme Federal right, is forced back a short distance, but soon reinforced by the Twenty-ninth, Seventh, and Fifth Ohio; the Federals, having the advantage of the terrace, hold their position and receive Winder's troops with a storm of musketry and shell. A most determined and stubborn conflict now takes place. The Ohio troops repel every attempt to drive them back, while the Confederates continue for a time their efforts under a storm of fire. At last the Confederates begin to waver and break. The Thirty-first Virginia regiment (Elzey's brigade) reaches Winder at this moment. Using it to cover his guns, Winder orders them to the rear, and tries to form his line again. Stopping one of Poague's guns, he turns it on the advancing enemy, and for a moment checks the disorder. But it is only for a moment; the enemy dash forward; the horses are shot down at the gun, and the Fifth Ohio, charging, drive back the half-formed Confederates across a wheat-field and seize the piece, which they carry off. Steuart's and Elzey's brigades* are next to Taylor's in reaching the battle-field. One regiment of Steuart's (Fifty-second Virginia) is sent to aid Winder, but arrives only in time to be involved in his repulse. Two others (Forty-fourth and Fifty-eighth Virginia) are stationed near the main road, in the wood, and are under Gen. Ewell's own eye. As the Federals advance to drive Winder, they expose their flank, and Ewell leads these two regiments forward. They make a vigorous dash on the enemy, drive him some distance, and, though in turn driven back to the woods, the result of the diversion is to check the farther advance against Winder, and give the latter an opportunity to rally a part of his troops, and to place two of Poague's guns

---

* Elzey's brigade, except the Thirty-first Virginia, was sent under Col. Walker to the right to help Gen. Taylor, but became lost in the woods, and only arrived at the proper point after the enemy had been broken.

where they had been before the Confederate advance.

Jackson, finding the resistance of the enemy so much more stubborn than he had expected, and that his first attacks had failed, determined to concentrate his whole force and give up all intention of recrossing the river. He therefore sent orders to Trimble and Taliaferro to leave Fremont's front, move over the bridge, burn it, and join the main body of the army as speedily as possible.

Meantime, Taylor has been moving as rapidly as the tangled forest would permit towards the Federal left. He reaches the point of attack at the time that the loud shouts of the Federals proclaim their success on the other wing. The infantry supporting the six guns that had played so important a part in the battle had been partly withdrawn to reinforce the troops engaged with Winder [111], and before they can be returned to their former place Taylor has charged and taken the battery. Most stubborn, however, has been the resistance, and so soon as reinforcements can be hurried over from the other wing, where the repulse of Winder relieves the Federals for a time, Taylor is in turn attacked, and his brave Louisianians are forced to yield the ground they had won. Once more the guns are in Federal possession. They attempt to carry them out of danger, but the horses are killed, and the removal requires time. One piece is gotten off, but before any more can be removed Taylor renews the charge. Ewell leads the two regiments under Col. Scott, which had so opportunely checked the pursuit of Winder, to Taylor's assistance. Winder renews the attack from his wing with Poague's guns; Chew's battery arrives and is placed in front, and with guns from the batteries of Brockenbrough, Raines, and Courtenay, opens on the enemy. Once more Taylor, thus aided, carried the position. The Federals have made a most gallant fight, both with the guns and to save them, but they cannot resist the combined attack now made. They are pushed back at every point, and are soon in full retreat. Not a moment too soon have they yielded the field, for the remainder of Jackson's force is arriving, and in a short time they must have been entirely overwhelmed. Taliaferro, who had just reached the field, is sent with Winder in pursuit. They press the retreating enemy in a confused mass for several miles [112], and then hand over the pursuit to the cavalry under Munford, who follow for three miles more. About four hundred and fifty prisoners, a few wagons, one piece of abandoned artillery (in addition to the five captured by Taylor in his final charge), and eight hundred muskets are the trophies of the pursuit. Some two hundred and seventy-five of the Federal wounded are paroled in the hospitals near the battle-field.* About two hundred others are carried off [113].

Jackson's losses were, killed, wounded, and missing, in Taylor's brigade, 290; Winder's,

* Jackson's report.

199 ; Steuart's, 199 ; Elzey's, 128 ; total, 816. The official reports in the Adjutant-General's office make the Federal loss 66 killed, 382 wounded, 382 missing ; total, 830. In the *Medical and Surgical History of the War* they are stated as 67 killed, 361 wounded, 574 missing ; total, 1002 [114].

During the forenoon Fremont had advanced against Trimble on the north side of the river, and was driving him slowly back, when the latter was ordered to rejoin Jackson at Lewiston. He, with Taliaferro, then withdrew as rapidly as possible, crossed the bridge without loss, and succeeded in burning it in the face of the advancing Federals. Fremont's army arrived on the heights overlooking Lewiston only in time to witness the retreat of Tyler, and were prevented by the river from giving him any assistance. In the afternoon Fremont placed some batteries in position and shelled the parties engaged in attending to the wounded on the field [115].

The Confederate trains had been moved in the course of the day across South River towards Brown's Gap, and during the afternoon and night the weary Confederates returned from the battle-field and pursuit, to camp in the cove at the foot of this mountain-pass. It was midnight before some of them lay down in the rain to rest.

Thus the day ended with the complete defeat of the two brigades under Tyler. Most gallant and determined had been their resistance, and

Jackson's impetuosity had made his victory
more costly than it otherwise would have been.
In sending in Winder's brigade before its supports
arrived, he had hurled this body of troops
against more than twice their number. Taylor
next attacked, but the repulse of Winder enabled
the Federal commander to concentrate his forces
against Taylor and drive him from the battery
he had taken. It was then that Jackson renewed the attack with the combined forces of
three brigades, and speedily forced the enemy
from the field. Had he attacked with this
force at first, it is probable that one charge
would have given him the victory at less cost
of life.

Next day the Confederates rested in camp.
Exhausted nature demanded repose, and Jackson
now gave it to his tired and battle-worn
troops. His enemies were effectually disposed of.
Shields, who had advanced to support Tyler
when the broken and defeated brigades rejoined
him [116], decided to return by the route by
which he had moved forward. Orders from
McDowell, sent on this day, caused him to
continue his retreat to Luray and Front Royal
[117], whence he was moved to Manassas to
rejoin McDowell's corps. Fremont, influenced
by his own repulse, the disaster sustained by
Shields, and the retreat of the latter, retired
from the vicinity of Port Republic on the morning of the 10th. On the 11th, Munford, with
the Confederate cavalry, once more crossed the
Shenandoah, and followed the retreating army.

Camping at Mount Crawford on the night of the 11th, he next day moved into Harrisonburg, which Fremont had evacuated, leaving two hundred wounded in the hospitals, some medicine and other stores, and about two hundred muskets. Fremont continued his retreat on the 11th and 12th. " Significant demonstrations of the enemy," as Gen. Fremont expresses it, caused him to withdraw farther, and on June 14 he joined Banks and Sigel * at Middletown. Banks and Sigel had not advanced beyond Middletown while Fremont and Shields were pursuing Jackson.

Jackson, on the 12th, moved out from his confined bivouac at the foot of Brown's Gap, and, crossing the South River near Weyer's Cave, camped in the noble, park-like forest between the latter place and Mount Meridian [118]. Here for five days of that splendid June he rested and refreshed his army. He says : " For the purpose of rendering thanks to God for having crowned our arms with success, and to implore His continued favour, divine service was held in the army on the 14th.

" The army remained near Weyer's Cave until the 17th, when, in obedience to instructions from the Commanding General of the department, it moved towards Richmond " [119].

His order of June 13 to his troops is as follows : " The fortitude of the troops under fatigue and their valour in action have again, under the

* Gen. Sigel had superseded Gen. Saxton in command of the forces gathered at Harper's Ferry to oppose Jackson.

blessing of Divine Providence, placed it in the power of the commanding general to congratulate them upon the victories of June 8 and 9. Beset on both flanks by two boastful armies, you have escaped their toils, inflicting successively crushing blows upon each of your pursuers. Let a few more such efforts be made, and you may confidently hope that our beautiful Valley will be cleansed from the pollution of the invader's presence. The Major-General commanding invites you to observe to-morrow evening, June 14, from 3 o'clock P.M., as a season of thanksgiving, by a suspension of all military exercises, and by holding divine service in the several regiments."

The battles of Cross Keys and Port Republic closed the Valley campaign of 1862. Just three months had passed since Jackson, with about four thousand six hundred (4600) troops, badly armed and equipped, had fallen back from Winchester before the advance of Banks with thirty thousand (30,000) men. So feeble seemed his force, and so powerless for offence, that when it had been pushed forty miles to the rear, Banks began to send his force towards Manassas to execute his part of " covering the Federal capital " in McClellan's great campaign. While a large part of the Federal troops are on the march out of the Valley, and their Commander is himself *en route* from Winchester to Washington, Jackson, hastening from his resting-place by a forced march, appears most unexpectedly at Kernstown, and hurls his little army with

incredible force and fury against the part of
Banks's army which is yet behind. He is mistaken as to the number of the enemy. Three
thousand five hundred (3500) men, worn by a
forced march, are not able to defeat the seven
thousand (7000) of Shields. After a fierce
struggle he suffers a severe repulse ; but he
makes such an impression as to cause the recall
of Banks and his corps, and to lead to the detachment of a strong force from McClellan to protect
Washington. The Federal Administration cannot believe that he has attacked Shields with
a handful of men.

Falling back before his pursuers to New
Market, and thence to Harrisonburg, he there
leaves the main road, and crossing over to
Elk Run Valley, at the foot of the Blue Ridge,
he takes a position in which he cannot be readily
attacked, and which yet enables him so to
threaten the flank of his opponent as effectually
to check his further progress up the Valley.
Here he gains ten days' time for the reorganization of his regiments, the time of service of
most of which expired in April, and here, too,
he finds that the return of furloughed men and
the accession of volunteers in the past month
has doubled his numbers.

Finding that no more troops could be obtained
besides those of Ewell and Edward Johnson, he
leaves the former to hold Banks in check, while
he makes a rapid and circuitous march, by way
of Port Republic and across the mountains at
Brown's Gap, to Mechum's River station, on the

Virginia Central railroad. Hence he goes *via* Staunton to Gen. Edward Johnson's position at West View. Uniting Johnson's force with his own, he appears suddenly in front of Milroy at McDowell, only eight days after having left Elk Run Valley. He has marched a hundred miles and crossed the Blue Ridge twice in this time, and now repulses Milroy and Schenck, and follows them up to Franklin. Then, finding Fremont within supporting distance, he, on May 12, begins to retrace his steps. He hastens on through Harrisonburg, New Market, Luray, —Ewell joining him on the road and swelling his force to sixteen thousand (16,000) men,— and on May 23 unexpectedly appears at Front Royal (a distance by his route of nearly one hundred and twenty miles from Franklin) and surprises and completely overwhelms the force Banks has stationed there. Next day he strikes with damaging effect at Banks's retreating column between Strasburg and Winchester, and follows him up all the night. At dawn (May 25) he attacks him on the heights of Winchester, forces him from his position, and drives him in confusion and dismay to the Potomac, with the loss of immense stores and a large number of prisoners. Resting but two days, Jackson marches to Harper's Ferry, threatens an invasion of Maryland, and spreads such an alarm as to paralyse the movement of McDowell's forty thousand (40,000) men at Fredericksburg, and to cause the attempted concentration of the greater part of this force, together with Fremont's command, in his rear. The militia of the adjoining States is called out. Troops are hurried to Harper's Ferry in his front. Nearly sixty thousand (60,000) troops in all are hastening under the most urgent telegrams to close in around him. Keeping up his demonstrations until the last moment, until, indeed, the head of McDowell's column was already crossing the Blue Ridge, and but twelve or fourteen miles from his line of retreat, at a point nearly fifty miles in his rear, he, by a forced march of a day and a half, traverses this distance of fifty miles and places himself at Strasburg. Here he keeps Fremont at bay until his long train of prisoners and captured stores has passed through in safety and his rear guard closed up. Then he falls back before Fremont, while, by burning successively the bridges over the Main Fork of the Shenandoah, he destroys all co-operation between his two pursuers. Arrived at a point when he thinks there is no further need for retreat, he turns off from Harrisonburg to Port Republic, seizes the only bridge left south of Front Royal over the Shenandoah, and takes a position which enables him to fight his adversaries in succession, while they cannot succour each other. By wonderful celerity and daring, he has extricated himself from the dangers which a week before gathered around him at Winchester. Then, nearly sixty thousand (60,000) men were encircling him. In a day or two he must have been overwhelmed. Now he has left the great mass of these troops fifty miles in the rear. Fremont alone is for the moment within reach. Jackson deals him a staggering blow, and next morning, withdrawing suddenly from his front and destroying the bridge to prevent his following, attacks the advance brigades of Shields and completely defeats them, driving them several miles from the battle-field.

With a force at no time exceeding seventeen thousand (17,000) men Jackson has beaten all his adversaries in succession, and, though they so largely exceeded him in strength, he has managed everywhere, except at Kernstown, to concentrate equal or superior numbers upon the point attacked. Thus at McDowell he throws double their force on Milroy and Schenck. When he leaves Fremont's front at Franklin, on May 12, he is much farther from Banks at Strasburg than any of the large bodies of Federal troops at Fredericksburg or around Washington, and yet he succeeds in overwhelming Banks with greatly superior numbers. Again, when he has completely outmarched the armies which attempt to surround him and turns at bay at Port Republic, he is ready to receive Fremont's attack with equal forces, and next day can concentrate two or three times their own strength against Shields's brigades, if it be necessary.

Now followed a week of rest, the first since the army had left Swift Run Gap on April 30. But to the indefatigable Commander it was but a week of preparation for another series of great deeds on a different theatre. The great soldier

who at this time commanded the Confederate
armies had already (see note 119, page 275,
Lee's letter, June 8) informed Jackson of the
intended union of his forces with those near
Richmond.   On June 11, in congratulating him
on his recent successes, Gen. Lee informs him
that Lawton's and Whiting's commands had
been sent to his assistance, but at the same
time directs that Jackson move rapidly with
the whole force to Ashland, and thence between
the Chickahominy and Pamunky Rivers, on
McClellan's communications [120].

Every precaution was taken to deceive the
enemy and produce on their part the expectation of an advance along the Valley in stronger
force than before.   Whiting's and Lawton's troops
were sent from Richmond for this purpose, and
Jackson manœuvred his cavalry so as to create
the same impression.   The prisoners sent to
Richmond by Jackson met the reinforcements
coming up.   The paroled Federal officers soon
carried this news to Washington, while Federal
spies confirmed it.   An amusing *ruse de guerre*
of Col. Munford, commanding the cavalry, upon
receiving a flag of truce from Gen. Fremont
asking for his wounded, strengthened the impression.   The Federal officers bearing the flag
were brought to Col. Munford's quarters, and
while awaiting an answer from Gen. Jackson it
was arranged that they should overhear a pre-
tended report, brought to the Colonel by Mr.
W. W. Gilmer, who assumed the *rôle* of orderly,
in which the road from Staunton was represented

as being filled with the troops coming to join Jackson. The news was spread through the town (Harrisonburg), and in the midst of the excitement consequent upon it the Federal officers were returned to their own lines, their request having been declined [121]. The Confederate lines were made as close as possible to prevent information getting through, and all passing was prohibited [122]. These and such like were the " significant demonstrations " which caused Gen. Fremont to retreat until he finally joined Banks's troops at Middletown, on June 24. They were thoroughly effective, for Gen. Banks telegraphed to Washington on the 12th that " Jackson is heavily reinforced and is advancing," and on the 19th he says : " No doubt another immediate movement down the Valley is intended with a force of thirty thousand (30,000) or more." He opposed the withdrawal of Shields strongly, in the same telegram. On the 22nd he is still on the alert for Jackson's and Ewell's movements, and on the 28th, when Jackson was fighting at Richmond, Banks telegraphs that he believes Jackson meditates an attack in the Valley ! *

Gen. McDowell had been ordered † as early as June 8 to collect his forces with a view to resuming his march by way of Fredericksburg to join McClellan, but in consequence of the

* See Federal official telegrams, Adjutant-General's office, Washington.

† McDowell's testimony, *Report on Conduct of the War*, Part I., p. 275.

victories of Cross Keys and Port Republic, and of the strong conviction wrought in the minds of Fremont and Banks of another advance by Jackson, he was delayed in getting his troops out of the Valley; and when they did move, it was towards Manassas and not Richmond. Rickett's division left Front Royal for Manassas on June 17, and it was followed by Shields's.

On this same day Jackson, having disposed of his various enemies and effected the permanent withdrawal of the greater part of McDowell's corps * from the forces operating against Richmond, again began to march, and, while Banks, Fremont, and McDowell were disposing their broken or baffled forces to cover Washington, hastened to throw his sword into the scale in that great series of battles which, during the last days of June and the early ones in July, resulted in the defeat of McClellan's army and the relief of the Confederate capital.

But here our present work ends. Brilliant as were the achievements of Gen. Jackson during the succeeding months of his too brief career, it was his Valley campaign which first lifted him into great fame; nor do any of his subsequent deeds show more strikingly the characteristics of his genius.

* The division that McDowell had left at Fredericksburg (McCall's) was sent to McClellan, but the other three divisions were retained, and became, later in the summer, a part of Gen. John Pope's "Army of Virginia."

NOTES

[1] The first battle of Manassas was fought on Sunday, July 21, 1861, between the Federal army, under Gen. Irwin McDowell, and the Confederate forces, under Gens. J. E. Johnston and Beauregard. The latter commanded the army which had gradually gathered at Manassas to resist the Federal advance from Washington, while Gen. Johnston, with the " Army of the Shenandoah," confronted Gen. Patterson, who was advancing from the Potomac, at Williamsport, towards Winchester, in the " Valley of Virginia." A forward movement by McDowell being imminent, Gen. Johnston was ordered to unite "if practicable " with Beauregard to resist it. Slipping away from Patterson's front on July 18, he arrived with a part of his command, including Jackson's brigade, at Manassas on the 20th, and, after consultation with Beauregard, determined to attack McDowell the next day, in order to fight him before Patterson could join him. McDowell, however, who was moving without reference to Patterson, had determined upon an advance on the same day. Johnston's plan was to throw forward his right across Bull Run and advance directly upon Centreville, the heart of the Federal position. For this purpose the mass of the Confederates were placed in the vicinity of the lower fords of Bull Run, near the direct road from Manassas to Centreville, while the upper fords, opposite the Confederate left, were guarded by small bodies. McDowell, on the other hand, determined, by a wide circuit, to cross the stream entirely beyond the Confederate left and thus turn and overwhelm that flank. A miscarriage of orders delayed the Confederates until McDowell's march to their left was discovered, when new dispositions became necessary. On the Confederate left Evans, reinforced by Bee and Bartow, and still later by

217

Hampton, threw his command in the path of the Federal army (which, having crossed Bull Run unopposed at Sudley's Ford, was pouring down on the flank), and stubbornly contested the ground until forced to retreat before the mass of McDowell's troops. As the Confederates were being borne back Jackson's brigade reached the field, and, promptly forming, checked the Federal advance and gave the broken commands time to rally. Then succeeded an hour or two of severe fighting. A bold effort on the part of the Confederates was made to drive back the Federals and regain the lost ground. They succeeded in sweeping back McDowell's lines and capturing a number of guns, but the Federals soon made a countercharge and retook the position and artillery. Again, mustering all his strength, Beauregard, who commanded in person on this part of the field, hurled it against the Federal lines. Fresh troops were arriving, which he sent against the Federal right flank. Jackson firmly held the centre of the advance. The Federal lines were again broken, the guns again captured. The arrival of Kirby Smith's and of Early's troops enabled Beauregard to press his advantage, to drive back McDowell's right flank, and to throw it into confusion. The defeat quickly changed into a rout, and this rout into one of the most remarkable panics on record. It was in the last successful effort of the Confederates that Bee and Bartow were slain; and it was just before the former fell that, to animate his thinned and wavering lines, he pointed to Jackson's brigade, and said, " See, there is Jackson standing like a stone wall; let us determine to die here and we will conquer." Such was the origin of the sobriquet of " Stonewall." It is now immortal.

[2] Gen. Lee was sent to Western Virginia immediately after the first battle of Manassas, which occurred on July 21. (Taylor's *Four Years with General Lee*, p. 16.) At that time Gen. Loring commanded the forces lately under Garnett, and Gens. Floyd and Wise each had a brigade in the Kanawha Valley. The three were independent of each other.

[3] Gen. Loring, after the withdrawal of Gen. Lee, had command of all the troops west of Staunton, except those under Floyd, in the Kanawha Valley. Gen. Wise had

been ordered to duty elsewhere about October 1. When
Loring was ordered to Winchester to join Jackson, Gen.
Edward Johnson was left with a brigade and some artillery
and cavalry at Camp Alleghany, where the Staunton and
Parkersburg turnpike crosses the Alleghany Mountains.

[4] Gen. J. E. Johnston says (Johnston's *Narrative*, pp.
83, 84) the " effective total " of troops in the Valley district
at the end of November was 3,700. Add 9 per cent. for
officers, and Jackson's force at that time (consisting of the
militia and the " Stonewall " brigade) may be placed at
about 4,000. At the end of December the " effective
total " under Jackson, from the returns, was 10,241, or,
adding officers, about 11,200.

[5] Jackson's notions of discipline are illustrated by an
incident of this time. Immediately after the arrival of
the " Stonewall " brigade in the Valley, a stringent order
was issued which prevented officers of even the highest
grades from passing the pickets around the camps except
upon passes from headquarters, and it was required that
these passes should specify whether the officer was on
public or private business. This order led to the following
protest and reply :

" Camp near Winchester, Virginia,
" *November* 16, 1861.

" Major :—The undersigned, having read General Orders
No. 8, transmitted from the headquarters of the Army of the
Valley, so far as it includes and relates to officers of their
rank, respectfully submit : That it is an unwarranted
assumption of authority, and involves an improper inquiry
into their private matters, of which, according to the official
usage and courtesy of the army, the Major-General commanding has no right to require information ; it implies
their abuse of the privileges according in every other department of the army to officers of their rank, which there
has been nothing in their conduct to justify ; it disparages
the dignity of the offices which they have the honour to
hold, and, in consequence, detracts from that respect of
the force under their command which is necessary to
maintain their authority and enforce obedience. There-

fore they complain of the order, and ask that it may be modified.

"Respectfully submitted."

(Signed by all the regimental commanders of the brigade.)

"MAJ. A. H. JACKSON,

"A. A. Gen'l."

"HEADQUARTERS VALLEY DISTRICT,

"*November* 17, 1861.

"The Major-General commanding desires me to say that the within-combined protest is in violation of the Army Regulations and subversive of military discipline. He claims the right to give his pickets such instructions as in his opinion the interests of the public service require.

"Colonels —— ——, on the day that their regiments arrived at their present encampment, either from incompetency to control their commands or from neglect of duty, so permitted their commands to become disorganized and their officers and men to enter Winchester without permission, as to render several arrests of officers necessary.

"If officers desire to have control over their commands, they must remain habitually with them, and industriously attend to their instruction and comfort, and in battle lead them well, and in such a manner as to command their admiration.

"Such officers need not apprehend loss of respect resulting from inserting in a written pass the words ' on duty,' or ' on private business,' should they have occasion to pass the pickets.

"By command of Maj.-Gen. Jackson.

"A. H. JACKSON,

"A. A. Gen'l."

[6] The *Record of Events* on Banks's division return for this period says that on December 18 the Fifth Connecticut, Twenty-ninth Pennsylvania, and First Maryland regiments, Company F of the Fourth United States artillery, and two companies of Maryland cavalry were ordered to Williamsport.

[7] Gen. Edward Johnson, with from 1,200 to 1,500 men

and two batteries, occupied Camp Alleghany, which is fifteen miles west of Monterey, on the Staunton and Parkersburg turnpike. He was attacked by Gen. Milroy, with from 1,700 to 1,800 men, on December 13. After a fierce struggle, lasting the greater part of the day, the Federals were repulsed at every point, and retreated to their camp on Cheat Mountain. (*Rebellion Record*, vol. iii., Doc. 226.)

[8] Jackson's letter, dated December 23, and sent both to Gen. J. E. Johnston and Adjt.-Gen. Cooper, is as follows : " I respectfully recommend that such of Brig.-Gen. Loring's forces as are on or near the Alleghany Mountains be ordered to march forthwith to Moorefield, in Hardy county, with a view to forming a junction with the troops now at or near this point (Winchester). If it is the design of the Government to commence offensive operations against Romney soon, the troops asked for should move to my aid at once. Recent intelligence from Romney gives reason to believe that the force of the enemy in Hampshire county is about 10,000, and that reinforcements are continuing to arrive. I regret to say that the occupation of Hampshire county by the enemy is exercising a demoralizing influence upon our people, who are gradually yielding to outward pressure and taking the oath of allegiance to the United States. There are noble spirits in and about Romney who have given up their earthly all, and are now, for our cause and institutions, exiles from their homes. I have endeavoured to cheer them, and to deter those who remained behind from taking the oath of allegiance to the enemy, by holding out to them the prospect of a speedy deliverance ; but this, I fear, will prove a delusion, unless the asked for forces, or their equivalent, come soon. I fear that the forces that were recently defeated on the Alleghany will be in Romney before Gen. Johnson leaves his position."

[9] Troops were indeed being hastened to Lander as Jackson foresaw. Gen. Williams (of Banks's corps) left Frederick, Maryland, with his brigade for Hancock at five on the morning of the 6th, and camped at Hagerstown the same night, and the remainder of Banks's forces were ready to march. Williams continued to Hancock,

and on January 8 assumed command at that point, Gen. Lander having gone to Romney the day before. Rosecrans had also hurried troops to Hancock, and Williams found there when he arrived " the Eighty-fourth and One Hundred and Tenth Pennsylvania, Thirty-ninth Illinois, four companies of the Thirteenth Massachusetts, two companies of the First Virginia, a company of sharpshooters, a detachment of 261 cavalry, and 8 guns, with 92 men from Best's, Hampton's, Knapp's, and Mathews's batteries." There were also six companies of the First Maryland regiment of infantry at Milestone Point, five miles below Hancock. To these forces he added his brigade of four regiments. (See *Record of Events* on return of Williams's brigade, Assistant Adjutant-General's office.)

[10] Col. Dunning, in his report, says he had six companies each of the Fourth, Fifth, Seventh, and Eighth Ohio, First Virginia, and Fourteenth Indiana infantry; Daum's battery and one section of Baker's, three companies of the First Virginia cavalry, and the Ringgold and Washington cavalry, in all " not over 2,000 men." He and Gen. Kelly report the movement as made on the night of the 7th, though all other authorities place it on the night of the 6th. (See also Doc. 8, vol. iv., *Rebellion Record.*)

[11] Col. (then Lieut.) Cutshaw says, in a letter to the author: " On January 7, 1862, a force from Romney surprised our camp at daylight, their advance coming in with part of our pickets. Instead of attempting a passage of the gap the enemy hurried immediately to the more accessible ridge on our right, and were there as soon as our militia, and with a volley scattered them." Cutshaw's guns were left without support, the gunners shot down or put to flight, and the pieces captured.

[12] Jackson's report of this affair to Gen. J. E. Johnston, dated Unger's Store, January 11, 1862, says: " Though on the 4th instant Bath and all that part of Morgan county east of the Big Capon River was recovered from the enemy, . . . yet on the 7th the enemy surprised our militia at Hanging Rock pass, distant fifteen miles from Romney, drove back our troops from their fortifications, burnt their huts, captured two pieces of artillery (one a four-

pounder rifle, the other a four-pounder smooth-bore). . . . As soon as they had accomplished this and burnt the buildings of Col. Charles Blue, near by, and killed his live-stock, leaving it on the ground, they returned to Romney."

Col. Dunning, in his report, says: "Seven prisoners were taken and seven dead were found."

[13] Jackson says in his official report: "I do not feel at liberty to close this report without alluding to the conduct of the reprobate Federal commanders, who, in Hampshire county, have not only burned valuable mill-property, but also many private houses. Their track from Romney to Hanging Rock, a distance of fifteen miles, was one of desolation. The number of dead animals lying along the roadside, where they had been shot by the enemy, exemplified the spirit of that part of the Northern army." (Dabney's *Life*, p. 271.)

Col. Dunning says in his report that he ordered the mill and hotel (Col. Blue's house) to be burned, and adds: "I am sorry to say that some straggling soldiers burnt other unoccupied houses on their return march." (Federal official reports, Adjutant-General's office.)

[14] Jackson, on January 10, reported the distribution of his forces as follows:

183 infantry .	.	.	at Winchester.
650 ,,	56 cavalry .		at Hanging Rock.
	50 ,,	.	at North River Mills.
100 ,,	56 ,,	.	at Martinsburg.
	60 ,,	.	at Shepherdstown.
100 ,,	26 ,,	.	at Duffield's Depot (Baltimore and Ohio railroad).
400 ,,	.	.	. at Moorefield.
8,000 ,,	375 cavalry .		at Unger's Store.

And adds that "Brig.-Gen. Meem left here this morning for Moorefield with 545 infantry, and Brig.-Gen. Carson for Bath, sixteen miles off, with 200 infantry and 25 mounted militia."

Jackson's artillery consisted at this time of:

McLaughlin's (Rockbridge) battery	.	6 guns
Waters's battery	.	4 ,,
Carpenter's battery	. . .	4 ,,

Shumaker's battery . . . . 4 guns
Marye's battery . . . . . 4 „
Cutshaw's section (lost January 7) . . 2 „

and a section of heavy guns (twenty-four-pounder Parrotts)
sent out to Bath under Capt. Wood McDonald, but afterwards returned to Winchester because of the difficulty of
transporting them over the bad roads.

The organization of the regular infantry under Jackson
(which was all at Unger's Store) was as follows :

Garnett's Brigade.	LORING'S TROOPS : Taliaferro's Brigade.
2nd Virginia regiment	23rd Virginia regiment
4th „ „	37th „
5th „ „	3rd Arkansas „
27th „ „	
33rd „ „	

LORING'S TROOPS :

Gilham's Brigade.	Anderson's Brigade.
21st Virginia regiment	1st Tennessee regiment
42nd „ „	7th „ „
48th „ „	14th „ „
Irish battalion.	

[15] Gen. Jackson had written on the 14th to Secretary
Benjamin as follows :

"BLOOMERY GAP, *January* 14, 1862.

" HON. J. P. BENJAMIN :

" SIR :—Through the blessing of God I regard this district
as essentially in our possession.

" There is reason to believe that there are medical and
other stores in Cumberland which would, if in our possession,
be of great value to our Government. If you desire them
to be secured, in addition to the other advantages resulting
from the occupation of Cumberland and the dispersion or
capture of their army near there, please send me at once
4,000 infantry and 350 cavalry. An engineer officer is
much needed.

" T. J. JACKSON,
" Major-General."

[16] Gen. Jackson's views are thus given in a letter to the Secretary of War, Hon. J. P. Benjamin, dated January 20, 1862 : " Though the enemy have retreated to the Potomac, yet they continue in possession of the frontiers of this district from seven miles below Cumberland to the Alleghany. On the first of this month there was not a single loyal citizen of Morgan county who, in my opinion, could with safety remain at home, and the same may be said respecting the most valuable portion of Hampshire county. A kind Providence has restored to us the entire county of Morgan, and nearly the entire county of Hampshire, but so long as the enemy hold possession of the railroad bridge, five miles below Cumberland, and the two railroad bridges above Cumberland, they can make dangerous inroads upon us. On last Friday night I designed moving rapidly, with my old brigade and one of Loring's, for the purpose of destroying one of the railroad bridges across the North Branch of the Potomac west of Cumberland, and thus cutting off their supplies from the west, and consequently forcing them to reduce their army in front of me ; but as Gen. Loring's leading brigade, commanded by Col. Taliaferro, was not in a condition to move, the enterprise had to be abandoned. Since leaving Winchester, the 1st instant, the troops have suffered greatly, and Gen. Loring has not a single brigade in a condition for active operations, though in a few days I expect they will be much improved, and will, if placed in winter quarters, be able to hold this important portion of the Valley ; but these quarters should be well selected and the position strengthened, and hence the great importance of having an engineer officer. It will not do for me to remain here much longer, lest Gen. Banks should cross the Potomac ; consequently, in a few days I expect to leave this place, taking with me Garnett's brigade. I have written to Gen. J. E. Johnston that, unless otherwise directed, Gen. Loring's command will go into winter quarters in the South Branch valley, Gen. Carson's at Bath, Gen. Meem's at Martinsburg, and Gen. Garnett's at Winchester. The cavalry will be distributed at various points along the northern frontier. Gen. Boggs's brigade, which principally belongs to the South Branch Valley, will be distributed

over the section of country to which it belongs. It is very desirable that the troops should go into winter quarters as soon as possible, so I trust you will send me the best engineer officer you can, though it be for only ten days."

[17] Gen. Johnston's letter is as follows :

" MY DEAR FRIEND :—I have just read, with profound regret, your letter to the Secretary of War, asking to be relieved from your present command, either by an order to the Virginia Military Institute or the acceptance of your resignation. Let me beg you to reconsider this matter. Under ordinary circumstances, a due sense of one's own dignity, as well as care for professional character and official rights, would demand such a course as yours. But the character of this war, the great energy exhibited by the government of the United States, the danger in which our very existence as an independent people lies, require sacrifices from us all who have been educated as soldiers. I receive my information of the order of which you have such cause to complain from your letter. Is not that as great an official wrong to me as the order itself to you ? Let us dispassionately reason with the government on this subject of command, and if we fail to influence its practice, then ask to be relieved from positions the authority of which is exercised by the War Department, while the responsibilities are left to us.

" I have taken the liberty to detain your letter to make this appeal to your patriotism, not merely from warm feelings of personal regard, but from the official opinion, which makes me regard you as necessary to the service of your country in your present position." (*Johnston's Narrative,* p. 88.)

Many soldiers and citizens added their efforts to those of Gen. Johnston and Governor Letcher.

[18] From a communication of Governor Letcher to the " Richmond Whig." Jackson's reply referred to is in the Archive Office in Washington, and is as follows :

" *February* 6, 1862.

" GOVERNOR :—Your letter of the 4th inst. was received this morning. If my retiring from the army would produce the effect upon our country that you have named in your letter, I, of course, would not desire to leave the service. And if, upon the receipt of this note, your opinion remains unchanged, you are authorized to withdraw my resignation, unless the Secretary of War desires that it should be accepted. My reasons for resigning were set forth in my letter of the 31st ult., and my views remain unchanged ; and if the Secretary persists in the ruinous policy complained of, I feel that no officer can serve his country better than by making his strongest possible protest against it, which, in my opinion, is done by tendering his resignation, rather than be a willing instrument in prosecuting the war upon a ruinous principle. I am much obliged to you for requesting that I should be ordered to the Institute.

" Yours, etc.,

" T. J. JACKSON."

[19] Col. Gilham and Maj. Ship had been ordered back to the Virginia Military Institute, where they held professorships, and Col. J. T. L. Preston, who had acted as adjutant-general and chief of staff for Jackson during the past few months, was ordered away for the same reason on February 1.

[20] The ideas of military efficiency in some of these commands were droll, and no doubt vexatious enough to the General. In the absence of Gen. Carson the command of his brigade devolved on Col. Sincindiver, a corpulent and good-humoured Dutchman, whose military training had been gained entirely at the annual militia musters which before the war constituted a feature of Virginia life. We find Jackson writing to him on February 11 : " I regret to hear from an officer that it is *impossible* to execute an order. If your cavalry will not obey your orders you must *make them* do it, and, if necessary, go out with them yourself. I desire you to go out and post your cavalry where you want them to stay, and arrest any man who leaves his post, and prefer charges and specifications against him, that he may be court-martialed. It will not do to say that your men cannot be induced to perform their duty. *They must be made to do it.* When you hear of marauding parties, send out and bring them in as prisoners of war." The affair of February 14 can hardly be wondered at.

[21] Gen. G. H. Gordon, then of the Second Massachusetts regiment, of Abercrombie's brigade, says the Federal troops were at that time disposed as follows : " While our brigade moved on and to Charlestown from Harper's Ferry, Gen. Williams moved from Hancock through Martinsburg to Bunker Hill. . . . Gen. Hamilton, passing through Charlestown, stopped at Smithfield, midway between Charlestown and Bunker Hill. Gen. Shields halted at Martinsburg, and Gen. Sedgwick at Charlestown." Abercrombie, Williams, and Hamilton then commanded the three brigades which constituted Banks's division. (*History of Second Massachusetts Regiment*, Third Paper, p. 15.)

On March 2, Banks, at Charlestown, was informed by a negro scout sent out by Col. Strother (of his staff) of the preparations for the evacuation of Winchester, etc. Strother says Banks was held back from advancing rapidly by the fear of a concentration from Manassas at Winchester against him, thus reversing the Manassas campaign of July, 1861. (*Harper's Magazine*, January, 1867.)

[22] Jackson's vigour in enforcing discipline is illustrated by an order on February 25 to prevent the introduction of liquors into his command, which had been done by means of boxes sent to the soldiers by their friends. He directed " that every wagon that came into camp should be searched, and if any liquor were found, it was to be spilled out, and the wagon and horses turned over to the quartermaster." (*Hotchkiss's Diary*.)

[23] In J. E. Johnston's field return of February 28, 1862, the force in the " Valley District " under Jackson is as follows (after correcting some mistakes in the addition) :

Present for duty, officers and men : infantry, 4,297 ; artillery, 369 ; cavalry, 601 ; total, 5,267.

An examination of such regimental returns as are on file among the Confederate archives in Washington shows that the strength (present for duty, officers and men), on March 1, of the Twenty-third and Thirty-seventh Virginia regiment (Fulkerson's brigade), and of the Twenty-first, Forty-second, and Forty-eighth Virginia regiments and the Irish battalion (Burks's brigade), was 1,837. No returns of Garnett's brigade of that date are to be found there ; but the returns of the Fourth, Fifth, Twenty-seventh, and Thirty-third Virginia regiments for February 1 give their strength as 1,403. These regiments, with the Second Virginia, constituted Garnett's brigade. Estimating the Second at the average of the other four, the brigade numbered at that date 1,754. Adding this to the sum given above for the other brigades on March 1, we have 3,591—say 3,600—as the infantry under Jackson on March 1. The difference (about 700) between this and the infantry strength as given by Gen. Johnston is to be accounted for either by supposing that some of the fragments of the militia commands were included in the return used by Johnston, or that some of the non-Virginian regiments ordered elsewhere had not gone at the date of the making of that return. The last of these regiments did not leave Jackson's district until February 22 or 23. Taking the artillery and cavalry from Gen. Johnston's return, Jackson's effective strength (excluding some remnants of militia) was—infantry, 3,600 ; artillery, 369 ; cavalry, 601 ; total, 4,570—say 4,600—men.

[24] McClellan says, " The whole of Banks's division and two brigades of Sedgwick's division were thrown across the river at Harper's Ferry, leaving one brigade of Sedgwick's division to observe and guard the Potomac from Great Falls to the mouth of the Monocacy." This last brigade of Sedgwick's (Gorman's) was subsequently sent forward, March 11, and joined those in advance at Berryville on the 14th. Jackson having retired and Winchester having been occupied, the whole of Sedgwick's division was sent back to Bolivar on March 15. Gen. McClellan's morning report, dated March 2, 1862, gives Banks's strength as follows :

Officers and men present for duty :

Banks's division	15,398
Lander's division (Shields's) . . .	11,869
Sedgwick's division	11,217
Total	38,484

This, no doubt, included railroad guards and other detachments in the rear, but his movable column could hardly have been less than 30,000 men, and was probably more, up to March 15, when Sedgwick's division was ordered to the rear.

[25] Jackson had ordered his trains into camp immediately south of Winchester, but, by some mistake on the part of those in charge, they were taken between Kernstown and Newtown, some five miles or more from Winchester, and the troops had to march that distance to get supper. The General, who had remained behind and was ignorant of this, called a council, consisting of Gen. Garnett and the regimental commanders of the " Stonewall " brigade, to meet in Winchester after dark, and to them he proposed a night attack upon the portion of Banks's troops near Stephenson's. He proposed, after the troops had eaten supper and rested for some hours, that they should march to the neighbourhood of the enemy and make the attack before daylight. The plan was not approved by the council, and Jackson learned from those present that the troops, instead of being in the suburbs of Winchester, were already five or six miles away. A march of ten miles would thus be needed to bring them into contact with the enemy. This last fact and the disapproval of the council caused him to abandon the plan. He followed the troops and bivouacked in a fence-corner. The foregoing is understood to have been Jackson's first and last council of war. (For the above account I am indebted to Gen. John Echols, of Staunton, Virginia, then colonel of the Twenty-seventh Virginia regiment, who was present at the conference.)

[26] McClellan says (p. 546 of his report, in *Rebellion Record*), in a letter dated April 1, 1862, to the adjutant-general U.S.A. : " If Shields's division, leaving out the cavalry, consisted of only 7,000, the other division, under Williams, must have contained over 12,000 men."

[27] The forces under Gen. Jackson at Kernstown were as follows (I have appended strength given in the regimental reports of the battle as far as it could be found) :

First brigade, under Gen. Garnett :

Second Virginia regiment . .	320 rank and file.
Fourth Virginia regiment . .	203 ,, ,, ,,
Fifth Virginia regiment . .	not found.
Twenty-seventh Virginia regiment	170 muskets.

Thirty-third Virginia regiment . 275 rank and file.

McLaughlin's battery . . not found, 8 guns.

Waters's battery . . . 90 men, 4 „

Carpenter's battery . . . 48 „ 4 „

Second brigade, under Col. Burks :

Twenty-first Virginia regiment . 270.

Forty-second Virginia regiment . 293.

Forty-eighth Virginia regiment . not found.

First battalion of regulars (Irish battalion) . . . . 187.

Marye's battery . . . 4 guns.

Third brigade, under Col. Fulkerson :

Twenty-third Virginia regiment . 177 Officers and men.

Thirty-seventh Virginia regiment 397 „ „ „

Shumaker's battery . . . 4 guns.

Ashby's regiment of cavalry . . 290.

Chew's battery . . . . 3 guns.

The Forty-eighth Virginia regiment and the batteries of Shumaker and Marye were not engaged.

[28] Gen. Shields says he " had 6,000 infantry and a cavalry force of 750, and 24 pieces of artillery." His organization was as follows :

First (Kimball's) brigade :

8th Ohio regiment.

67th „ „

14th Indiana „

84th Pennsylvania reg't.

Second (Sullivan's) brigade :

13th Indiana regiment.

5th Ohio „

62nd „ „

39th Illinois „

Third (Tyler's) Brigade :

7th Ohio regiment.

29th „ „

1st Virginia „

7th Indiana „

110th Pennsylvania reg't.

Daum's artillery.

Jenks's battery (" A," First Virginia).

Clark's „ (" E," Fourth artillery).

Davis's „ (" B," First Virginia).

Robinson's „ (" L," First Ohio).

Huntington battery (" H," First Ohio).

Broadhead's cavalry :

4 companies First Michigan cavalry.

2   ,,   Ohio   ,,

2   ,,   Maryland   ,,

6   ,,   First Virginia   ,,

2   ,,   Ringgold and Washington cavalry.

There were also a company of Massachusetts sharpshooters and Company B, First Maryland infantry (Federal), present.

Gen. McClellan's return for March gives Shields's strength (officers and men present for duty) as 12,255, and enumerates 203 companies as composing his division. From the above it appears that about 152 or 153 of these companies were present at Kernstown. At the average Gen. Shields would have had over 9,000 men present.

[29] This church carries one back to the first settlement of the Valley of Virginia. The first regular settlement in this Valley was made in 1732 by a party of colonists, consisting of sixteen families, under Joist Hite, from Pennsylvania, who settled on the Opequon. They were Scotch-Irish Presbyterians. In 1735, William Hoge joined them, and having settled on the land about Kernstown, gave the lot on which the church stands for the use of the first Presbyterian congregation ever organized in Virginia west of the Blue Ridge. Mr. Hoge was the ancestor of the family of that name distinguished in Church and State in Virginia. (*Foote's Sketches.*)

[30] Maj. R. M. Copeland, assistant adjutant-general to Gen. Banks, says, in his report : " The centre and right wing (Federal) were composed of three batteries and about five regiments of infantry, with a considerable force of cavalry. A high and commanding position on our right was occupied by the enemy at about 3 o'clock p.m., and a severe fire opened on our centre, which compelled the withdrawal of a portion of our force into a more secure position.

" At about 3.30 p.m. Col. Tyler was ordered to attack the enemy's new position on our right, and to take their battery. He moved immediately forward, with three or four regiments, a battery, and about 400 cavalry, through a dense wood, which covered the enemy's centre and left wing. In about half an hour after Col. Tyler's movement his skirmishers exchanged shots with the enemy, who were posted behind high stone walls, a rocky hill, and some woods, a quarter of a mile in front of his battery. The enemy reserved their fire until our line was very near. They then rose and poured a very heavy volley. The suddenness and strength of their fire caused our lines to falter, and the extreme left, composed mainly of the One Hundred and Tenth Pennsylvania Volunteers, broke and ran. The rest of the line soon rallied and maintained a steady fight (falling back on the right and advancing on the left) for at least half an hour, when two regiments came to their assistance up the left flank and through a very severe fire. They advanced steadily, and soon gained a position from which they could flank the enemy delivering their fire. When they received this new fire the enemy fell back rapidly, but still fighting, to the woods nearest the hill, from which the battery had been in the meantime withdrawn.

" Having in vain attempted to rally the One Hundred and Tenth Pennsylvania Volunteers (which, with such company officers as I could see, was in a shameful rout), I gained the advance on the first field which the enemy had held, where there were many dead and wounded." Maj. Copeland says that Tyler then moved slowly forward, supporting Kimball and Sullivan.

[31] Maj. Copeland says of this second stand : " The enemy now opened on our line with a heavier fire than before. We maintained our position from the first, and soon drove them in utter confusion down the hill ; but the near approach of night forbade further pursuit."

See reports of Cols. Harman and Burks.

[32] Jackson's report. The brigade and regimental reports of the losses at Kernstown make them a little greater. Thus :

	Killed.	Wounded.	Missing.	Total.
Garnett reports for his brigade .	41	162	158	361
Burks's losses by regimental reports	24	114	39	177
Fulkerson's losses by regimental reports	15	76	71	162

700

Ashby's loss was not reported, but it was slight. The total Confederate loss may have reached 725.

[33] After the war, the ladies of Winchester, from the midst of the saddened and desolate homes, continued their self-denying care for the ashes of the brave men to whose comfort and encouragement they had contributed so freely in life, and by whose suffering cots they had often watched in sorrow, danger, and death. Under the leadership of Mrs. Philip Williams, they gathered the thousands of Confederate dead from the surrounding battle-field and placed them in the "Stonewall Cemetery,"—a monument not more to the patriotism of man than to the devotion of woman.

[34] Brig.-Gen. Garnett was relieved on April 1, and Brig.-Gen. C. S. Winder assigned to the command of the First brigade. Gen. Garnett was subsequently assigned to one of Pickett's brigades, and fell, gallantly leading it, in the famous charge of that division on the heights of Gettysburg, July 3, 1863.

Whether Garnett's judgment at Kernstown was correct will perhaps always remain a question; not so his splendid courage and unselfish patriotism.

[35] Jackson followed his troops, and when near Newtown halted at a camp-fire and warmed himself for some time. He then remounted and rode back towards the Opequon, followed by several of his staff, who, overcome by weariness, dropped away one by one, until only Maj. W. J. Hawks (chief commissary) remained with the general. Then turning from the road into an orchard, he fastened his horse, and asked the major if he could make a fire, adding: "We shall have to burn rails to-night." The major soon had a roaring fire, and was making a bed of rails, when the general wished to know what he was doing. "Fixing a place to sleep," was the reply. "You seem determined to make yourself and those around you comfortable," said Jackson. Knowing the general had fasted all day, the major soon obtained some bread and meat from the nearest squad of soldiers, and after they had satisfied their hunger, they slept soundly on the rail-bed in a fence-corner.

[36] The "Mountain Department" embraced the territory

between Banks's districts and Halleck's. It had the Alleghanies for its eastern boundary and embraced the present State of West Virginia. A few days before the end of March, President Lincoln informed Gen. McClellan that he had resisted the pressure brought upon him to detach Blenker's division; yet, on March 31, the President writes: "This morning I felt constrained to order Blenker's division to Fremont, and I write this to assure you that I did it with great pain, understanding that you would wish it otherwise." (McClellan's report.)

[37] McClellan's orders to Banks on April 1 were as follows:

"HEADQUARTERS ARMY OF THE POTOMAC.
"ON BOARD THE COMMODORE, *April* 1, 1862.

"GENERAL:—The change in affairs in the Valley of the Shenandoah has rendered necessary a corresponding departure, temporarily at least, from the plan we some days since agreed upon.

"In my arrangements I assume that you have with you a force amply sufficient to drive Jackson before you, provided he is not reinforced largely. I also assume that you may find it impossible to detach anything towards Manassas for some days, probably not until the operations of the main army have drawn all the rebel force towards Richmond. . . . I will order Blenker to march on Strasburg, and to report to you for temporary duty, so that, should you find a large force in your front, you can avail yourself of his aid as soon as possible. Please direct him to Winchester, there to report to the adjutant-general of the army for orders; but keep him until you are sure what you have in front.

"In regard to your own movements, the most important thing at present is to throw Jackson well back, and then to assume such a position as to enable you to prevent his return. As soon as the railway communications are reestablished, it will be probably important and advisable to move on Staunton; but this would require secure communications, and a force of from 25,000 to 30,000 for active operations. It should also be nearly coincident with my own move on Richmond; at all events, not so long before it as to enable the rebels to concentrate on you and then return on me. I fear that you cannot be ready in time, although it may come in very well with a force less than that I have mentioned after the main battle near Richmond. When Gen. Sumner leaves Warrenton Junction, Gen. Abercrombie will be placed in immediate command of Manassas and Warrenton Junction, under your general orders. Please inform me frequently, by telegraph and otherwise, as to the state of things in your front.

" I am very truly yours,
" GEO. B. McCLELLAN,
" Major-General Commanding.
" MAJ.-GEN. N. P. BANKS, Commanding Fifth Corps."

[38] McClellan evidently thought that with Banks occupying Jackson, and with over 36,000 men distributed at Warrenton and Manassas, and around Washington itself, the Federal President and capital were reasonably safe! But Mr. Lincoln thought otherwise. On April 4, Gen. Banks was placed in chief command of that portion of Virginia and Maryland lying between the Mountain Department (Fremont's) and the Blue Ridge. This region, composed principally of the valley of the Shenandoah river, was to be styled the " Department of the Shenandoah." Gen. McDowell, on the same day, was put in chief command of the portion of Virginia east of the Blue Ridge and west of the Richmond, Fredericksburg and Potomac railroad, including the District of Columbia and the country between the Potomac and Patuxent. His department was to be known as that of the Rappahannock. Henceforth these officers were to be independent of Gen. McClellan and of each other.

[39] On the day that Ashby first took position along Stony Creek (April 1), he was at one time riding along the edge of the woods held by his skirmishers, reconnoitring the enemy, followed by a little boy named " Dixie," a sort of pet of the camp. A bullet from a sharpshooter, aimed at Ashby, struck Dixie's horse in the head and killed it. The boy rolled off, and was jumping up to run, when Ashby called him back and told him to get his saddle and bridle, coolly waiting for him, though a mark for a continual fire.

[40] They reached the vicinity of Mount Jackson on

March 20. On March 21 we find Jackson writing to Col. S. Bassett French, aide-de-camp to Governor Letcher, as follows :

" COLONEL :—Please request the Governor to order three thousand muskets to Staunton at his earliest convenience for the militia of this district. None of the militia beyond this county, except five hundred from Augusta, have yet arrived, but they are turning out encouragingly. There are three religious denominations in this military district who are opposed to war. Eighteen were recently arrested in endeavouring to make their escape through Pendleton county to the enemy. Those who do not desert will, to some extent, hire substitutes, others will turn out in obedience to the Governor's call, but I understand some of them say they will not ' shoot.' They can be made to fire, but can very easily take bad aim. So, for the purpose of giving to this command the highest degree of efficiency, and securing loyal feelings and co-operation, I have, as these non-combatants are said to be good teamsters and faithful to their promises, determined to organize them into companies of one hundred men each, rank and file, and after mustering them, with the legal number of company officers, into service, assign them to the various staff departments without issuing arms to them ; but if at any time they have insufficient labour, to have them drilled, so that, in case circumstances should justify it, arms may be given them. If these men are, as represented to me, faithful labourers and careful of property, this arrangement will not only enable many volunteers to return to the ranks, but will also save many valuable horses and other public property in addition to arms. . . . All I have pledged myself is that, as far as practicable, I will employ them in other ways than fighting, but with the conditions that they shall act in good faith with me, and not permit persons to use their names for the purpose of keeping out of service. . . ."

On March 29 the Governor ordered all the militia to be drafted into existing organizations until these were full. The execution of this order was begun on April 4. On April 14, Gen. Jackson writes to Gen. W. B. Richardson,

Adjutant-General of Virginia, that " the militia have not turned out as well as I was induced to believe, but those who are here are a fine body of men, and bid fair to render good service. . . . I fear there will not be enough militia to fill up the old companies. . . ." He advised stringent measures to bring them out, but the Conscription Bill, passed two days later, made all further action on the part of the State unnecessary.

[41] Col. (then Capt.) Cutshaw says this force marched into the mountain recesses, but the people fled or hid themselves. From high points the woods were shelled, and this greatly increased the panic among the simple mountaineers. Many came in and surrendered, and no further trouble was had.

[42] General Order No. 36, April 4, from Jackson's headquarters, announced the organization of the Army of the Valley. Brig.-Gen. C. S. Winder was assigned to the First brigade (" Stonewall "). The Second brigade remained under Col. John Campbell, and the Third brigade under Col. Fulkerson (Gen. Taliaferro not having yet reported). McLaughlin's and Carpenter's batteries were assigned to the First brigade, Marye's and Waters's to the Second brigade, and Shumaker's to the Third. All the cavalry was placed under Ashby.

[43] Gen. Edward Johnson, whose force was on Shenandoah Mountain, came to confer with Gen. Jackson while he was at Peale's. In his absence Gen. Johnson's troops fell back towards Staunton, in consequence of information having reached them of Jackson's movement towards Swift Run Gap.

[44] Gen. Banks, in a despatch to the Federal War Department, April 19, says : " To-day I have been to the bridges on the south fork of the Shenandoah, in the Massanutton Valley, with a force of cavalry, infantry, and artillery, to protect the two important bridges that cross the river. We were within sight of Luray at the south bridge. A sharp skirmish occurred with the rebels, in which they lost several men taken prisoners. Their object was the destruction of the bridges. . . . I believe Jackson left this Valley yesterday. He is reported to have left Harrisonburg yesterday for Gordonsville by the mountain road. He encamped last

night at McGaheysville, eleven miles from Harrisonburg."
(*Rebellion Record*, vol. iv. p. 93.)

[45] Jackson writes to Gen. Lee on April 23 : " Banks's
main force is still in the vicinity of New Market, extending
from one mile below to three above the town.   Yesterday
he had near one hundred wagons twelve miles above New
Market, and a part of his force even entered Harrisonburg,
seventeen miles from New Market.   My object has been
to get in his rear at New Market or Harrisonburg if he gives
me an opportunity, and this would be the case if he should
advance on Staunton with his main body.   It appears to
me that if I remain quiet a few days more he will probably
make a move in some direction, or send a larger force towards Harrisonburg, and thus enable me, with the blessing
of Providence, to successfully attack his advance ; and if
I am unsuccessful in driving back his entire force, he may
be induced to move forward his commands from New
Market and attempt to follow me through this gap, when
our forces would have greatly the advantage.

" Without Gen. Ewell's division, Banks can march on
to Staunton, though, if he attempts it, I design threatening
his flank and rear, and this may prevent his reaching
Staunton ; but without doing this he could advance so
far as to threaten Gen. Edward Johnson's rear so seriously
as to make him fall back, and thus let Staunton fall into
the hands of the Federal force in his front. . . ."

Later on the same day Jackson writes that the news
from Fredericksburg induces him to believe that Ewell's
division may be more needed there than with him, and
says he will "make arrangements so as not to be disappointed
should he (Ewell) be ordered to Fredericksburg."

A few days later the news from Fredericksburg was more
reassuring, and this led Jackson to apply for troops from
that point.   (See next chapter.)

The letters from which the above extracts are taken are
in the Confederate archives at Washington.

[46] Gen. Edward Johnson, in a letter dated March 18.
reports his strength as :

Aggregate present for duty	.	.	.	2,425
Aggregate present	.	.	.	.	2,784

This is the latest report (giving his strength) I could find among the Confederate archives.

[47] Gen. Fremont says that he relieved Rosecrans on March 29, 1862, that the total troops then turned over to him consisted of thirty-five and two-tenths regiments of infantry, thirty-six companies of cavalry, and nine batteries of artillery; total number of men, 34,271. A few days after, the troops in South-west Virginia and Eastern Kentucky, amounting to 9,195, were detached from his command. He adds to this 6,269 as the usual percentage " for sick, etc., and not available for duty," and states 18,807— " say in round numbers 19,000 men "—as his effective force left. " A small but not appreciable increase of this was made by enlistments in the department, but the policy of the War Department did not foster this." He continues: " When sent to the department I was promised 17,000 men as reinforcements. On April 1 was despatched that Blenker's division was *en route* to join me; as it had not reached Harper's Ferry by April 12, I asked what had become of it, and that it be sent to Moorefield by the shortest route." Rosecrans was temporarily conducting it. It was dreadfully in want of horses and transportation. On April 21, Fremont was informed it could not move for want of shoes. It was thus greatly delayed, but finally joined him at Petersburg, Hardy county, May 11. Fremont's plan of campaign, submitted to President Lincoln on April 21, was as follows: " The first base of operations being the Baltimore and Ohio railroad, the division of Gen. Blenker, which, from the best information I can obtain, numbers about 9,000 men, will take position at Moorefield. At this point, or at Franklin, it will unite with the troops now under command of Gen. Schenck, numbering about 3,000 men. With these, acting in conjunction with Gen. Banks, I propose to move up the Valley of Virginia by a course which you will see on the accompanying map, over roads which are as dry and as good at all seasons of the year as any in Virginia, and through a country where forage is easily obtained. At Monterey I shall be joined by the troops under Gen. Milroy, numbering 3,500 effective men, and can then strike the railroad at or near Salem, while

Gen. Cox (in command along the Kanawha), with his 7,000 men, takes possession of Newburn; or can first effect a junction with Gen. Cox and seize the railroad with a force thus increased to about 22,000 men.

" The base of operations will then be changed to Gauley. To this place, by the Ohio and Kanawha Rivers, abundant supplies for the army can be transported with the means now at hand and being prepared. Having thus destroyed the connection between Knoxville and the army in Eastern Virginia, and perhaps seized some rolling-stock, we can advance rapidly along the railroad towards Knoxville, turning the position at Cumberland Gap. The forces now under Gen. Kelly, and the Virginia troops will be left, as we proceed, to guard the Baltimore and Ohio railroad and to protect the loyal inhabitants of the State from guerrillas."

This plan was approved by President Lincoln, but with the " view of the ultimate closing in of my (Gen. Fremont's) column towards Richmond rather than Knoxville."

[48] Jackson's report. On April 29, Jackson wrote to Gen. Lee as follows : " As I do not believe that Banks will advance on me in my present position, I am disposed, unless you send me large reinforcements, to adopt one of three plans, viz., either to leave Gen. Ewell here to threaten Banks's rear in the event of his advancing on Staunton, and move with my command rapidly on the force in front of Gen. Edward Johnson ; or else, co-operating with Gen. Ewell, to attack the enemy's detached force between New Market and the Shenandoah, and if successful in this, then to press forward and get in Banks's rear at New Market, and thus induce him to fall back. The third is, to pass down the Shenandoah to Sperryville, and thus threaten Winchester *via* Front Royal. I believe that this would cause the enemy to fall back. From Sperryville I could move either in the direction of Front Royal or Warrenton, or, if my command should be opposed by too large a Federal force, it could turn off towards Culpeper Court House.

" To get in Banks's rear with my present force would be rather a dangerous undertaking, as I would have to cross the river and immediately cross the Massanutton Mountains, during which the enemy would have decidedly the advantage of position. Of the three plans I give the preference to attacking the force west of Staunton, for if successful I would afterwards only have Banks to contend with, and in doing this would be reinforced by Gen. Edward Johnson, and by that time you might be able to give me reinforcements, which, united with the troops now under my control, would enable me to defeat Banks; and if he should be routed and his command destroyed, nearly all our forces here could, if necessary, cross the Blue Ridge to Warrenton, Fredericks-burg, or any other threatened point. I have written to Gen. Edward Johnson to know what force, in addition to his command, would be required for a successful blow in his vicinity. If I receive an answer justifying a move in that direction, I may leave here to-morrow *via* Port Republic." Gen. Lee replies, May 1 : " I have carefully considered the three plans of operations proposed by you. I must leave the selection of the one to be adopted, to your judgment."

[49] West View is six or seven miles west of Staunton, on the Parkersburg turnpike, and four miles from Buffalo Gap, a water-way in the Little North Mountain, through which passes this turnpike, as well as the Chesapeake and Ohio railroad.

[50] Johnson, in the afternoon of Tuesday, May 6, marched through Buffalo Gap and up the eastern slope of the Great North Mountain, resting his advance in the notch known as Dry Branch Gap, fifteen miles from Staunton. Here, between Crawford's Mountain and Elliot's Knob, he bivouacked part of his troops in line on the crest of the mountain. Milroy's advance was at the eastern base of the Shenandoah Mountain, on the opposite side of the Big Calf-Pasture Valley.

[51] Gen. Schenck says : " By leaving my baggage-train under a guard in my last camp on the road, fourteen miles from McDowell, I was able to push forward so as to make the whole distance, thirty-four miles, in twenty-three hours." As he reached McDowell at 10 a.m. on May 8, he must have left Franklin at 11 a.m. on the preceding day. (Schenck's report, *Rebellion Record,* vol. v. p. 35.)

[52] Fremont, in his official report, already quoted, says

that Milroy and Schenck had together 6,500 men. His official return for May 10 gives as present for duty, officers and men :

Under Milroy	**3,694**
„ Schenck	**2,335**
Total	**6,029**

On April 30 the return gives the strength of the two as 6,422.

[53] The troops actually engaged at McDowell, with the losses in detail, so far as the regimental reports give them, are as follows :

CONFEDERATE

Edward Johnson's brigade:

	Strength.	Killed.	Wounded.	Missing.	Total Loss.
Twenty-fifth Virginia .		1			
Thirty-first „ .					
Twelfth Georgia . .	540	40	140		180
Forty-fourth Virginia .					
Fifty-second „ .		6	47		53
Fifty-eighth „ .					

Taliaferro's brigade :

Tenth Virginia . .		1	20	21
Twenty-third Virginia .		6	35	41
Thirty-seventh „ .		5	34	39

	Wounded.	Total Loss.
Campbell's brigade :		
Forty-second Virginia .	3	3
Forty-eighth „ .	4	4
Twenty-first „ .		
Irish battalion : . .	1	1

Total strength, about 6,000. Total loss, 461.

FEDERAL

	Strength.
Of Milroy's brigade, parts of the :	
Twenty-fifth Ohio	469
Seventy-fifth „	444

Strength.

Thirty-second Ohio   416
Third Virginia   439

Of Schenck's brigade, part of the
    Eighty-second Ohio   500
    Also, some of Second Virginia, as skirmishers.
    Part of Hyman's battery, and part of Johnson's
        Twelfth Ohio) battery.
    Strength, about 2,500.   Loss, 256.

[54] Fremont had been joined by Blenker's division at Petersburg, in Hardy county, May 11. Next day he set out for Franklin, which place he reached on the 14th. On the 16th, Secretary Stanton telegraphs to know if he still designs to move on the Virginia and Tennessee railroad, and how long it will take him to reach it. Fremont says he was then busy trying to equip his destitute men, and he did not move until the news of the overthrow of Banks was sent to him. Fremont seems to have been very largely occupied in "equipping his destitute men," and from his and Rosecrans's reports, this division of Blenker must have been the most improvident or unfortunate set of poor devils that ever took up arms. They were detached from McClellan about April 1, and ordered to Fremont. Their route lay through one of the finest countries in the world. They were probably never more than thirty miles from a railroad which put them within from two to five hours of Washington. They were not at any time within fifty miles of an enemy, and yet it took them until May 11 to reach their destination,—a distance not more than one hundred and sixty or one hundred and seventy miles. At one time they seem to have lost themselves, for Gen. Rosecrans was sent by the Federal Secretary of War about the middle of April to hunt them up and lead them to Fremont. He says he went to Winchester *via* Harper's Ferry, "despatching messengers from two or three points in my route in search of Gen. Blenker's division"; found that a boatload had drowned themselves in crossing the Shenandoah at Berry's Ferry, and ordered the division to Snicker's Ferry,

where there was a " flying bridge." He says they were " unfed, unclothed, and unpaid, between 8,000 and 10,000 men, bare-footed," etc. He had them supplied, and finally delivered them to Gen. Fremont. The latter says that Blenker reported his effective force when they reached him at 8,000, but that " subsequent investigation placed the number of men and officers actually present and fit for duty at considerably below 7,000." They had left Alexandria 10,000 strong.

[55] McClellan says, in his report, p. 546 : " From the following letter to the Adjutant-General, dated April 1, 1862, it will be seen that I left for the defence of the national capital and its approaches, when I sailed for the Peninsula, 73,456 men, with 109 pieces of light artillery, including the 32 pieces in Washington alluded to, but not enumerated in my letter to the Adjutant-General." (This includes Blenker's division, 10,028 strong, with 24 guns.) " It will also be seen that I recommended other available troops in New York (more than 4,000) to be at once ordered forward to reinforce them." (See p. 57, *ante.*)

[56] The returns of Gens. Williams and Hatch for May 1 show that Banks then had in these commands " present for duty " at Harrisonburg 6,032 infantry and artillery (under Williams), and about 2,000 cavalry (under Hatch). McDowell states that Shields's strength (effective) was at this time 11,000 men.

[57] This confidence was no doubt increased by the falling back of the Confederate army from Yorktown on May 3, the battle of Williamsburg on the 5th, and the subsequent advance of McClellan to the line of the Chickahominy.

[58] President Lincoln would not allow McDowell to join McClellan by way of the Peninsula, but adopted the middle course by ordering the former to advance on Richmond by way of the Fredericksburg and Richmond railroad. By this route McDowell would still be between Washington and the enemy, and it was thought could unite with McClellan's right wing in four days. (See *McClellan's Report*, p. 565.)

[59] Two days after, instructions received from Gen. J. E. Johnston seemed to Jackson to seriously restrict his

operations. We find the following telegram in the Confederate archives, Washington :

"Camp near New Market, *May* 20,
"*via* Staunton, *May* 21.

"Gen. R. E. Lee :—I am of the opinion that an attempt should be made to defeat Banks, but under instructions just received from Gen. Johnston I do not feel at liberty to make an attack. Please answer by telegraph at once.

"T. J. Jackson."

The reply to this and the letter of Gen. Johnston giving the instructions have not been found. Gen. Johnston (p. 129 of his Narrative) says his instructions to Gen. Jackson " were to advance and attack unless he found the enemy too strongly intrenched." It was perhaps some emphasis on the last clause that made the instructions appear to Jackson to hamper him.

[60] On May 21 the First Maryland and Brockenbrough's battery were constituted the " Maryland Line," intended as the nucleus of a brigade to be commanded by Gen. George H. Steuart, who had been recently commissioned by the Confederate government to collect the Maryland troops into one body. Elzey was put in command of a brigade composed of the Thirteenth Virginia regiment and three of Gen. Edward Johnson's regiments (Twelfth Georgia and Thirty-first and Twenty-fifth Virginia regiments). The remaining three regiments of Johnson (Forty-fourth, Fifty-second, and Fifty-eighth Virginia) continued under command of Col. Scott, of the Forty-fourth Virginia, until early in June, when, on the retreat from Strasburg, they were united with the other troops under Steuart, and were commanded by him at Cross Keys.

[61] I have been able to find no complete returns of Ewell's, Jackson's, or Johnson's forces for the period between March and July, 1862, in the Confederate archives ; hence the Confederate strength has been deduced from various *data*.

I. Gen. Ewell writes to Gen. Lee, April 16 (see letter on file among Confederate archives) : " This division numbered, on the 12th, 6,500 men *aggregate*. Large accessions have been and are coming in, and the strength is now somewhat over 8,000, exclusive of two regiments of cavalry, mounting over 500 men. I have 14 pieces of artillery."

In Gen. J. E. Johnston's return for February 28, Ewell's division (the Third) is given as: effective, 4,918; total, 5,251; aggregate, 5,598.

" Effective " means all the privates and non-commissioned officers *present for duty*; " total " all the privates and non-commissioned officers *present*, including those sick, in arrest, and on extra duty; " aggregate," all the officers and men *present*. The difference between the " total " and the " aggregate " equals all the officers present, both for duty and sick, etc. The real strength for action is to be gotten by adding to the " effective " strength the officers " present for duty." The above return does not give this last, but it was of course less than 347 (the difference between " total " and " aggregate "). The difference between " effective " and " total " (equal 333 above) represents the men sick, on extra duty, or in arrest, and was equal to about 6 per cent. of the aggregate. Now deducting from Ewell's *aggregate* (8,000) for April 16, 6 per cent. for sick, etc., we have, say, 7,500, for his effective strength, including all officers present at that time. Add the cavalry, and we get the 8,000 estimated in the text. Between April 16 and the middle of May, Ewell lost Bowyer's battery, ordered elsewhere, and the Tenth Virginia regiment, transferred to Taliaferro's brigade, of Jackson's division; but I suppose these losses to have been made up by men joining. (This estimate of the strength of Ewell's division agrees with that furnished me by Maj. G. Campbell Brown, of Spring Hill, Tennessee, then assistant adjutant-general on Gen. Ewell's staff.)

II. Gen. Edward Johnson's return for February, 1862, shows his officers and men then present for duty to have been 2,418, and a letter of his, dated March 18, reports his " present for duty " at that time as 2,425.

In a letter of Gen. Lee to Jackson, April 29, he speaks of Gen. Edward Johnson as having a " present force of upwards of 3,500," and Col. A. Smead, assistant adjutant-general

to Gen. Johnson, says that the latter had an effective strength
of 3,000 at McDowell. Deducting the losses at that battle,
the total strength of this brigade may have been about
3,000 at the middle of May.

III. Jackson's division consisted of three brigades, containing eleven and a half regiments of infantry, five batteries
of artillery, and Ashby's cavalry. Five of these regiments
were in the " Stonewall " (Winder's) brigade. The strength
of this brigade at Winchester, on May 25, was 1,529, rank
and file, and adding in officers, it could not have exceeded
1,700 in all, or an average of 340 per regiment. Col. Campbell's brigade of three and a half regiments in the same
division numbered, officers and men present for duty,
April 1, 1,391, an average strength of nearly 400 per regiment.
Taking the larger average, the division may have contained
say 4,600 infantry, and adding from 300 to 400 for artillery,
and say 700 for cavalry (Ashby had twenty-three companies),
Jackson's division, including his cavalry, must have numbered about 5,500 or 6,000. The sum of his forces then
did not exceed 17,000 men. Dr. Dabney (then adjutant-
general to Gen. Jackson) puts his force at 16,000 men, and
so does Gen. Banks, in a telegram to his government dated
May 21. (See below.)

[62] At Asbury Chapel, four and one-half miles from Front
Royal. At this point the main road approaches the river
and runs along under the river bluffs for some three
miles. At the Front Royal end of this defile, and about
a mile from the town, was stationed the principal Federal
picket.

[63] Banks telegraphed his government, May 21 : " My
force at Strasburg is 4,476 infantry (two brigades), 2,600
cavalry, 10 Parrott guns, and 6 smooth-bore. On the
Manassas railroad, between Strasburg and Manassas, 2,500
infantry, 6 companies of cavalry, and 6 guns. There are
five companies cavalry of First Maine near Strasburg,
belonging to Col. Miles's command. Jackson is within eight
miles of Harrisonburg. He and Ewell have 16,000 men
together." (Federal official telegrams.)

The Federal troops concerned in Banks's operations were
distributed as follows, May 23 :

At Strasburg :

2 brigades of infantry	4,476
Hatch's and Broadhead's cavalry . . .	2,600
5 companies First Maine cavalry . . .	300*
3 companies artillery, 16 guns . . .	280†

At bridge near Strasburg :

1 company of Second Massachusetts regiment .	60‡

At Buckton :

1 company of Twenty-seventh Indiana and 1 company Third Wisconsin	100§

At Front Royal :

9 companies First Maryland infantry	
2 companies Twenty-ninth Pennsylvania	
Mapes's pioneers (56 men)	900‖
2 guns Knapp's battery (38 men)	

At Linden Station :

1 company of First Maryland infantry .	80

At Winchester :

Tenth Maine infantry	856¶
5 companies Maryland cavalry (estimated) .	300
5 companies Eighth New York cavalry (estimated)	300**
	———
	10,252

The troops at Winchester and the First Maine cavalry belonged to Col. Miles's command. Col. Miles was at Harper's Ferry.

[64] Company E of Kenly's regiment, on guard duty at Linden station, was not present. Capt. Smith and other officers of the First Maryland regiment, who escaped, report officially on May 28 that the troops at Front Royal were as follows : nine companies First Maryland, containing 775

* Estimated.   † Banks's return, May 1.
‡ Estimated from Gen. Gordon's report.
§ Estimated from Gen. Gordon's report.
‖ Camper and Kirkley.
¶ This regiment lost 83 on the 25th, and had 773 at Williamsport on May 31.
** Arrived at Winchester on May 24.

available rank and file; two companies Twenty-ninth Pennsylvania, containing about 120 men; Mapes's pioneers, 40 men; the New York cavalry detachment, 90 men; artillery, 38 men; total, 1,063. Of these, as above stated, but 8 officers and 120 men had reported up to the date of the report.

[65] Dabney says: " At the time of the combat of Front Royal the duty of couriers was performed for Gen. Jackson by a detachment from one of Ashby's undisciplined companies, of whom many· were raw youths just recruited, and never under fire.· As soon as the first Federal picket was driven in, and free access to the village won, orders were despatched to the rear brigades to avoid the laborious and circuitous route taken by the advance, and to pursue the direct highway to the town, a level tract of three miles, in place of a precipitous one of seven or eight. The panic-struck boy, by whom the orders were sent, thought of nothing but to hide himself from the dreadful sound of the cannon, and was seen no more." As a consequence, the whole of Ewell's division followed the advance and made the long circuit, only reaching Cedarville at dark. Jackson's division, however, followed the main road, but, after a march of twenty-four miles from Luray, camped at Front Royal.

[66] The quartermaster and commissary supplies referred to (except the train of Kenly's command) were chiefly stored in the railroad depot and an adjoining store-house at Front Royal. They were so great in amount and value as to be estimated by the Confederate quartermasters as worth three hundred thousand dollars. They were only partially removed before the recapture of the town, a week later, by the advance of Gen. Shields's division, when the remainder were burned by the retiring Confederates. (See Maj. John A. Harman's official report. Maj. Harman was chief quartermaster for Gen. Jackson.)

[67] The following account by Col. Kenly's courier is found in *Rebellion Record*, vol. v., Incidents, p. 22 :

" WILLIAMSPORT, MD., *May* 26, 1862.
" DEAR FATHER AND MOTHER :—You have probably heard

by this time of the three days' fighting from Strasburg and Front Royal to Martinsburg. Our company and Company B were ordered to Front Royal, in the mountains, twelve miles from Strasburg, last Friday, and when we got within two miles of our destination we heard cannonading. The Major ordered the baggage to stop, and our two companies dashed on, and found several companies of our infantry and two pieces of artillery engaged with several thousand of the enemy. Just as we arrived on the field, Col. Parem, who had command of our forces, rode up to me and ordered me to take one man and the two fastest horses in our company, and ride for dear life to Gen. Banks's headquarters, in Strasburg, for reinforcements. The direct road to Strasburg was occupied by the enemy, so I was obliged to ride round by another, seventeen miles. I rode the seventeen miles in fifty-five minutes. Gen. Banks didn't seem to think it very serious, but ordered one regiment of infantry and two pieces of artillery off. I asked Gen. Banks for a fresh horse to rejoin my company, and he gave me the best horse that I ever rode, and I started back. I came out on the Front Royal turnpike, about two miles this side of where I left our men. Saw two men standing in the road and their horses standing by the fence. I supposed they were our pickets. They didn't halt me, so I asked them if they were pickets. They said no. ' Who are you ? ' ' We are part of Gen. Jackson's staff.' I supposed they were only joking. . . . I left them and rode towards Front Royal, till I over-took a soldier and asked him what regiment he belonged to. He said he belonged to the Eighth Louisiana. . . . I turned back. . . . The officers in the road did not stop me, and I was lucky enough not to meet any of their pickets. . . . When I got out of the enemy's lines I rode as fast as the horse could carry me to Gen. Banks, and reported what I had seen and heard. He said I had saved the army, etc.

" CHARLES H. GREENLEAF,

" Company D, Fifth New York Cavalry."

[68] Banks's report, *Rebellion Record*. Donelly and Gordon commanded the two infantry brigades, which, with Broadhead's First Michigan cavalry, constituted Williams's

division.   Hatch commanded all the cavalry except Broadhead's.

[69] Gen. Gordon (commanding one of the Federal brigades) criticizes Banks's hesitation and delay with great severity.   He says he twice urged Gen. Banks, early in the night of the 23rd, to retreat to Winchester, but without effect.   He left Banks to put his own brigade in readiness to move at a moment's notice, and continues : " It was eleven o'clock at night when I left him.   As I returned through the town I could not perceive that anybody was troubled with anticipations for the morrow.   The sutlers were driving sharp bargains with those who had escaped from, or were not amenable to, military discipline ; the strolling players were moving crowds to noisy laughter in their canvas booth, through which the lights gleamed and the music sounded with startling shrillness.   I thought, as I turned towards my camp, how unconscious all are of the drama Jackson is preparing for us, and what *merriment* the morning will reveal !   As my troops were aroused from their slumbers a low murmur ran through camp, followed by the louder noise of packing camp equipage and baggage, the harnessing of artillery horses, and hitching-up of trains. We were ready for action.   But the night sped on ; silence fell upon the town, and slumber was as deep that night in Strasburg as if without there was no cause for watchfulness. My brigade, however, found little comfort sitting around dismal camp-fires, reduced to expiring embers by the falling rain.   Unsheltered and unprotected, in a damp clover-field, the morning dawned upon a cheerless group.   Some unimportant steps had been taken for the security of the sick and for the safety of public property.   I had ordered my brigade and regimental trains forward to Winchester, and they were saved.   After three o'clock in the morning Banks had sent off some ambulances with sick and disabled, and this was all.

*   *   *   *   *

" After daylight of the 24th, we remained inactive until between ten and eleven o'clock in the morning, at which time I received the following note from Gen. Banks :

" ' Headquarters Department of Shenandoah.
" ' Strasburg, Va., *May* 24, 1862.

" ' Col. Geo. H. Gordon, Commanding Brigade.

" ' Sir :—Our information this morning shows that the enemy returned to Front Royal last night, and will not, now at least, attempt our rear. Our force will remain in Strasburg, therefore, until further orders.

     *   *   *   *   *

" ' Respectfully yours,
" ' N. P. Banks,
" ' Major-General Commanding, etc.' "

Immediately after, however (says Gen. Gordon), information was received of the attack on the Federal train beyond Middletown, and orders were at once issued for the movement of all the Federal forces towards Winchester.

[70] Gen. Hatch had under his command this day the Fifth New York cavalry (Col. De Forrest), First Vermont (Col. Tompkins), five companies of the First Maine (Lieut.-Col. Douty), Hampton's battery, and a section of Best's battery. The half regiment of the First Maine and two companies of the First Vermont had accompanied the infantry column, and at Middletown were sent towards Front Royal to observe Jackson's advance. They were driven back to Middletown just as Hatch, at the head of the remainder of his force, was coming into it from Strasburg.

[71] Banks's report. De Forrest was behind Tompkins, and found the way into Winchester blocked when he approached the town. He then made a circuit and attempted to enter it next morning by the Romney road, only to find Banks retreating and the Confederates in possession. He then marched in the direction of Hancock, and crossed the Potomac at Cherry Run Ford.

[72] The road was lined with captured wagons from Cedar Creek to Newtown. Nearly all the transportation of Hatch's cavalry, besides a large number of other wagons, were captured at this time. (See Gordon's *History of Second Massachusetts Regiment*, Third Paper. He speaks of " six miles of wagons " as captured on this occasion.)

[73] Gen. Ewell's report. Gen. Trimble informs the author

that Ewell's division was ordered to halt at the point mentioned (near Nineveh) until Jackson, after having struck the enemy and discovered his intentions, should send orders for Ewell's further movements. These orders (to move on Winchester), Gen. Trimble says, were sent by Jackson early in the afternoon, but in consequence of the courier's losing his way and not finding Gen. Ewell promptly, they did not reach the latter for several hours.

[74] Banks's report, *Rebellion Record*, vol. v.

Gen. Banks states his force at Winchester as follows : " My own command consisted of two brigades of infantry of less than 4,000 men, all told, with 900 cavalry, 10 Parrott guns, and one battery of six-pounders, smooth-bore cannon. To this should be added the Tenth Maine regiment of infantry and five companies of Maryland cavalry, stationed at Winchester, which were engaged in the action." To this should be added also five companies of the Eighth New York cavalry, which arrived in Winchester from Harper's Ferry on the evening of the 24th, and which were involved, if not in the action, at least in the rout of the next day. (See report of Lieut.-Col. Babbitt.) Banks's force at Winchester, from the above, must have been about 6,400. Jackson's was about 15,000.

The organization of the Federals was as follows (the strength and losses being given in detail so far as they have been found) :

WILLIAMS'S DIVISION

Infantry.

Donelly's (First) brigade :

	Strength.	Killed.	Wounded.	Missing.	Total Loss.
Forty-sixth Pennsylvania					
Twenty-eighth New York	1,700	3	47	251	301
Fifth Connecticut		(7)	(51)	Medical report.	

Gordon's (Third) brigade :

	Strength.	Killed.	Wounded.	Missing.	Total Loss.
Second Massachusetts		7	28	133	168
Third Wisconsin					
Twenty-seventh Indiana	2,102	(25)	(71)	Medical report.	
Twenty-ninth Pennsylvania					

	Strength.	Killed.	Wounded.	Missing.	Total Loss.
Tenth Maine regiment .	856		6	77	83

Cavalry.

Broadhead :

	Strength.	Killed.	Wounded.	Missing.	Total Loss.
Part of First Michigan .	..	10	10	34	54

Hatch :

Part of First Vermont .	900				
Part of Fifth New York .					
5 companies First Maryland	600 (Estimated).				
5 companies Eighth New York . . .	..	2	0	24	26

Artillery.

Best's battery, 6 guns .	250 (Estimated).				
Cothran's battery 6 ,, .					
Hampton's battery, 4 ,, .					

———

6,408

The Confederate organization was as follows :

JACKSON'S DIVISION

Infantry.

Winder's (First) brigade :

	Strength.	Killed.	Wounded.	Total Loss.
Second Virginia . .	1,529 (r.&f.)	4	14	18
Fourth ,, .				
Fifth ,, .		1	3	4
Twenty-seventh Virginia.		1	3	4
Thirty-third ,, .		1	7	8

Campbell's (Second) brigade :

	Killed.	Wounded.	Total Loss.
Twenty-first Virginia .			
Forty-second ,, .		3	3
Forty-eighth ,, .	2	7	9
Irish battalion ,, .		4	4

Taliaferro's (Third) brigade :

	Strength.	Killed.	Wounded.	Total Loss.
Tenth Virginia . .		1	8	9
Twenty-third Virginia .			7	7
Thirty-seventh ,, .	300	1	19	20

EWELL'S DIVISION

	Strength.	Killed.	Wounded.	Missing.	Total Loss.
Taylor's brigade :					
Sixth Louisiana					
Seventh ,,					
Eighth ,,		15	90		105
Ninth ,,		(Whole brigade.)			
Wheat's battalion					
Trimble's brigade :					
Twenty-first North Caro-lina		22	65		87
Twenty-first Georgia		1	18		19
Fifteenth Alabama					
Sixteenth Mississippi					
Elzey's brigade :					
Thirteenth Virginia					
Thirty-first ,,					
Twenty-fifth ,,					
Twelfth Georgia					
Scott's brigade :					
Forty-fourth Virginia					
Fifty-second ,,					
Fifty-eighth ,,					
Maryland line :					
First Maryland					

Cavalry

Under Geo. H. Steuart :
  Munford's Second Virginia
  Flournoy's Sixth ,,
Ashby's Seventh Virginia .

Artillery.

	Strength	Killed.	Wounded.		Total Loss.
Poague's battery, 6 guns .	89(r.&f.)	2	16		18
Carpenter's ,, 4 ,, .	52	1	5		6
Cutshaw's ,, 4 ,, .					
Wooding's ,, 4 ,, .					

Strength. Killed. Wounded. Missing. Total Loss.

Caskie's battery, 4 guns .
Raine's   ,,   4   ,, .
Rice's   ,,   4   ,, .
Lusk's   ,,   4   ,, .
Courtenay's ,,   6   ,, .
Brockenbrough's,,4   ,, . (with Maryland line.)
Chew's   ,,   4   ,, . (with cavalry.)

―――

48

Total strength about 15,000 or 16,000.

[75] Donelly's regiments were placed, the Twenty-eighth New York on the left, Fifth Connecticut in the centre, and Forty-sixth Pennsylvania on his right, the wings thrown forward crescent-like. As the Twenty-first North Carolina advanced against the centre,—not seeing the position of the Forty-sixth Pennsylvania in the midst,—they received a raking flank fire at close quarters from that regiment as well as the front fire from the Fifth Connecticut, to which was added as they retired that of the Twenty-eighth New York. The Twenty-first North Carolina lost 87 men killed and wounded. (See Donelly's and Trimble's reports.)

[76] Gen. Jackson says in his report: " The public property captured in this expedition at Front Royal, Winchester, Martinsburg, and Charlestown was of great value, and so làrge in quantity that much of it had to be abandoned for want of necessary means of transportation. Maj. Harman, my chief quartermaster, had but one week within which to remove it; and, although his efforts were characterized by his usual energy, promptitude, and judgment, all the conveyances that within that short period could be hired or impressed were inadequate to the work. The medical stores, which filled one of the largest storehouses in Winchester, were fortunately saved. Most of the instruments and some of the medicines, urgently needed at that time by the command, were issued to the surgeons. The residue were sent to Charlottesville and turned over to a medical purveyor. Two large and well-furnished hospitals, capable of accommodating some 700 patients, were found in the town, and left undisturbed, with all

17

their stores, for the use of the sick and wounded of the enemy.

"Commissary supplies, consisting of upwards of 100 head of cattle, 34,000 pounds of bacon, flour, salt, sugar, coffee, hard bread, and cheese, were turned over to the proper authorities, besides large amounts taken by the troops and not accounted for. Sutler's stores valued at $25,000, and for want of transportation abandoned to the troops, were captured. Quartermasters' stores to the value of $125,185 were secured " (at Winchester), " besides an immense amount destroyed. Many horses were taken by the cavalry.

"Among the ordnance stores taken and removed in safety were 9,354 small arms, and 2 pieces of artillery and their caissons." A large amount of ammunition was also among the ordnance captures.

[77] Jackson's report.

Gen. Banks's report of his losses is apt to mislead, and has done so, at least in the case of the Comte de Paris, the distinguished French historian of the war. Banks says (see his report, vol. v., *Rebellion Record*) : " Our loss is stated in detail, with the names of the killed, wounded, and missing, in the full report of Brig.-Gen. A. S. Williams, commanding division, to which reference is made.

"The whole number of killed is 38 ; wounded, 155 ; missing, 711 ; total loss, 904.

"It is undoubtedly true that many of the missing will yet return, and the entire loss may be assumed as not exceeding 700. It is also probable that the number of killed and wounded may be larger than that above stated, but the aggregate loss will not be changed thereby. All our guns were saved.

"Our wagon-train consisted of nearly 500 wagons. Of this number, 55 were lost. They were not, with but few exceptions, abandoned to the enemy, but were burned upon the road. Nearly all of our supplies were thus saved. The stores at Front Royal, of which I had no knowledge until my visit to that post on the 21st instant, and those at Winchester, of which a considerable portion was destroyed by our troops, are not embraced in this statement."

In this statement Gen. Banks confines himself to the losses reported by Gen. Williams. Gen. Williams says that his report embraced a " complete list of killed, wounded, and missing of the troops under my (his) command, except that of the First Maryland (infantry), detached on duty at Front Royal." I could not find this list, but from subordinate reports it appears that the losses of his troops in *killed* and *wounded* were :

	Killed.	Wounded.	Killed.	Wounded.
Donelly's brigade (official report)	3	47 (Med.)	7	51
Gordon's ,, ,, ,,	.	report	25	71
Broadhead's cavalry,, ,,	. 10	10		
Artillery—no report found.				
The least sum of the above is . . .			38	128
Banks reports			38	155

The troops just enumerated constituted Gen. Williams's command. That command did *not* include Hatch's cavalry brigade, nor the parts of the First Maryland cavalry and Eighth New York cavalry present, nor the Tenth Maine infantry. The last-named regiment lost in all 83 men, and the five companies of the First Maine cavalry lost 127. The other cavalry, under Hatch, no doubt lost in proportion. Again, Gen. Banks says there were nearly 1,000 sick and disabled soldiers of Shields's division left behind at Strasburg. Several hundreds of these were " put upon the march " towards Winchester early on the 24th. A number of them were captured. If the losses of prisoners at Front Royal (expressly omitted by Gen. Williams), and those of the troops not under Gen. Williams's command, and those of Gen. Shields's convalescents, were added to Gen. Banks's report, it would, no doubt, agree with Jackson's. In the same way, the artillery lost at Front Royal is not reported by Banks, and the wagons he reports as lost, and which, no doubt, represent the loss in Williams's division, constituted but a small part of those that actually fell into the hands of the victors. Hatch, for instance, according to Gen. G. H. Gordon, lost all his baggage. (See *History Second Massachusetts*, Third Paper, pp. 100, etc.)

[78] Jackson's report. He reports his loss as 68 killed, 329 wounded, and 3 missing. This, probably, does not include Ashby's loss at Buckton, or the infantry loss at Front Royal. No report of Ashby's loss has been found. It may have been 20 or 30. The loss in the Louisiana troops at Front Royal was 10 (Gen. Taylor's report). That in the First Maryland not reported. It was slight, if any. Hence possibly about 40 should be added to the number in Gen. Jackson's report.

[79] President Lincoln telegraphed McClellan on May 24 : " I left Gen. McDowell's camp at dark last evening. Shields's command is there, but it is so worn that he cannot move before Monday morning, the 26th. . . . McDowell and Shields both say they can and positively will move Monday morning. I wish you to move cautiously and safely. You will have command of McDowell after he joins you, precisely as you indicated in your long despatch to us of the 21st." (McClellan's report.)

[80] Secretary Stanton's despatch to McDowell is as follows : " In view of the operations of the enemy on the line of Gen. Banks, the President thinks the whole force you designed to move from Fredericksburg should not be taken away, and he therefore directs that one brigade, in addition to what you designed to leave at Fredericksburg, should be left there. This brigade to be the least effective of your command." (McDowell's testimony.)

[81] There was no force after him except possibly some guerrillas. Tenney, in his *Military and Naval History of the Rebellion*, p. 235, says : " When the news of the attack on the Maryland regiment at Front Royal on the 23rd reached Gen. Geary, who, with his force, was charged with the protection of the Manassas Gap railroad, he immediately began to move to Manassas Junction. His troops hearing the most extravagant stories of the fate of the Maryland regiment, and supposing that they were about to be swallowed up, burnt their tents and destroyed a quantity of arms. Gen. Duryea, at Catlett's Station, became alarmed on learning of the withdrawal of Gen. Geary, took his three New York regiments, leaving the Pennsylvania one behind, and hastened back to Centreville, and telegraphed to Wash-

ington for help. He left a large quantity of army stores behind, and also, for two days, his camp equipage. A panic prevailed at Catlett's Station and Manassas Junction for two days. At night the camps were kept in constant alarm by the sentinels firing at stumps or bowing bushes, which they mistook for Confederate guerrillas. The alarm spread to Washington, and Secretary Stanton issued orders calling for the militia of the loyal States to defend that city."

It is hard to see how any " stories " as to the fate of the Maryland regiment could have been " extravagant." It was very nearly " swallowed up."

[82] The Government of the United States, on the same day, May 25, called for additional troops, and issued an order taking " military possession of all the railroads in the United States," for the transportation of troops and munitions of war.

" The news of Gen. Banks's defeat and the sudden call of the Secretary of War upon the State militia created the utmost excitement at the North, not only among the military themselves, but among the thousands connected with them." (*Rebellion Record*, vol. v., Diary, p. 17.)

The following is Secretary Stanton's despatch, dated May 25, to the Governor of Massachusetts :

" Intelligence from various quarters leaves no doubt that the enemy in great force are marching on Washington. You will please organize and forward immediately all the militia and volunteer force in your State."

Tenney says : " This alarm at Washington, and the call for its defence, produced a most indescribable panic in the cities of the Northern States on Sunday, the 25th, and two or three days afterwards. . . .

" Governor Curtin, of Pennsylvania, issued the following order, May 26 :

" ' On pressing requisition of the President of the United States in the present emergency, it is ordered that the several major-generals, brigadier-generals, and colonels of regiments throughout the Commonwealth muster, without delay, all military organizations within their respective divisions or under their control, together with all persons willing to join their commands, and proceed forthwith to the city of Washington, or such other points as may be indicated by future orders.'

" The Governor of Massachusetts issued the following proclamation :

" ' Men of Massachusetts ! The wily and barbarous horde of traitors to the people, to the government, to our country, and to liberty, menace again the national capital. They have attacked and routed Maj.-Gen. Banks, are advancing on Harper's Ferry, and are marching on Washington. The President calls on Massachusetts to rise once more for its rescue and defence.

" ' The whole active militia will be summoned by a general order, issued from the office of the Adjutant-General, to report on Boston Common to-morrow ; they will march to relieve and avenge their brethren and friends, and to oppose with fierce zeal and courageous patriotism the progress of the foe.

" ' May God encourage their hearts and strengthen their arms, and may He inspire the government and all the people !

" ' Given at headquarters, Boston, eleven o'clock, this (Sunday) evening, May 25, 1862.

" ' John A. Andrew.'

" The Governor of Ohio began his proclamation as follows :

" ' To the Gallant Men of Ohio : I have the astounding intelligence that the seat of our beloved government is threatened with invasion, and am called upon by the Secretary of War for troops to repel and overwhelm the ruthless invaders.' " . . .

But enough of gubernatorial rhetoric. The effect of Jackson's movement was unmistakable. " Almost half a million of men offered themselves for the defence of Washington within twenty-four hours after the issue of the proclamation."

Tenney adds that this " panic " was " extremely disastrous to the Federal cause."

[83] McDowell was moving towards Front Royal and Strasburg with the divisions of Shields, Ord, and King,

containing 30,000 men (see his return for May 17, and his testimony before the Committee on the Conduct of the War). Fremont was marching towards the same points, by way of Wardensville, with a force of 14,672 (officers and men for duty, by return of May 30). Saxton had at Harper's Ferry 7,000 troops (Saxton's report), and Banks was at Williamsport, where the remains of his army had grown to over 7,000 men (see his return for May 31). All were to join in the general movement against Jackson.

[84] Shields's division entered Front Royal first; Ord's (Rickett's) division followed. King, who was in the rear, sent two of his brigades (Augur's and Patrick's) as far as Front Royal, which they entered June 1. The other brigade (Gibbons's) stopped at Haymarket, to which point the advance brigades of King returned on June 2.

[85] Fremont says: "With the intelligence of these events" (Jackson's attack on Banks), "despatched to me under date of May 24, came also an order from the President directing me to break camp and march against Jackson at Harrisonburg.

"Of the different roads leading from Franklin to Harrisonburg, all but one had been obstructed by Jackson in his retreat. . . . The road still left open ran southwardly, reaching Harrisonburg by a long detour."

Fremont was afraid to lengthen his line of supply, and especially was fearful, if he went to Harrisonburg, that Jackson might go from Strasburg or Winchester to Romney or Moorefield. A despatch from Secretary Stanton, May 25, left him free to choose his route, and he chose to go back from Franklin to Petersburg, and then to go by way of Wardensville to Strasburg. He reached Petersburg on the afternoon of May 26, resumed his march at daybreak on the 27th, reached Moorefield at night, and on the 28th went to Fabius, ten miles east of Moorefield, on Branch Mountain. Here he halted on the 29th, because, he says, of the urgent representations of his surgeon and others that the men needed rest, and could not properly go on. On the 30th he moved forward, and on the 31st reached Cedar Creek.

[86] On Thursday night a messenger brought him information of the movement of Fremont towards Strasburg,

and on the morning of the 30th he received definite information of the progress of Shields and McDowell towards Front Royal, and of the condition of Banks's troops at Williamsport.

[87] A Federal account in the *Rebellion Record*, vol. v., puts the number of Confederates captured at 156, and so does the report of the Surgeon-General in the *Medical and Surgical History of the War*. The latter puts the Federal loss at 14. I have found no official reports of the officers engaged.

It is said that when the officer in command reported to Gen. Jackson, at Winchester, in the evening, and gave a rather sensational account of the recapture of Front Royal and the repulse of his own regiment, Gen. Jackson looked up and, in his quick, nervous way, asked : " Colonel, how many men had you killed ? " " None, I am glad to say, General." " How many wounded ?" " Few or none, sir." " Do you call that fighting, sir ? " said Jackson, and a few minutes afterwards the Colonel was put under arrest.

[88] The following despatches are from Gen. Fremont's report :

" WASHINGTON, *May* 29.
" MAJ.-GEN. FREMONT :
" Gen. McDowell's advance, if not checked by the enemy, should, and probably will be, at Front Royal by 12 noon to-morrow. His force, when up, will be about 20,000.

" Please have your force at Strasburg, or, if the route you are moving on does not lead to that point, as near Strasburg as the enemy may be by that time. . . .

" A. LINCOLN."

" WASHINGTON, *May* 30, 4 P.M.
" MAJ.-GEN. FREMONT :
" Yours saying you will reach Strasburg or vicinity by 5 p.m. Saturday, has been received and sent to Gen. McDowell, and he directed to act in view of it. You must be up to time of your promise if possible.

" A. LINCOLN."

[89] Capt. Hotchkiss says that Gen. Jackson sent him,

at 10 p.m., to Winder, saying : " I want you to go to Charlestown and bring up the First brigade. I will stay in Winchester until you get here, if I can ; but if I cannot and the enemy gets here first, you must conduct it around through the mountains."

[90] Saturday having been lost, Shields could not have reached Strasburg in time to " intercept " any portion of Jackson's command, as Winder was only nine or ten miles from that place on Sunday morning with the Confederate rear guard, while Shields was twelve miles off, with a hilly country road to move on and a river to cross.

[91] Gen. Shields says he was ordered up the Luray Valley, June 1, to fall on Jackson's flank while Fremont attacked him in rear. He continues : " About 5 p.m. next day my advance reached the Shenandoah at Honeyville, but found the Whitehouse Bridge and the Columbia Bridge both burned, thus cutting off all hope of attacking his flank at New Market. . . . I then pushed forward the advance as rapidly as possible in hope of finding the bridge at Conrad Store still standing, but that bridge was also found burned." (Shields's report.)

[92] There was a tremendous rain in the afternoon. Fremont replaced the burnt bridge by a pontoon, but the rapidly rising river broke it, and thus delayed him one day. On the night of the 2nd, Jackson sent Capt. Hotchkiss, with a party of signal-men, to the south end of the Massanutton Mountain, to keep him advised of the movements of both Shields and Fremont.

[93] " Two arms of the mountain, lofty and rugged as the mother-ridge, project from it on the right and left hand, embracing a deep vale of many miles' circuit, watered by a copious mountain stream ; and while the mighty rim of this cup is everywhere impracticable for artillery and cavalry, the narrow gorge through which the road enters it from the west affords scarcely room to set a regiment in battle array between the two promontories of the mountain. Here was obviously the place for a small army to stand at bay against superior numbers." (Dabney, p. 403.)

[94] " After all the sad rites were completed Gen. Jackson came to the room where he lay and demanded to see him.

They admitted him alone. He remained for a time in silent communion with the dead, and then left him with a solemn and elevated countenance. It requires little use of the imagination to suppose that his thoughts were in part prophetic of a similar scene, when his corpse was to receive the homage of all the good and brave." (Dabney, p. 401.)

[95] Fremont's return for May 30 gives the " present for duty " of Schenck's, Milroy's, Cluseret's, and Blenker's commands as 14,672. Yet Gen. Fremont, without explaining this " stubborn fact," says that on May 29 he had " something over 11,000 " effectives (official report written long after), and estimates this force as 10,500 on June 8. Adding Bayard's cavalry, which he says numbered 800, and Kane's Bucktails (about 125 or 150), his effective strength by this estimate was about 11,500 at Cross Keys.

Shields's division numbered 10,000 effectives May 17. See McDowell's return. McDowell did not send Ord's or King's divisions farther than Front Royal, so that Shields had but one-third of the force that had been sent from Fredericksburg against Jackson.

Jackson had moved against Banks, on May 19, with a total effective force of 16,000 or 17,000 men, and since that time his troops had been subjected to a series of forced marches far exceeding anything endured by those of Shields or Fremont, and which had diminished his strength in a much greater degree than battle. His effective force could not have exceeded 13,000, even if it reached that amount, as is apparent from the strength of the commands reported. Thus Ewell says the three brigades of Trimble, Elzey, and Steuart numbered less than 5,000 on June 8, at Cross Keys. Winder reports his brigade as 1,313 rank and file, and, adding officers, it did not exceed 1,450. Patton's (Campbell's) brigade had about 800 men present (the Twenty-first Virginia having gone off as an escort to prisoners). There were besides these but Taylor's (the strongest in the army) and Taliaferro's. Putting Taylor's four and one-half regiments at 2,500 effectives and Taliaferro's three regiments at 1,200, we have a total infantry force of about 11,000. Add 1,000 for cavalry and 500 or 600 for artillery, and we see that Jackson's strength for battle was short of 13,000. The only addition made to Jackson's force between May 23 and June 8 was Carrington's battery (four guns).

[96] Ed. Johnson's brigade had been incorporated into Ewell's division, the Twelfth Georgia, Twenty-fifth and Thirty-first Virginia having been assigned to Elzey's brigade, and the Fifty-second, Fifty-eighth, and Forty-fourth Virginia to Gen. George H. Steuart, commanding the Maryland line.

[97] Col. Crutchfield and Lieut. Willis. Crutchfield was left in the town as the Federals retreated. Willis was carried over the river and placed in care of a soldier, whom he captured in turn a few hours later and brought back with him.

[98] A pretty story has been often told about the recapture of this bridge, in which Jackson, cut off from his troops, and on the Port Republic side, is made to ride up to the Federal artillery officer and order his gun forward. For a moment the officer is deceived, and prepares to obey, while Jackson, taking advantage of the confusion, spurs his horse forward and crosses the bridge unharmed by the shots fired after him. The foundation for this story is thus given by Col. (then Capt.) W. T. Poague, in a letter dated February 25, 1879 : " I recollect well the incident you ask about. Gen. Jackson finding one of my guns ready to move, directed me to hasten with it towards Port Republic, he himself going along and posting it in the field overlooking and commanding the bridge. I was surprised to see a gun posted at the farther end of the bridge. For I had just come from army headquarters, and, although I had met a cavalryman who told me the enemy were advancing up the river, still I did not think it possible they could have gotten any guns into the place in so short a time. It thereupon occurred to me that the gun at the bridge might be one of Carrington's, who was on that side and whose men had new uniforms something like those we saw at the bridge. Upon suggesting this to the General, he reflected a moment, and then riding a few paces to the left and front of our piece, he called, in a tone loud enough to be heard by them, ' Bring that gun up here ; ' but getting no reply, he raised himself in his stirrups and in a most authoritative and seemingly angry tone he shouted, ' Bring that gun up here, I say ! ' At this they began to move the trail of the gun so as to

bring it to bear on us, which when the General perceived, he quickly turned to the officer in charge of my gun and said, in his sharp, quick way, ' Let 'em have it.' The words had scarcely left his lips when Lieut. Brown, who had his piece charged and aimed, sent a shot right among them, so disconcerting them that theirs in reply went far above us, and in a few minutes, seeing our infantry approaching, they left the place, and, as I was informed, abandoned their gun before crossing South River."

[99] It was about the time of Carroll's repulse that Shields was despatching Fremont as follows :

"Luray, *June* 8, 9½ a.m.

" I write by your scout. I think by this time there will be 12 pieces of artillery opposite Jackson's train at Port Republic, if he has taken that route. Some cavalry and artillery have pushed on to Waynesboro' to burn the bridge. I hope to have two brigades at Port Republic to-day. I follow myself with two other brigades from this place. If the enemy changes direction you will please keep me advised. If he attempts to force a passage, as my force is not large there yet, I hope you will thunder down on his rear. Please send back information from time to time. I think Jackson is caught this time.

" Yours, etc.,
" Jas. Shields.

" Maj.-Gen. Fremont."

[100] Gen. Fremont's column, June 8, moved as follows : I. In advance : Cluseret's brigade of Sixtieth Ohio and Eighth Virginia infantry, reinforced by Thirty-ninth New York (Garibaldi Guard).

II. Main column, comprising :

1. Dickel's Fourth New York cavalry.

2. Stahl's brigade : Eighth, Forty-first, and Forty-fifth New York, and Twenty-seventh Pennsylvania infantry, and Dilger's, Buell's, and Schermer's batteries. (Kane's Bucktails reported to Stahl and fought with him.)

3. Bohlen's brigade : Fifty-fourth and Fifty-eighth New York and Seventy-fourth and Seventy-fifth Pennsylvania infantry, and Wiedrich's battery.

NOTES 269

4. Milroy's brigade: Twenty-fifth Ohio and Second, Third, and Fifth Virginia infantry, and Hyman's, Johnson's, and Ewing's batteries.

5. Schenck's brigade: Thirty-second, Seventy-third, Seventy-fifth, and Eighty-second Ohio infantry, and De Beck's and Rigby's batteries, and a small detachment of cavalry.

III. Rear guard following trains:

Steinwehr's brigade, under Col. Kolte: Twenty-ninth and Sixty-eighth New York and Seventy-third Pennsylvania infantry, and Dickmann's battery.

IV. Bayard's cavalry was left at Harrisonburg in charge of trains, but came forward later. (Fremont's report.)

[101] Gen. Ewell says: " The general features of the ground were a valley and rivulet in my front, woods on both flanks, and a field of some hundreds of acres, where the road crossed the centre of my line; my side of the valley being more defined and commanding the other." (Ewell's report.)

[102] Gen. Steuart had commanded temporarily the Second and Sixth Virginia cavalry at Winchester, but was subsequently returned to the command of the Maryland line, to which were added the Forty-fourth, Fifty-second, and Fifty-eighth Virginia regiments, in order to form a brigade.

Ewell's division was organized as follows on June 8 and 9:

Trimble's brigade:
21st Georgia regiment
21st N. Carolina regiment
15th Alabama ,,
16th Mississippi ,,

Elzey's brigade: *
13th Virginia regiment
25th ,, ,,
31st ,, ,,
12th Georgia ,,

G. H. Steuart's brigade:
1st Maryland regiment
44th Virginia ,,
52nd ,, ,,
58th ,, ,,

Taylor's brigade: *
6th Louisiana regiment
7th ,, ,,
8th ,, ,,
9th ,, ,,
Wheat's battalion.

* Not engaged on the 8th.

Artillery : Courtenay's, Brockenbrough's, Lusk's, Raines's and Rice's batteries.

The organization of Jackson's (Winder's) division was the same as at Winchester (see page 92, note), with the addition of Carrington's battery. After the death of Ashby, Col. Munford became commander of the cavalry.

[103] In a letter to the author, dated February, 1880, Gen. Trimble thus describes the action on his front : " . . . The enemy had crossed the valley and were advancing gallantly up the slope towards Gen Trimble's position, thus receiving the full fire of the two right regiments at about sixty paces distant. They wavered, and then fell back in disorder. . . . Then a charge was ordered, but before the men advanced over the crest of the ridge Gen. Trimble arrested it, as he saw the enemy reforming with supports on the opposite ridge. He waited twenty minutes for another attack, but as the enemy did not move, though formed to do so, he went to the right regiment, Col. Canty's, and marched it by the right flank to the right, as if moving from the field. When concealed by the woods the regiment was marched to the left, and gained, unobserved, the ridge occupied by the enemy at a point not over fifty paces from his left flank in the woods. Before making this flank movement Gen. Trimble had ordered the two regiments left on the ridge to charge across the valley as soon as they heard a brisk fire opened by Col. Canty. As soon as Col. Canty got into position he was ordered to charge. A sharp conflict of a few minutes ensued. The Twenty-first Georgia charged across the valley, followed by Col. Posey, with the Sixteenth Mississippi, when the enemy were driven back in front of our whole line. It was here that Col. Posey, in advancing, did not look to his left, and was attacked on his flank by a force which was stationed in the woods, throwing his regiment into some disorder. Col. Mercer, with much presence of mind and judgment, came to his aid with the Twenty-first Georgia, and, by a charge, drove off the enemy. Gen. Trimble then gave orders to charge a battery on a high plain, but by the time the Fifteenth Alabama reached the top of the hill the battery was moving off with precipition. A few minutes before this Col. J. A.

Walker, with the Thirteenth and Twenty-fifth Virginia regiments, had been sent over by Gen. Ewell, and was directed by Gen. Trimble to advance on the right of the Fifteenth Alabama. Col. Walker, passing too far to the right, was observed by a battery, and for a few moments was under a warm fire ; but his troops gallantly advanced, and as the battery drove off rapidly we saw the infantry force in full retreat towards the Keezletown road. Thus the enemy's force in front of our right was driven by three successive charges from the field to a mile in rear of their first position. . . ."

[104] Seventh and Eighth Louisiana. Patton and Taylor had been sent up from Port Republic to reinforce Gen. Ewell. Patton was in command of Campbell's brigade (Second of Jackson's division), and had but about 800 men for duty. (See Dabney.)

[105] Ewell's force was less than 5,000 in the morning. Patton added 800 and Taylor possibly 2,500 more. The latter was not engaged. Fremont reports his force present at over 11,000, but, as already said, his returns show a much larger number.

[106] Trimble earnestly urged a night attack, but Ewell decided against it. (Trimble's report.) Ewell says : " I did not push my success at once, because I had no cavalry, and it was reported and reaffirmed by Lieut. Hinrichs, topographical engineer, sent to reconnoitre, that the enemy was moving a large column two miles to my left. As soon as I could determine this not to be an attack I advanced both my wings, drove in the enemy's skirmishers, and when night closed was in position on the ground previously held by the enemy, ready to attack him at dawn." (Ewell's report.)

[107] Probably written by one of Gen. Schenck's staff, Capt. Piatt. It does not include the loss in Von Steinwehr's brigade or in the cavalry. (*Rebellion Record*, vol. v., p. 109.) The *Medical and Surgical History of the War* reports Fremont's loss in killed and wounded (without prisoners) as 625.

[108] " It has been already explained that he did not arrest the pursuit of Fremont at once by burning the bridge

across the Shenandoah, because he was unwilling to deprive himself of the ability to take the aggressive against that general. He now formed the bold purpose to concentrate his army and fight both Shields and him, successively, the same day. Hence his eagerness to begin his attack on the former at an early hour. Stronger evidence of this design will be given. During the night he held an inter-view with Col. Patton, commanding the Second brigade, which he then proposed to employ as a rear guard to cover the withdrawal of Gen. Ewell's forces from the front of Fremont. This officer found him at two o'clock in the morning of the 9th actively engaged in making his disposi-tions for battle. He immediately proceeded to give him particular instructions as to the management of his men in covering the rear, saying : ' I wish you to throw out all your men if necessary as skirmishers, and to make a great show, so as to cause the enemy to think the whole army are behind you. Hold your position as well as you can ; then fall back when obliged ; take a new position ; hold it in the same way ; and *I will be back to join you in the morning.*' Col. Patton reminded him that his brigade was small, and that the country between Cross Keys and the Shenandoah offered few advantages for protracting such manœuvres. He therefore desired to know for how long a time he would be expected to hold the army of Fremont in check. He replied : ' By the blessing of Providence I hope to be back by ten o'clock.' " (Dabney.)

[109] Tyler's report, *Rebellion Record,* vol. v. His force consisted of the Eighty-fourth and One Hundred and Tenth Pennsylvania and Sixty-sixth Ohio on his left, and of the First Virginia, Seventh Indiana, and Fifth, Seventh, and Twenty-ninth Ohio on the right, and of a detachment of the First Virginia cavalry, and 16 guns.

[110] Strength of his four regiments now in action: Twenty-seventh Virginia, 150 ; Fifth Virginia, 447 ; Second Virginia, 224 ; Fourth Virginia, 317 ; total, rank and file, 1,138.

Gen. Tyler says the Federal forces " could not have exceeded 3,000 men."

[111] " Additional reinforcements of the enemy were

coming up on our right, having abandoned their position on the left, and I ordered the Eighty-fourth and One Hundred and Tenth (Pennsylvania) down to the right, but before they reached the position assigned them the enemy was in full retreat before our brave men, and I at once ordered them back into the wood again. Under cover of the engagement on our right the enemy had thrown another force into the woods, and pressed them down upon our batteries on the left. So rapid was this movement that they passed the line on which the Eighty-fourth and One Hundred and Tenth were ordered, unobserved, making a dash upon the battery so sudden and unexpected as to compel the cannoneers to abandon their pieces.

" Col. Candy met the enemy with his regiment with great coolness, his men fighting with commendable bravery. The Seventh and Fifth Ohio were soon supporting him, driving the enemy from their position and retaking the battery. The artillery officers made a strong effort, and used great exertions to remove their guns, but, the horses having been killed or disabled, found it impossible. The enemy had given way along the whole line, but I saw heavy reinforcements crossing from the town that would have been impossible for us to resist. After consulting Gen. Carroll, I ordered the troops to fall back under his direction, with a view of retreating until we should meet the reinforcements of Gens. Kimball and Terry." (Tyler's report, *Rebellion Record*.)

[112] Col. Carroll, who covered the Federal rear, says: " As soon as we commenced the retreat the enemy turned and opened upon us portions of Clark's and Huntington's batteries that they had taken from us on the left, which threw the rear of our column in great disorder, causing them to take to the woods and making it, for the earlier part of the retreat, apparently a rout. . . . Their cavalry also charged upon our rear, increasing the confusion."

[113] On June 13, Surgeon Cox telegraphed the Federal surgeon-general that 180 of the wounded of Shields's division had just arrived at Front Royal. Surgeon Stidger, one of the surgeons in charge, puts the number at " perhaps 200." (*Report on Conduct of the War*, Part III., 1863, p. 493, etc.)

[114] In the series of engagements on June 6, 8, and 9, the losses were :

Confederate.		Federal.	
On June 6 .	70	On June 6 over	155
„ 8 .	287	„ 8	704 (including Carroll's)
„ 9 .	816	„ 9 (say)	916
	1,173		1,775

[115] Jackson's report. Fremont thus describes the scene when he reached the heights overlooking the field from which Tyler had been driven : " The battle which had taken place upon the farther bank of the river was wholly at an end. A single brigade sent forward by Gen. Shields " (there were two, Tyler's and Carroll's) " had been simply cut to pieces. Col. Carroll in command had for his own reasons failed to burn the bridge, though occupying it in time with his guards. Jackson hastening across had fallen upon the inferior force, and the result was before us. Of the bridge nothing remained but the charred and smoking timbers. Beyond, at the edge of the woods, a body of the enemy's troops was in position, and a baggage-train was disappearing in a pass among the hills. Parties gathering the dead and wounded, together with a line of prisoners awaiting the movements of the rebel force near by, was all in respect to troops of either side now to be seen. A parting salvo of carefully aimed rifled guns duly charged with shell hastened the departure of the rebels, with their unlucky though most gallant convoy, and the whole were speedily out of sight." (Fremont's report.) In returning from the battle-field to Brown's Gap, Jackson took a road through the forest and away from the river to avoid Fremont's guns.

[116] Shields says he marched on the night of the 8th, and, reaching Conrad's Store on the morning of the 9th, learned that Tyler was within two miles of Port Republic. He pressed forward as fast as he could, and some miles in advance of Conrad's met the routed and flying brigades.

[117] Gen. Shields is disposed to attribute his immediate

retreat from Conrad's Store not to the defeat of Tyler, but to Gen. McDowell's positive orders to return. He says he desired, in co-operation with Fremont, to again attack Jackson, and anticipated success in such an attempt. McDowell's orders hardly bear Gen. Shields's interpretation. On June 9, McDowell's chief of staff wrote : " If, however, you are in hot pursuit and about to fall on the enemy, and can do so with reasonable chances of success without relying on the troops at Front Royal, who are too far in rear to support you in your extended movements, the General is not disposed to recall you. . . ." Gen. McDowell says : " Both the condition of Gen. Shields's division and that of the roads and rivers as represented by him indicated anything than the success he anticipated."

[118] Dr. Dabney thus speaks of this camp : " The troops were encamped in a range of woodland groves between the two rivers, surrounded with the verdure of early summer and the luxuriant wheat-fields whitening to the harvest. In this smiling paradise they solaced themselves five days for their fatigues, the men reposing under the shade or bathing in the sparkling waters of the Shenandoah, and the horses feeding in the abundant pastures. The Saturday following the battle was proclaimed by Gen. Jackson as a day of thanksgiving and prayer, and all the troops were called to join with their general and their chaplains in praises to God for His deliverances. The next day a general communion was observed in the Third Virginia brigade, at which the Lord's Supper was dispensed, in the wood, to a great company of Christian soldiers from all the army. At this solemnity the General was present as a worshipper, and modestly participated with his men in the sacred feast. The quiet diffidence with which he took the least obtrusive place and received the sacred elements from the hands of a regimental chaplain was in beautiful contrast with the majesty and authority of his bearing in the crisis of battle."

[119] Jackson's report. Gen. Lee (now in immediate command of the Confederate forces in Virginia, in consequence of the wounding of Gen. J. E. Johnston on May 31) wrote to Jackson as follows on June 8 : " Your letter of the 6th has been received. I congratulate you upon defeating and

then avoiding your enemy. Your march to Winchester has been of great advantage, and has been conducted with your accustomed skill and boldness. I hope you will be able to rest and refresh your troops for a few days before compelled to enter upon active service. I desire you to report the probable intentions of the enemy and what steps you can take to thwart them. Should there be nothing requiring your attention in the Valley so as to prevent your leaving it in a few days, and you can make arrangements to deceive the enemy and impress him with the idea of your presence, please let me know, that you may unite at the decisive moment with the army near Richmond. Make your arrangements accordingly ; but should an opportunity occur for striking the enemy a successful blow do not let it escape you."

When this letter reached its destination the " blow " had been " struck," and Jackson was free to join Lee.

[120] Gen. Lee's letter is as follows :

" HEADQUARTERS NEAR RICHMOND,
" *June* 11.

" MAJ.-GEN. JACKSON, ETC. :—Your recent successes have been the cause of the liveliest joy in this army as well as in the country. The admiration excited by your skill and boldness has been constantly mingled with solicitude for your situation. The practicability of reinforcing you has been the subject of earnest consideration. It has been determined to do so at the expense of weakening this army. Brig.-Gen. Lawton, with six regiments from Georgia, is on the way to you, and Brig.-Gen. Whiting, with eight veteran regiments, leaves here to-day. The object is to enable you to crush the forces opposed to you. Leave your enfeebled troops to watch the country and guard the passes covered by your cavalry and artillery, and with your main body, including Ewell's division and Lawton's and Whiting's commands, move rapidly to Ashland by rail or otherwise as you may find more advantageous, sweep down between the Chickahominy and Pamunky rivers, cutting up the enemy's communications, etc., while this army attacks Gen. McClellan in front. He will thus, I think, be forced to come out of his entrenchments, where he is strongly posted on the Chickahominy, and apparently preparing to move by gradual approaches on Richmond. Keep me advised of your movements, and if practicable precede your troops, that we may confer and arrange for simultaneous attack.

" R. E. Lee."

On June 16, Gen. Lee again wrote :

" I have received your letter by the Hon. Mr. Boteler. I hope you will be able to recruit and refresh your troops sufficiently for the movement proposed in my letter of the 11th. . . . From your account of the position of the enemy, I think it would be difficult for you to engage him in time to reunite with this army in the battle for Richmond. Fremont and Shields are apparently retrograding, their troops shaken and disorganized ; some time will be required to set them again in the field. If this be so, the sooner you unite with this army the better. . . . In moving your troops you could let it be understood that it was to pursue the enemy in your front. Dispose those to hold the Valley so as to deceive the enemy. . . ."

[121] Dabney, p. 432, etc. Gen. Jackson says, in a despatch to Col. Munford, June 13 : " Please impress the bearers of the flag of truce as much as possible with an idea of a heavy advance on our part, and let them return under such impression." (See Paper of Col. Munford in *Southern Historical Papers*, November, 1879.)

[122] In despatches dated June 17, Jackson says to Col. Munford : " Do all you can to cut off communication across the lines between us and the enemy ; also let there be as little communication as practicable between your command and that of the infantry. Let your couriers be men whom you can trust, and caution them against carrying news forward, as it may reach the enemy." Again : " I will be at Mount Sidney to-night about ten o'clock. Can you meet me there ? I will be on my horse at the north end of the town, so you need not inquire after me. I do not desire it to be known that I am absent from this point. . . . Say to those who come on this side (the lines) that for a few days they will have to remain on this side, as no one is permitted to pass the lines to the enemy's side." (See Col. Munford's Paper.)

LIST OF OFFICERS

THE following is a list of the officers who served during parts or during the whole of the Valley Campaign on Gen. Jackson's staff. They were not all on duty at the same time, but, from the loss of the order books of the command, the dates of assignment and the periods of service are in many cases not known.

As Adjutant-General	Lieut.-Col. J. T. L. Preston (to February 1, 1862).
	Maj. A. H. Jackson.
	Maj. R. L. Dabney (assigned April 24, 1862).
As Assistant Adjutant-General	Lieut. A. S. Pendleton.
As Inspector-General	Lieut.-Col. W. S. H. Baylor (to April 24, 1862).
	Col. A. Smead.
	Lieut. H. Kyd Douglas.
As Chief of Artillery	Maj. D. Trueheart.
	Lieut.-Col. S. Crutchfield.
As Assistant to Chief of Artillery	Lieut. Ed. Willis.
As Engineer	Lieut. J. K. Boswell.
As Topographical Engineer	Mr. Jed. Hotchkiss.
As Medical Director	Surgeon Hunter McGuire.
As Acting Medical Director	Surgeon H. Black.
As Ordnance Officer	Lieut. Jas. M. Garnett.
	Lieut. H. H. Lee.
	Lieut. R. H. Meade.
As Chief Quartermaster	Maj. John A. Harman.
As Acting Chief Quartermaster	Lieut.-Col. M. G. Harman (in January, 1862).
	Capt. T. R. Sharp (in January, 1862).
As Chief Commissary	Maj. Wells J. Hawks.
As Aide-de-Camp	Lieut. A. S. Pendleton (throughout the campaign).
	Lieut. George G. Junkin.
(Volunteer)	Col. Charles J. Faulkner.
	Col. W. L. Jackson.

INDEX

Alleghany Camp, Milroy's repulse at, 220

American Civil War, leading causes of the, 1 *et seq.*

Ashby, Gen., C.S.A., drives Federals from Bloomery Gap, 34 ; covers retirement from Winchester, 42 ; extraordinary activity of, 47 *et seq.* ; smart action with Federals near Buckton, 120 ; cuts off part of Banks's force at Middletown, 127 ; his activity during Jackson's retreat from Winchester, 172 ; fight with Fremont's cavalry near Harrisonburg, 175 ; killed, 180 ; his character, 181 ; his coolness under fire, 236

Banks, Gen., U.S.A., occupies Harper's Ferry, 36 ; strength and composition of his command, April 1, 1862, 41, 229 ; occupies Winchester, 42 ; strength of his forces there, 254 ; McClellan's instructions to, March 16, 1862, 46 ; orders to, on April 1, 1862, 235 ; given an independent command, 103, 236 ; takes up position at Strasburg, 105 ; dispositions on May 24, 1862, 122, 248, 252 ; his movements before, during, and after the battle of Winchester, 107 *et seq.*

Bath, capture of town by Confederates, 18

Baylor, Col., C.S.A., at capture of Bath, 18

Benjamin, Hon. J. P., Confederate Secretary of War, Jackson's letter of resignation to, 28, 226 ; other correspondence with, 224, 225

Bloomery Gap, Confederates surprised at, 34 ; recovered by Ashby, *ibid.*

Bunker's Hill, occupied by Federals, 37

Carroll, Col., U.S.A., at Port Republic, 187 *et seq.*

Charlestown, Federals driven from, 154

Confederate States Army, condition of, 67

Conner, Col., C.S.A., abandons Front Royal, 161 ; Jackson's rebuke of, 264

Council of War, Jackson's first and last, 230

Cross Keys, Jackson's dispositions at, 185 ; battle of, 192 *et seq.* ; casualties, etc., 197

Davis, Jefferson, inaugurated as first President of the Confederate States, 35

Discipline, relaxation of, among Confederate troops, 26, 227 ; Jackson's ideas of, 219, 228

Dunning, Col., U.S.A., drives Confederates from Hanging Rock Gap, 22, 222, 223

Ewell, Gen., C.S.A., joins forces with Jackson, 113 ; composition of his command, *ibid.*, 246 ; his dispositions at Cross Keys, 193 ; strength of his command there, 269

Faulkner, Hon. C. J., appointed A.D.C. to Jackson, 12 (note)

Fredericksburg, McClellan ordered to advance from, 106

Fremont, Gen., U.S.A., moves on Strasburg, 157 ; his dispositions for the battle of Cross Keys, 192, 194, 268

Front Royal, Confederate advance on, 114 ; Federals driven from, 115 *et seq.* ; Confederate and Federal casualties, 119 ;

281